Frank R. Kemerer

J. Victor Baldridge

UNIONS

ON

CAMPUS

98223

 Jossey-Bass Publishers

San Francisco · Washington · London · 1975

UNIONS ON CAMPUS
A National Study of the Consequences of Faculty Bargaining
by Frank R. Kemerer and J. Victor Baldridge

Copyright © 1975 by: Jossey-Bass, Inc., Publishers
                      615 Montgomery Street
                      San Francisco, California 94111
                      &
                      Jossey-Bass Limited
                      3 Henrietta Street
                      London WC2E 8LU

Library of Congress Catalogue Card Number LC 75-24009

International Standard Book Number ISBN 0-87589-268-X

Manufactured in the United States of America

JACKET DESIGN BY WILLI BAUM

FIRST EDITION

Code 7522

The Jossey-Bass

Series in Higher Education

*To Barbara Kemerer
and Patricia Miller*

Preface

A number of critical events and movements have influenced decision making and academic governance during the history of modern universities and colleges. In all likelihood, the mushrooming growth of faculty collective bargaining is such a major movement.

Most books currently available on academic governance have not dealt explicitly with the problem of unionization. In addition, most books on unionization have not taken into account the larger aspects of academic decision making. For these reasons, we know little about the *impact on governance* of the faculty collective bargaining movement. Important questions are often left unanswered: What effect will unionization have on personnel decisions? What will happen to academic senates when union contracts are signed? Will broad-scale union contracts cause power to become more and more centralized at the state administrative level? Will unionization increase the power of the faculty over curriculum, or will that power be substantially reduced? How will students make their demands known if faculty members are unionized? Will strong unions hinder change and innovation, or will they promote it?

Starting in 1971, the Stanford Project on Academic Governance, financed by the National Institute of Education and sponsored by the Stanford Center for Research and Development in Teaching, undertook a major research effort to study the impact that this new force would have on governance and decision making in higher education. The project was conducted in two phases. For Phase One, we selected 240 institutions at which to study general issues of academic governance. In this phase, collective bargaining was only one issue among many. We used a variety of research tools, including gathering information about the colleges from published sources, sending question-naires to the presidents of the institutions (with 100 percent response after several series of coaxing letters and phone calls), and sending another questionnaire to 17,293 randomly selected faculty members and administrators (with a 53 percent response rate).

Phase Two, begun in 1974, focused on collective bargain-ing. We resampled the original 240 institutions, of which 29 were by then unionized; and, in addition, we surveyed all other unionized institutions, except for a few which we excluded because of their extremely specialized character. This unionized group included 300 institutions for a total of 511 (240 plus 300, minus the overlapping 29). These two samples provided valuable contrast between a random sample of all colleges and universities and those institutions with faculty unions. In this second phase, we again used two questionnaires: one for presi-dents and the other for the faculty chairpersons of the local campus bargaining units at the unionized institutions. Taken together, these questionnaires had a response rate in excess of 65 percent. Further information about the surveys can be ob-tained from us or from the Center for Research and Develop-ment in Teaching, Stanford University.

In addition, we conducted intensive case studies at seven institutions, diverse in background and governance, where col-lective bargaining was in different stages of development: Cen-tral Michigan University, a public four-year institution un-attached to a larger system, which has had a union since 1969; the City Colleges of Chicago, a two-year system that has had a militant union since 1966; Rutgers, the State University of New Jersey, with three campuses in close proximity to one another; the State University of New York and City University of New

York systems, both with several years of strong collective bargaining experience; the University of Hawaii, a public institution with one main campus, several outlying units, and a stormy, inconclusive history of attempted collective bargaining that did not result in a ratified contract until mid-1975 after several union elections and the ouster of one union by another; and finally, to help round out the picture, Hofstra University, a private university in the New York City suburb of Hempstead, Long Island.

From these survey data and case study data, we have tried to go beyond merely reporting facts about collective bargaining to an understanding of the implications of unionism for the future of academic governance. The specific facts change from day to day, but some major themes and trends are now becoming evident. For example, the number of state systems that are unionized is a fact that changes rapidly, but the connection between increasing systemwide unionization and increasing state authority is likely to become a long-term and constant trend. The fact that most unionization has occurred in community colleges may be only a passing statistic; however, the great appeal of unionism to people in the disadvantaged sections of the academic hierarchy will most likely remain a stable theme. The fact that unions have grown where faculty members believe their senates are weak may be only a first-stage development, but the increasing formalization of relationships between faculty and administration when unions are chosen will probably be an enduring condition. Our purpose in this book is to alert those in higher education to the relationships and intersections between the union movement and the governance of higher education, concentrating on those themes that will endure even as specific facts and statistics change.

A number of books on faculty collective bargaining are available today, several of them excellent. We believe, however, that *Unions on Campus* has unique features that make it substantially different from anything currently available in the literature. First, it is an integrated monograph rather than a collection of readings. Most of the books are edited collections of papers, as is common in a fast-breaking field. Only a handful of

integrated monographs exist at this time, such as Carr and Van
Eyck (1973), Ladd and Lipset (1973), and Garbarino (1975),
with the Garbarino book not only the most recent but the most
comprehensive. Early edited collections such as Duryea and
Fisk (1973), Tice and Holmes (1972, 1973), and Vladeck and
Vladeck (1975) performed a great service for the field by calling
attention to the topic; however, collected articles usually vary
substantially in quality, and collections tend to lack overall inte-
gration and sequence as well as an overarching theoretical perspective. In contrast, this book grows out of research with a
theoretical underpinning: that academic governance is a decision-making process largely in the political arena and that collective bargaining is a logical extension of long-existing political
processes.

Second, *Unions on Campus* is based on the strongest set
of empirical data yet collected on faculty collective bargaining.
Most early work on collective bargaining was essentially descriptive rather than analytic; in many ways, the Garbarino book is a
bridge between the descriptive volumes and second-generation
analytical studies. Our data support many of the propositions
advanced in earlier books but refute others. Indeed, since our
findings do refute some propositions, we have deemed it vital to
include a chapter on the causes of faculty unionization.

Third, apart from that chapter, *Unions on Campus* shifts
the focus of research from the causes of collective bargaining to
its consequences. Most research on faculty collective bargaining
so far has examined the causes that have promoted unionism,
and there has been little opportunity to observe its impact.
Now, however, we believe that preliminary conclusions about
the consequences of collective bargaining can be made, based on
systematic survey data and our intensive case studies at seven
diverse institutions. Thus, this book makes a fairly radical shift
in perspective within the literature on collective bargaining, for
it moves beyond causes to the impact of bargaining on academic
governance.

Finally, *Unions on Campus* carefully examines the legal
issues that surround faculty collective bargaining. We did extensive research on the impact of the law at both the federal and

state levels, and the resulting data are woven throughout the volume. In addition, we have compared precedents and patterns from collective bargaining experiences in other sectors of the economy with our data on faculty collective bargaining.

Among the colleagues who aided the development of this book are the senior researchers on the Stanford Project on Academic Governance: David Curtis, now at Governors' State University in Illinois; George Ecker, now at Ohio State University; and Gary Lee Riley, at the University of California, Los Angeles. Much credit is due them for their work on other segments of the project that supplements and supported this effort. In addition, Jeanette Wheeler contributed invaluable editing services, and typing was done by Helen Leamy, Elizabeth Herring, and Marion Holys.

A number of experts in the field of academic governance and collective bargaining contributed valuable information and thorough reviews of the manuscript. Special thanks go to Philip W. Semas of *The Chronicle of Higher Education*; Matthew Finkin, associate professor of law at Southern Methodist University; Joseph W. Garbarino, director of the Institute of Economic and Business Research at the University of California, Berkeley; Ronald P. Satryb, assistant vice-president of business affairs at SUNY/Geneseo; Kenneth P. Mortimer, professor and research associate at Pennsylvania State University; George W. Angell, director of the Academic Collective Bargaining Information Service, Washington, D.C.; Maurice C. Benewitz and Thomas Mannix of the National Center for the Study of Collective Bargaining in Higher Education at CUNY/Bernard Baruch College.

Geneseo, New York   Frank R. Kemerer
Fresno, California   J. Victor Baldridge
October 1975

Contents

Unions
on Campus

A NATIONAL STUDY OF THE
CONSEQUENCES OF FACULTY BARGAINING

Summary
of Findings

Faculty collective bargaining in higher education is a phenomenon of the 1970s. In 1965, there were virtually no unionized institutions; since then, the number of campuses with faculty bargaining units has increased yearly, as the following figures demonstrate:

1966	11
1967	25
1968	65
1969	130
1970	160
1971	230
1972	290
1973	330
1974	360
mid-1975	430

These figures mean that nearly one eighth of the 3038 colleges and universities in the country have faculty bargaining agents. Nearly 12 percent of all professional staff and over 20 percent of the full-time teaching faculty in American higher education are now represented by unions.

A total of 266 bargaining units cover these 430 campuses, the largest representing the 26 campuses of the State University of New York. As of mid-1975, these 266 units had negotiated 212 contracts. In the public institutions of several eastern states, unionization has practically reached the saturation point. For example, in New York and New Jersey—both states with strong collective bargaining laws—almost 95 percent of state institutions are unionized.

A few important facts about faculty unionism can be summarized briefly. First, the vast majority of unionized faculty members are in public institutions, mainly two-year colleges. Little unionism exists in private, four-year colleges, though it is growing.

Second, most unionized institutions are in the handful of states with laws favoring collective bargaining among public employees, such as New York, New Jersey, Michigan, and Pennsylvania, because professors in public institutions are included under these laws. Third, the major national labor unions have been spending huge sums of money in attempts to organize higher education professionals. In 1975, the National Education Association (NEA) budgeted nearly two million dollars for unionizing professors. Albert Shanker, head of the American Federation of Teachers (AFT), an AFL-CIO affiliate, indicates that his organization will give top priority to organizing higher education. The American Association of University Professors (AAUP) has also committed increased resources toward this end.

Coupled with the general economic problems facing higher education in the 1970s, these facts demonstrate the potential of academic collective bargaining. Both the organizing efforts of national labor unions and changing collective bargaining laws across the nation are catalysts to the expansion of faculty unionism. Generally, laws are being liberalized so as to give public employees more bargaining rights. As this trend continues, a surge of unionism can be expected—such as in California, where new legislation is imminent. Further, as more and more faculty unions sign contracts, grow in membership, accumulate funds, and develop political skills, they will use these assets to help other unions organize and grow. Major social movements have a tendency to snowball as their visibility, power, skill, and money increase. It is likely that faculty unions will experience a similar development.

Given its rapid growth to date and its potential for future growth, we believe faculty collective bargaining will almost certainly be a major force in the governance of higher education. This prediction is the starting point for our discussion about how collective bargaining will affect academic governance. The following overview outlines the subject matter of Chapters Two through Eight and briefly sets forth some of our findings.

(1) *Three images dominate most discussions of academic governance: "collegial," "bureaucratic," and "political."* As we note in Chapter Two, a couple of the images are traditional: the *collegial* process, with scholarly professionals cooperating to make decisions, and the *bureaucratic* process, with a system of rules, regulations, and hierarchical communication patterns. A more recent perspective, however, suggests that academic governance is a *political* process involving a network of competing interest groups that exert pressure to gain favorable decisions. The interaction of collegial, bureaucratic, and political activities makes academic governance a complicated process.

(2) *Collective bargaining is a system of governance and decision making difficult to reconcile with the collegial image of academic governance.* Collective bargaining assumes there is conflict between the employees and the employer, that a union supported by a legal framework will be the exclusive representative of the employees, that group representation will supplant traditional individual negotiations, and that the terms of employment must be included in a binding contract between employer and union. Because a legal contract can ensure rights that informal collegial processes fail to secure, unionization may protect and enhance faculty rights and collegial governance at those institutions where they have been weak. At the same time, unionization undoubtedly undermines some of the central ideals of academic professionalism. Shared governance may become more adversarial and polarized; individual negotiations will be subsumed under group bargaining; the subjective proce-

dures of peer evaluation may be replaced by a more mechanical process; and seniority may be substituted for merit as the prime criterion for promotion and tenure.

(3) *Collective bargaining is more compatible with political and bureaucratic rather than collegial concepts of governance.* Unions are a logical outgrowth of the interest-group dynamics that have always occurred in higher education; in effect, organizing a union and bargaining over a contract are highly political activities that represent a formalizing of age-old informal processes. A routine bureaucratic process of contract administration and adjudication of grievances follows the signing of a contract. In essence, the bureaucratic mechanisms of contract administration and the channeling and resolution of conflict they provide help regularize the political dynamics that occur in unionization and collective bargaining. From this standpoint, a contract has much in common with a constitution or set of by-laws.

(4) *There are strong environmental forces that are promoting the growth of unions.* (See Chapter Three.) The seventies has been a period of economic crisis for the United States and the rest of the world. The dual curse of staggering inflation coupled with sluggish economic growth has cut into everyone's pocketbook. The economic ills felt in the larger society have been magnified in the depressed academic job market, where thousands of qualified people are underemployed or unemployed. As enrollments level off because of the economic downturn and fewer potential students in the post-baby boom population, opportunities in higher education are obviously curtailed. Fewer and fewer people can enter at the lower professional ranks since positions are filled with tenured faculty members. Faculty unions are organizing to fight tenure quotas, the dismissal of faculty, and what they consider to be arbitrary administrative actions over personnel. Based on union achievements in other sectors of the economy, it is reasonable for faculty members to expect that a strong union effort will recapture and preserve their own economic power and job security.

(5) *Faculty desire to influence governance is also a critical impetus in faculty unionization.* The economic downturn

combines with rising professional expectations on many campuses, particularly those that are less prestigious, to impel faculty to participate in decisions affecting them. Even on campuses where the faculty traditionally has played a large role in campus governance, many professors see collective bargaining as a way to halt the drift of power to administrators.

Finally, as demands for public funds in other sectors of the economy—health, social welfare, and other social services— have sharply reduced the priority of higher education in state and federal funding, some state legislatures have imposed new work rules, quotas for staff, and a host of other regulations. As these restrictions increase, it is likely that faculty will turn to unions as defenses against encroachments on their professional life.

Chapter Three uses data from both Phase One and Phase Two of the Stanford Project on Academic Governance to examine the environmental, institutional, and individual causes of faculty unionization—both nationally and on the campuses of the respondents. The data provide fresh information that sometimes differs with past assumptions, and we urge even the knowledgeable expert in the field of faculty unionization to at least skim this chapter before going on.

(6) *Several critical factors can influence the effect of faculty collective bargaining on campus governance, including the geographic extent and personnel composition of the bargaining unit, the scope of bargaining, union security agreements, and strike sanctions.* An expert in the field of academic labor relations may likewise wish to skim Chapter Four. We urge the layman reader, however, to read it carefully, for many of the outcomes of collective bargaining are affected by the shape it takes on a given campus. Since both American higher education and American government are largely decentralized and diversified, generalizations about how specific issues of unionism will be resolved in different situations are difficult to come by. Nevertheless, one generalization warranted by the rulings of regulatory agencies to date is that the geographic extent of unions should be as large as practical. For private institutions, the local campus is the largest reasonable unit. For public colleges, how-

ever, the units are often huge, with geographically scattered and different kinds of institutions in the same bargaining unit. Another generalization based on the rulings to date is that all types of academic employees should be lumped together in the same unit.

(7) *Unions adapt themselves to the existing structure and management of institutions.* Consequently, complex management systems will generate complex, statewide unions. This concentration of union power in turn produces more system-level management. The circle is complete—centralized systems produce centralized unions, which in turn generate more centralization. The dramatic shift toward state and system-level control that collective bargaining helps to produce is one obvious trend of unionism—one that weakens the local autonomy that has been considered a mark of excellence in the educational system; ironically, this trend undermines one of the reasons faculty turn to unions in the first place.

(8) *One of the most important factors shaping collective bargaining is the "scope of bargaining" that is allowed.* Restrictive laws, strong faculty governance bodies that jealously protect academic issues, and strong administrative pressure tend to restrict bargaining to wages and economic issues. On many campuses, however, these forces are weak or absent. Combined with the natural tendency of unions to expand the scope of bargaining, campus realities may help to increase union power and concerns. In the process, the power of traditional governance bodies such as senates, departments, and faculty committees is eroded.

Union "security" agreements (systems to collect dues through payroll deductions or other systems) take many forms, and one of the important conclusions of Chapter Four is that the degree of security helps determine union behavior. Although lack of security sometimes makes a union weak, "hungry" unions are likely to be particularly aggressive and obstructionistic, for they hope to call attention to issues that will elicit public concern and backing.

(9) *Since higher education has little union experience, it is not clear what the impact of strike threats will be.* The gener-

ally accepted assumption has been that these threats may not be very effective because few faculty believe in them and because the services that they disrupt are not urgent, time-bound activities affecting public convenience, health, or safety. However, the strength of strike threats may lie in administrative fear of service employees and other union members, including food and fuel suppliers refusing to cross picket lines; fear of immediate campus disruption; and, most significantly, fear of lasting campus bitterness engendered between students, faculty, and administrators.

(10) *Interestingly, the national affiliation of the union is one of the least important factors influencing governance.* In Chapter Four we suggest that contrary to all expectations and public position statements by the different unions, AFT, NEA, and AAUP affiliates act very similarly at the bargaining table. There are nuances of differences, to be sure, but hardly enough to make the agent affiliation a critical one.

Having set the theoretical framework for our analysis and examined the causes of unionization and the factors that shape the character of bargaining at the campus level, we turn to a discussion of the impact that collective bargaining has on academic governance. Chapter Five, the first of four on this subject, reaches several main conclusions about the impact on personnel decision making:

(11) *Unions have made impressive progress in affecting personnel policies in the short time they have been representing faculty.* Basic personnel policies in relation to hiring, firing, promotion, and tenure are usually included in initial union contracts. In addition, subsequent contract provisions tend to include such professional issues as merit pay, the composition of promotion committees, and faculty participation in governance. Both college presidents and union chairpersons agree that unions, like senates, strongly influence personnel issues.

(12) *Faculty unions may help to raise standards in institutions where professional practices, peer judgments, and faculty rights have had little foothold.* Probably the most positive function of unions is supporting reasonable and fair personnel practices in institutions that have been weak in those areas.

(13) *The positive effects on personnel matters may be offset by a number of negative consequences.* While struggling for job security, unions may harm the more traditional process of peer evaluation based on subjective criteria. Union attacks on traditional procedures and the thrust toward objective criteria have a tendency to encourage "promotion and tenure by default." Unions may ensure job security only by tying up the system with a burgeoning bureaucracy, rigid rules and procedures, and constant grievance actions; as a result, higher education may face a crisis of quality.

Chapter Six focuses on the long-term impact that collective bargaining will have on traditional academic senates. We acknowledge the problems inherent in our attempt to reach some conclusions on this issue. For one thing, with few exceptions, only institutions with weak senates have unionized; thus, it is difficult to project how unions might affect more developed senates. In our opinion, however, the importance of senates as manifestations of ideal "shared governance" has been overrated, and so we believe the following conclusions drawn from the current situation can be applied to most institutions of higher education:

(14) *Senates are unlikely to convert to unions successfully.* Collective bargaining laws hinder such a change, and senates lack the support of national union affiliations.

(15) *Senates and unions have different responsibilities, with unions addressing economic issues and working conditions, and senates dealing with curriculum, degree requirements, and admissions.* Areas of joint responsibility include such personnel issues as hiring, promotion, and tenure. Neither senates nor unions have much control over budgets, selection of administrators, overall staffing arrangements, physical plant, and long-range planning. In these areas administrators are in command.

(16) *Senates will not collapse with the arrival of collective bargaining, but as union influence continues to expand into areas of traditional senate responsibility, the current pattern of union and senate influence may not remain stable.* Where senates and unions presently coexist, unions curtail senate influence on economically related issues. Although unions and senates today share concurrent jurisdiction in relation to per-

sonnel decision making, how long this dual influence continues
will depend on many factors, of which unionism is only one.
Most senates are susceptible to problems of faculty apathy,
administrative interference, and changing legal conditions.
These realities will help determine the future viability of senates
in the face of union challenges.

(17) *One critical element in how unionization will affect
senates is the relationship of an institution to larger systems.*
For example, at Central Michigan University, the campus senate
and union have a reasonable though uneasy chance of coexistence, because the issues and major actors are confined to the
local situation. In contrast, at Hunter College within the City
University of New York, the senate has been seriously undermined by the twin threats of an off-campus central union contract and a powerful system administration. Local senates may
find themselves with little authority to oppose such potent
competition.

Our major conclusion in Chapter Six is that senates and
other mechanisms of faculty governance are fragile, and, if not
protected and supported, they will be destroyed by the political
winds sweeping the campus.

In Chapter Seven, we present considerable evidence that
despite the perceptions of administrators, power flows toward,
not away from, administrative groups. Our conclusions are summarized as follows:

(18) *Presidents on unionized campuses feel they have lost
power to unionized faculty,* and foresee a steady erosion of
administrative capacity by faculty unions. Presidents of campuses in state systems believe they are particularly vulnerable to
a two-directional power loss—to unionized groups and to central
headquarters.

(19) *Despite the presidents' feelings of vulnerability, evidence indicates that there is actually a shift toward greater
administrative power.* Internally, more and more decisions are
forced upward, away from departments to the central administration. Governing boards are certainly gaining power at individual campuses. In addition, systemwide collective bargaining
means that power accrues to the system administrators.

(20) *The nature and composition of administrations will*

gradually change in response to collective bargaining. In order to negotiate and administer contracts successfully, traditional faculty-related administrators are likely to be replaced with specialists such as lawyers, labor relation experts, and institutional researchers—a situation that will further widen the gap between administrators and faculty members. Despite increasing numbers, those who, like deans and assistant vice-presidents, serve as middle-level administrators are likely to feel that bargaining goes on at their expense.

(21) *The burdens of negotiating and administering the complex provisions of contracts compound the difficulties of administration.* Campuses are increasingly balkanized into "veto groups," and administrative discretion to respond to campus problems is increasingly circumscribed by contractual provisions, particularly in personnel areas.

(22) *A majority of both campus presidents and union chairpersons foresee outside arbitrators and courts playing a greater role in campus decision making.*

Chapter Eight draws all our previous discussions together by asking, Will collective bargaining help or hurt higher education? As with most simple questions, the answer is complex. Faculty unionization clearly seems to be a double-edged sword. Some of its consequences may provide important benefits for higher education in a time of crisis; other consequences may undermine cherished academic values and practices. In general, we can summarize five major effects of faculty collective bargaining:

(23) *Collective bargaining will realign many of the major power blocks in the traditional academic setting.* Traditionally, senior professors and administrators have dominated the decision-making practices of most colleges and universities. Faculty collective bargaining will seriously challenge that pattern of governance, because it is the junior faculty and part-time faculty who most frequently join unions to make their voices heard. If the "most aggrieved" members of the faculty are successful in their unionization efforts, they will upset the past political processes of academic governance. Further, students—who until now have been gaining more voice in governance practices at

most institutions—will be adversely affected. One of the most interesting aspects of this shifting political scene is the position of administrators. It is clear that their lives will be enormously complicated and more harried when faculty members unionize. But it is also clear that many decisions that formerly were made in faculty committees will now be pressed upward into the controlling hands of the administrators. In short, it seems likely that although the administrators will have more power because of faculty unionization, they will have a harder time using it.

A number of positive consequences stem from unionization. Because this is a time of financial stress for the academic profession, one of the major objectives of unionization is to preserve and extend economic benefits as well as to achieve job security. We anticipate that faculties across the nation will benefit economically from unionization.

(24) *Greater procedural protection for faculty promotions and tenure, less arbitrariness about administrative decisions, more job security and protection for nonteaching professionals, and greater economic security in general—all are more likely with unions than without.* These benefits would even apply to those faculties that do not unionize, for trustees and administrations are inclined to make concessions to ward off unionization just as much as to appease an already existing union.

(25) *Other major benefits of unionization are governance-related—faculties will use unions to establish stronger faculty participation in decision making in institutions that have never had a strong tradition of faculty governance and to preserve their role in governance where it is being challenged.* The administrative dominance that is so characteristic of many community colleges and small liberal arts colleges will undoubtedly be tempered by healthy faculty unions. Another possible advantage is that unions will work to eradicate discrimination against women and minority groups; however, this outcome is somewhat questionable because it is not clear whether minorities and women will be any more successful in mounting the necessary pressure within unions than they have been within institutions.

(26) *Although the advantages are real, on the negative*

side faculty unionization will add one more strong interest group to campus politics, further complicating the decision-making process and constituting a potential veto to beneficial organizational change. Unions, formed to fight administrative bureaucratization and the centralization of power, will themselves generate substantial amounts of red tape and concentrated control. Procedural regularity will often be balanced by endless procedural restrictions. The concentration of power in the hands of union executives will unquestionably undermine some traditional faculty governance processes. Moreover, off-campus administrative power will burgeon as state systems become unionized and state governments respond by building ever greater off-campus educational bureaucracies. All of these factors are serious ones that can be expected to accompany and complicate unionization.

(27) *Most disturbingly, unionization challenges one of the most cherished principles of the academic profession—merit judgments based on peer evaluation.* Unions are controlled by the majority of their members, and there is always a serious danger that unions will reduce the quality of the profession by substituting egalitarianism for meritocracy in personnel decision making. In our opinion, this possibility is the most serious negative aspect of faculty unionization. It stands in sharp contrast to many established and important academic traditions of quality.

In sum, academic unionism is on the threshold of becoming a major force in higher education, and it is difficult to predict its long-term impact on academic governance. Decades of traditional governance patterns are now confronted with the relatively new phenomenon of collective bargaining. In some respects, collective bargaining is a natural outgrowth of trends that have long existed in higher education, but in other ways it strongly contradicts some time-tested governance traditions. Whether the benefits outweigh the costs is a delicate question. Although its long-range effect is still largely unpredictable, the impact it has already had means that for better or worse academic governance will certainly never be the same.

2

Patterns of Academic Governance and Collective Bargaining

Two trends are converging in higher education today: traditional patterns of academic governance and emerging patterns of faculty collective bargaining. As these two trends start to come together, educators are faced with a classic dilemma—that of meshing two differing and often contradictory patterns of action. This chapter sets the stage for discussing that dilemma. First, basic patterns of academic governance are discussed. Second, the major characteristics of collective bargaining are outlined. Finally, the two—along with the drive to form unions—are examined for logical connections and similarities, as well as for tensions and contradictions.

Academic Governance

Academic governance is a complex and tangled web of decision making that translates scholarly goals and values into college and university policies and action. How we perceive that

13

process largely depends on which pair of analytical glasses we wear. Academic governance may be viewed as a collegial process where the values of scholarly professionals form the basis for decisions affecting the institution. From a different perspective, academic governance looks like a bureaucratic process with complex organizational procedures. Using another set of ideas, academic governance appears to be a political process composed of competing interest groups that pressure the decision makers so that the outcomes will be in line with their goals.

The following discussion explores these three perspectives and also points out the drawbacks in using any one of them individually as an exclusive model for academic governance. We would like to suggest that no one model accurately reflects the realities of academic governance today; rather, governing processes can best be understood by analyzing them from all three perspectives.

Many writers declare that the academic institution is a "collegium," or a "community of scholars." The collegial model views decision making as a process of deliberation by academic professionals. It presumes that (1) there is a consensus within the professional academic community as to the purposes and goals of higher education and as to the role of the faculty; (2) the faculty should be the key participant in governance because it alone has the necessary knowledge; and (3) administrators and faculty have common interests that transcend their role differences within academic institutions.

The supporters of this model argue that academic decision making should not be hierarchical but that members of the academic community should participate fully in its management. In other words, the community of scholars should administer its own affairs, and outsiders and bureaucrats should have little influence. According to the collegial model, educational decision making, particularly regarding curriculum and personnel issues, requires the deliberative abilities of professors, for "it is they who possess the special training, competence, experience, special understanding, and professional commitment necessary for sound and reliable decisions" (Kadish, 1972, p. 121). Since administrators are also academic professionals, they sup-

posedly share the same goals as the faculty and can thus be expected to support faculty decisions.

For all of the seemingly sound arguments in support of this model, there are cracks in the collegial armor. The experience of the late 1960s demonstrated that all members of the academic profession do not hold similar views about the purposes and goals of higher education. As one observer comments, "the modern university is most emphatically *not* a cloistered retreat for like-minded scholars" (Leslie, 1972, p. 709). In 1972, the president of the AAUP called attention to three claims that increasingly threaten the collegial view of the academy (Kadish, 1972): (1) that the professor is an employee, a claim that has led to an adversarial relationship between faculty and institution; (2) that the university and its faculty should be directly involved in social concerns, a claim that has split and embittered many faculties; and (3) that democratic political precepts should be applied in decision making within the university, a claim that has undercut the professor's elitist claim to authority based on expert knowledge.

Economic pressures and a trend toward egalitarianism in institutional membership have continued to threaten the collegial model. The growth of faculty collective bargaining in American higher education indicates that many faculty members lack faith in the ability of existing collegial governance mechanisms to satisfy their job-related needs.

The growing apathy of academicians to participate in governance, an apathy reinforced by the increasing complexity of campus management, also contributes to the breakdown of the collegial model. Many educators would probably agree with a well-respected English professor at Central Michigan University who admits, "My interests are to teach; I don't want to get involved in governance."

Admittedly, the collegial model is a value-laden conception of how higher education organizations should function. It seems less descriptive of what actually happens and more instructive of how decision making should be conducted. A more realistic picture of higher educational institutions is associated with a bureaucratic interpretation of organizational decision making.

The prominent characteristics of the bureaucratic model include the following: (1) Higher educational organizations have a formal hierarchy with by-laws and organizational charts that specify organizational levels and role relationships between members. (2) There are formal lines of communication to be observed. (3) Authority relationships, although sometimes unclear, are present nevertheless. (4) Specific policies and rules govern much of the work of the institution. There are deadlines to be met, records to be kept, periodic reports to be made, and so on. (5) Decision making often occurs in a relatively routine, formalized manner using decision councils and procedures established by institutional by-laws.

The bureaucratic characterization holds true for routine decision processes such as admissions, registration, course scheduling, and graduation procedures. The application of modern management techniques to solve financial problems facing colleges and universities helps to systematize decision making in a bureaucratic manner.

In relation to other processes, especially decision making, the bureaucratic paradigm falls short of explaining university governance. First, although the bureaucratic model says much about "authority"—that is, legitimate, formalized power—it neglects the nonformal power based on nonlegitimate threats, the force of mass movements, expertise, and appeals to emotion and sentiment. Second, the bureaucratic image covers the formal structure but not the dynamic processes that characterize the institution in action. Third, the bureaucratic model deals with the formal structure at one particular time, but it does not explain changes over time. Finally, the bureaucratic image does not thoroughly explore the crucial tasks of policy formulation. Although it explains how policies may be carried out most efficiently after they are set, it does not describe the process by which policy is initially established. It slights the political issues, such as the struggles of special interest groups within the university.

The third governance perspective, the political model of decision making, assumes that complex organizations can be studied as miniature political systems, with interest group dynamics and conflicts similar to those in cities, states, or other political situations. As Baldridge (1971) describes it, the political approach to governance examines several processes that center around policy formulation. Major policies commit the organization to definite goals, set the strategies for reaching those goals, and determine the long-range destiny of the organization. Policy decisions are critical decisions; they have a major impact on the organization's future because they bind the organization to important courses of action.

When policies directly affect their special interests, people try to ensure that their values are reflected in the outcomes. Policy making becomes the focal point for interest group activity permeating a college or university; it is also the focal point for those studying the governance process. With policy formulation as the key issue, several assumptions can be attributed to the political perspective:

(1) To say that policy making is a political process is not to say that everybody is involved—quite the contrary, because the "law of apathy" usually prevails. For most people, the policy-making process is often an uninteresting, unrewarding activity, and administrators run the show. This is not only true in colleges but also in the larger society. Voters do not vote, people do not attend city council meetings, school boards usually do what they please; the decisions of the society are usually made by small groups of elites. (2) Even when people participate in political decision making, they do not do so on a continual basis. Rarely do people sustain their interest; they become active when they are directly affected. Decisions, therefore, are usually made by those who persist, the small groups of political elites who invest time in the governance process.

(3) Colleges and universities, like most other social organizations, are fragmented into interest groups with different goals and values. These groups normally live in armed coexistence. When resources are readily available and times are generally good, these interest groups engage in minimal conflict. But when resources are tight, outside pressure groups attack, or internal groups try to take over their goals, interest groups mobilize and try to influence decisions. (4) Since conflict is

natural in a fragmented, dynamic social system, it does not necessarily signify a breakdown in the academic community. In fact, conflict helps to promote healthy organizational change.

(5) Formal authority as prescribed by a bureaucratic system is severely limited by the political pressure and bargaining exerted by groups. Decisions are not simple bureaucratic orders but negotiated compromises between competing groups. Officials cannot arbitrarily issue policy statements; rather, they must jockey between interest groups and build viable positions between the power blocs in an institution.

(6) Academic decision making does not occur in a vacuum. The external environment generates pressures that affect internal governance procedures. External interest groups and outside agencies—especially in the public sector—influence the policy-making process to a significant degree.

These assumptions may be translated into what we term a political process model of academic decision making. First, powerful political forces—interest groups, bureaucratic officials, influential individuals, organizational subunits—push a particular problem to the front and force the political community to consider it. Second, groups struggle over which person or group has the right to make decisions, for where the decision is made can determine the outcome. Third, decisions are often "preformed" by the time one person or group is awarded the decision-making right, which means that options are limited by previous conflicts. Fourth, political struggles are more likely to occur over "critical" decisions than "routine" decisions. Fifth, a complex decision network is developed to gather the necessary information and supply the critical expertise. Sixth, during the decision-making process, political controversy is likely to continue; thus, compromises, deals, and plain head-cracking are often necessary to get any decision made. Finally, because the political processes appear to unmake and confuse agreements, it is difficult to know when a decision is made, and thus controversies may continue for some time.

The political model basically describes the decision-making process within a loosely coordinated, fragmented academic institution. The decision model that emerges is more open, more dependent on conflict and political action than either the collegial or bureaucratic models. Although it is not as systematic or formal as the other models, it may be closer to the truth. Obviously, there are exceptions to this picture of colleges and universities; it is not intended to be an iron-clad characterization of institutions. Thus, the political image does not replace bureaucratic and collegial models, but we feel that it enlarges and enhances the picture offered by the other two.

Collective Bargaining

Although the traditional patterns of academic governance have not included union action, the collective bargaining movement has deep roots in other sectors of the society. By first examining patterns of unionization that have developed over 50 years of experience in industry, we can then look at those union patterns in terms of how they mesh with the various academic governance images.

What is a union? One of many definitions is offered by Charles Rehmus of the University of Michigan Institute of Labor and Industrial Relations. He suggests there are essentially three conditions that must be fulfilled for an organization to be a union (Rehmus, 1973, p. 93): (1) The assumption of conflict between those who are employed and those who administer. (2) The acceptance by the employee group of an organization that is its exclusive representative vis-à-vis management. (3) The willingness to protect the individual or a small group of individuals—in other words, "fair representation" of all groups even if they are a minority.

This definition can be misleading. In today's world of economic crisis, a campus-based senate may fulfill each of these conditions yet, because of its institutional ties, be prevented from becoming a union in the same class as the American Federation of Teachers. Therefore, in addition to Rehmus' points, a fourth should be added: (4) The employee group must win representative status as a collective bargaining agent within a legal framework that has authority beyond the employer and must not depend on the employer's good graces for its continued existence.

The basic difference between organizations such as academic senates and unions is that the latter exist because of legal authorization. In many states, the lack of a permissive legislative environment has retarded faculty collective bargaining. Industrial employees spent long years bitterly struggling to win the right to choose unions that could negotiate a binding contract with management. The first major piece of collective bargaining legislation was the Railway Labor Act of 1926. It was followed by the more encompassing National Labor Relations Act (NLRA) of 1935. Both made the clear refusal of an employer to bargain with the employee representative an unfair labor practice subject to fine and imprisonment. There continues to be no effective remedy to what has been labeled *surface bargaining* by an employer—continued discussion that does not result in agreement. The Supreme Court has denied the National Labor Relations Board the power to compel a concession from an intransigent employer.

The National Labor Relations Act conveys to the private sector employee, including most employees at private colleges and universities, a full complement of collective bargaining rights.

The NLRA defines collective bargaining as "the performance of the mutual obligation of the employer and the representative of the employees to meet at reasonable times and confer in good faith with respect to wages, hours, and other terms and conditions of employment, or the negotiation of an agreement, or any question arising thereunder, and the execution of a written contract incorporating any agreement reached if requested by either party." (Section 8d.)

In addition, the NLRA supports the employee's right to organize collectively. The obligation to bargain on the employer's side and the right to organize on the employee's side are the foundation for a full bargaining relation that also includes: (1) The right of employees to be represented by an exclusive agent. (2) Bilateral (management-labor) determination of wages, hours, and other terms and conditions of employment. (3) The right to a binding contract between the employer and the representative of his employees, a contract that does not depend on the employer's good graces but can be enforced by the courts. (4) The right to strike or to negotiate binding arbitration of both grievance disputes (those arising under the contract) and interests disputes (those arising from the negotiation of a new contract).

Although the NLRA extends these bargaining rights to the private sector, state or federal government employees are not included—and many faculty are employed by public institutions. For them, special state laws have been necessary for unionization, though most states have been reluctant to pass legislation offering the broad rights available under the federal NLRA.

The history of collective bargaining, both in the private sector and in the few instances of public sector activity, provides us with several generalizations about a collective bargaining system and its resulting agreements that can be compared with traditional academic governance patterns.

Group Rights. Under both federal and state legislation, employees have the basic right to organize and to bargain collectively with their employers. Collective bargaining does not confer these rights on the *individual* employee, however; rather, as the representative of all the employees, the *union* is the party to the collective agreement. Individual employees cannot deal directly with the employer to gain individual advantages but must work through the union representative. This stipulation departs radically from traditional individualistic practices in the more elite academic and other professional organizations. A collective agreement allowing individual contracts would, of course, modify this generalization; although some college and university union contracts allow individual and merit bargaining, these are exceptions to the rule.

When a faculty shifts from traditional informal practices to the formality of collective bargaining, many changes occur. First, the individual is no longer the negotiating agent and individual concerns are sublimated to group needs. Contracts are no longer negotiated on an individual basis but for the entire union. Second, personnel practices are no longer informal between the institution and the individual but are highly specified under a contractual relationship. What is permissible or necessary in terms of faculty behavior and institutional performance is often spelled out in minute detail. The individual's employment relationship to the institution is no longer direct but takes place through the intermediaries of the union.

Exclusivity and Fair Representation. Under a comprehensive collective bargaining law such as the NLRA, the union has "exclusivity" as the sole representative of all employees in the bargaining unit. The concept of exclusivity, long desired by unions, stems from a conviction that group members often have no incentive to contribute time and money to group activities; unlike the individual acting alone, they will still receive the collective benefit even if they do nothing (Olson, 1971). Thus, to prevent "free riders," unions have sought and usually won the right to be the exclusive representative of all employees in the unit. Additionally, exclusivity has traditionally been considered the best means of stabilizing employer-employee relations.

As a by-product of exclusivity, the union usually has a legally enforceable obligation to represent all employees fairly— whether or not they are union members. The union does not always have to press an individual's claim, of course. On the contrary, the union as a representative of group interests may well decide to settle an individual grievance early or simply to refuse to process it at all. However, the individual does have some recourse. Federal law gives the individual a conditional right to pursue grievances, and the individual has a constitutional right to petition the government for a redress of grievances (First Amendment).

The discretionary power to back grievants creates a dilemma for unions in higher education. For example, in a disputed tenure case, the union may incur the wrath of its membership by refusing to process a grievance. If it does support a grievant, the union may be challenging the decision of a tenure committee who may also be members of the bargaining unit. Under such circumstances, the ironic result is that the administration becomes the defender of faculty as faculty, and the union is open to administrative criticism as a violator of academic processes.

Union Democracy. Both potential bargaining topics and

disputes arising within the bargaining unit are resolved by majority vote of union members. Although majority rule is an efficient way to resolve policy disagreements, it does not take into account the different statuses of various people in the union. In other words, under a one-man, one-vote approach, seniority, rank, or special skills are not considered—a difficult situation for professional organizations that historically have been status-oriented.

The federal NLRA and many comprehensive state laws allow professional employees to form their own unit separate from a bargaining unit composed of nonprofessionals. Presumably, future legislation will do likewise. In practice however, the provision that allows a separate unit of professional employees is diluted, for the general principle—particularly in the public sector—is that regulatory agencies should create large units incorporating different or "unequal" positions. This large unit determination, combined with the industrial union principle of majority rule, clearly threatens academic elites who have held disproportionate power under traditional governance processes. "Majority rule" and "professional status" are two principles that are strange bedfellows in academic unions.

Pressure Toward Uniformity. Many commentators on faculty collective bargaining fear that the "industrial model" of bargaining will wipe out institutional autonomy and diversity if imposed on higher education. Frequently cited as leading examples of the pressure toward uniform collective bargaining practices are laws that vary little from state to state and that fail to establish separate provisions for higher education. In addition, public employment relations boards often introduce practices based on their experience in the industrial sector when they resolve higher education bargaining issues such as the geographic extent of units and the scope of bargaining.

Despite these pressures toward uniformity, collective bargaining can encourage diversity. Even where laws do not treat higher education differently from other institutions, administrative agencies often approve separate procedures for community colleges, senior colleges, universities, and other systems of higher education. Substantial differences remain between the private sector operating under the federal NLRA and the public sector, as well as between various states. Most significantly, the contractual nature of bargaining enables the parties themselves to tailor the process toward their needs, since they are the ones who decide what is to be included or excluded in the contract, based on the statutory provisions regarding bargainable issues. It should not be forgotten that collective bargaining has long served the interests of such diverse groups as airline pilots, steel workers, actors, truck drivers, football players, and symphony musicians.

American industrial collective bargaining is distinguished from that in most other countries by its highly decentralized nature. In 1970, 150,000 separate union-management agreements existed in the United States, most of them involving a single employer or plant. According to Bok and Dunlop (1970, p. 208), only 40 percent of the employees covered by these agreements involve multiemployer negotiations, and the bulk of them are limited geographically to single metropolitan regions. Thus, although there are tendencies toward uniformity, strong currents exist for diversity as well. To the extent that collective bargaining recognizes implicitly the differences between employees and employers, few noticeable differences will characterize bargaining in the industrial sector or in public employment, including higher education. Whether or not the outcomes of bargaining in higher education and among colleges and universities will be uniform is open to question. Despite pressures toward uniformity, collective bargaining may not be as threatening to institutional diversity as some critics fear.

Accommodating Management Prerogative and Union Control. Collective bargaining laws and rulings recognize the concept of "management prerogative"—the right of management to direct many activities of the organization in pursuit of its goals. In some cases, the management prerogative is used as a pretense for management to limit union influence, but there are also some craft agreements that give the union unilateral power over employee working conditions, thereby substantially diminishing the significance of management prerogative. Most collective bargaining agreements fall somewhere between strict management prerogative and strong craft union control. All agreements are similar in that they represent an uneasy accommodation between two basically differing interests—those of the employer and those of the employee.

Because collective bargaining practices recognize the differing interests of employers and employees, they could pose a threat to the concept of "shared governance." Professional employees, such as doctors, lawyers, and professors, function in part as managers and in part as employees; they often have considerable control over personnel and institutional decision making, matters usually considered management prerogative. For this reason, one might presume that collective bargaining would be directed toward professionals' interests as employees, not managers. In fact, this approach has been taken by several unions in higher education. The coalition of AAUP and NEA chapters at the University of Hawaii, for example, supports a "dual-track" system of bargaining—one track preserving traditional faculty governance, with the other using collective bargaining to deal with salary issues (UHPA flyer, March 5, 1974):

> The University of Hawaii Professional Assembly (UHPA) proposes the "Dual-Track" approach to collective bargaining for University of Hawaii faculty. Under the "dual-track" approach faculty members are viewed to have two roles—as academic professionals, and as State employees. These dual roles are peculiar to a university system. The contract must be formulated, therefore, to maintain them; otherwise, faculty self-government and participation in the University policymaking process will disappear. . . . UHPA believes that the dual-track approach to bargaining will preserve faculty rights as academic professionals, by using collective bargaining to assure these rights and will improve the economic status of the faculty.
>
> UHPA will insist upon *continuance of the present policies and procedures* including existing Faculty Handbooks, except as specifically modified by contract provisions. The Faculty Handbooks and procedures could be altered only by mutual consent between the Regents and represen-

tative faculty bodies, such as senates, in dealing
with academic freedom, due process and tenure,
personnel evaluation by peer review, faculty control over academic policies and goals, including curriculum. These academic matters would continue
as rights of faculty in their role as academic professionals. UHPA will support development and
acceptance of Faculty Handbooks covering these
matters where they do not now exist or require
improvement.

The AAUP is walking a fine line, upholding the faculty's union
control over economic issues and the faculty's management prerogative over curriculum issues. This delicate balancing act may
be jeopardized both by legal decisions based on traditional concepts of management prerogative and by the expansionist
tendencies of unions.

Unionism as an Instrument of Governance. Through collective bargaining, the involved parties arrive at an agreement
that has much in common with a government charter or treaty.
The agreement regulates the diverse activities and conflicting
interests of groups of individuals within the same organization.
In many instances, particularly in relation to the first few contracts negotiated by a new union, collective bargaining does not
replace past governance structures and procedures but is superimposed on them.

In the private industrial sector, the collective bargaining
agreement has been a charter through which workers have
gained influence over organizational policies. Collective bargaining, one authority writes, "is . . . the means of establishing
industrial democracy as the essential condition of political
democracy, the means of providing for the workers' lives in
industry, the sense of worth, of freedom, and of participation
that democratic government promises them as citizens" (Shulman, 1954-1955, p. 1002).

Not only does collective bargaining affect the *formulation* of organizational rules, it also affects their *interpretation*
and *adjudication* through grievance and arbitration procedures.
A majority of collective bargaining contracts in the industrial

sector contain a grievance system.* Most of the agreements in higher education contain similar provisions.

A grievance system consists of steps by which an individual employee, with union support, seeks a solution to a complaint. First, the grievance is brought to the attention of the employee's immediate superior. If no satisfactory adjustment is made, the employee may continue to appeal to higher levels. If agreement cannot be reached, most grievance procedures culminate in binding arbitration by a neutral third party. In return for binding arbitration, both the employer and the union usually relinquish economic weapons, such as the lockout and strike, over issues included within the scope of the grievance/arbitration clause. The collective agreement, through its grievance and arbitration provisions, helps organizations enforce rules and manage conflict. In short, the contract and its procedures become part of the governance process.

Now let us compare and contrast patterns of academic governance with collective bargaining. In some ways, the wedding of academic governance and collective bargaining will occur easily and naturally; in other ways, it will be troublesome.

Unionism Evolves from Academic Political Processes

From some perspectives, faculty collective bargaining may appear alien to higher education. More than a few people see unionization as a breakdown in the traditional academic and professional approach to managing academic organizations. From other perspectives, however, the process is less alien than it first seems; rather, it appears as a logical outgrowth of long-existing trends in academic governance. In other words, if aca-

---

*A recent study of contracts in the United States covering 1000 or more workers showed that 1314 of the 1339 agreements (98.1 percent) contained both grievance and arbitration provisions. Twelve had grievance provisions alone; only thirteen contracts made no reference to either grievance or arbitration. "Characteristics of Agreements Covering 1000 Workers or More, July 1, 1973," *U. S. Bureau of Labor Statistics Bulletin 1822* (1974):64.

demic governance is viewed as a dynamic "political" process, with competing interest groups trying to influence the decision process, then formal faculty collective bargaining is a natural progression from informal conflict processes to formal conflict expression.

Specialized interest groups, conflict, bargaining, and negotiation have always been part of decision making in large academic institutions. Further, the patterns of negotiation and conflict that characterize *informal* academic processes are vital to the dynamics of *formalized* collective bargaining. In short, the argument is that unionization is the formalization of the interest group dynamics that have continually occurred in higher education.

The early days of education in the United States were informal, and the collegial model was the dominant image of at least a few small liberal arts colleges. Later, complex institutional governance forms developed and came to include academic senates, rigid departmentalization, the national AAUP, and special interest groups that formed within the disciplines.

In the current phase of development, conflicts over wages and working conditions have risen to the surface as critical issues. Faculties today feel threatened by economic conditions and the growth of large bureaucracies. It should be no surprise, therefore, to find that interest groups have become more formalized and are structured around economic issues. In fact, it would be most unusual if this were not the case. We can project that future changes and environmental pressures will result in interest groups forming around other issues and concerns.

We believe that the political interpretation of decision making explains why collective bargaining has grown so rapidly in higher education. Political activity invariably means the formation of interest groups, and unions traditionally have been interest groups that have formed around economic issues. In higher education, the political activity that had centered around interest groups such as the AAUP has now generated unions concerned with economic issues. Of course, if we tend to view the college or university only as a collegial system or a complex bureaucracy, then the growth of faculty unions may seem to be an anomaly and an aberration. However, if academic governance is seen as a combination of collegial, bureaucratic, and political processes, then unionization appears as a normal, legitimate, and reasonable outcome.

In stating that unionization is a logical progression of an ongoing political process, we must make two important qualifications. First, although unionization in higher education has evolved from conditions similar to collective bargaining in the industrial sector, and although the two have similar characteristics, higher education should not necessarily adopt industrial union practices. There are some aspects of industrial unionization that could be detrimental to higher education. Faculty unionization must be sensitive to the peculiar values and cherished traditions of the academic community.

Second, although unionization may have evolved naturally from the political process, we should not enthusiastically embrace all the possible consequences. Although some of the results of unionization will undoubtedly be positive and will bring major benefits to higher education, it is possible that a high price will have to be paid for these benefits.

Unions and Collegiality

Is collective bargaining compatible with the concepts of collegiality, such as shared governance, professional expertise, and collegial decision making? This is a difficult question, for collective bargaining can support the goals of collegiality in some situations but undermine those goals in other instances.

In certain institutions, ideas of faculty participation in governance and shared, collegial decision making have always been fictional, for the institutions were actually managed by strong administrators and trustees. Such a pattern of administrative dominance is characteristic of many community colleges, state colleges, and private liberal arts colleges. In institutions where academic collegiality has been a myth, collective bargaining may promote faculty rights and collegial decision making. Most observers have argued that collective bargaining will undercut collegiality, but we feel that in many situations strong union contracts will produce greater faculty participation in governance. In one sense, then, collective bargaining may bring some semblance of collegial management to institutions that never had such a tradition. The helpful role that unionization can play in extending faculty rights is noted by no less a collegial organization than the AAUP, whose comments sum up this argument (AAUP Policy Documents and Reports, 1973, p. 52): "The longstanding programs of the Association are means to achieve a number of basic ends at colleges and universities; the enhancement of academic freedom and tenure; of due process; of sound academic government. Collective bargaining, properly used, is essentially another means to achieve these ends, and at the same time to strengthen the influence of the faculty in the distribution of an institution's economic resources. The implementation of Association-supported principles, reliant upon professional traditions and upon moral suasion, can be effectively supplemented by a collective bargaining agreement and given the force of law."

Despite the benefits that unionization may bring to some institutions, it is nevertheless true that collective bargaining may threaten some collegial practices. In institutions with long histories of faculty rights, shared governance, and peer judgment, unionization may weaken faculty professionalism, because many collective bargaining practices are in opposition to academic collegiality. In particular, collective bargaining does not accept the presumption of shared governance, which is central to academic collegiality. Instead, collective bargaining divides the world into a we-they dichotomy, recognizing that people's perceptions and interests depend largely on their positions within organizations. The best way to guarantee shared decision making, according to many union advocates, is to mandate it in a legally binding contract.

Frequently proponents of this view stress that the relationship between administration and faculty is essentially adversarial. Donald Wollett, director of employment relations for New York State, comments (1973, p. 32): "Collective bargaining amounts to a turning away from collegiality and self-governance and a moving toward an adversary system which recognizes that the central fact of life in the academy is that there are those who manage and those who are managed, that there are employers and employees, that conflicts arise from these relationships, and that in a collective-bargaining system they are resolved by a process predicated upon the proposition that people whose interests conflict are, at least in respect of those conflicts, adversaries." Others acknowledge that occasionally administrators and faculty do have different viewpoints but believe bargaining can be a catalyst toward accommodation and can thus reduce, not increase, polarity. As we shall see, this view has commanded a good deal of attention within the Massachusetts State system.

At its best collegial governance has enhanced faculty participation in decision making, but at the same time it has masked the differences between administrators and faculty. In contrast, collective bargaining brings those differences into the open. While bargaining may be a means of increasing joint decision making, it may also lead to polarization, with the administration controlling certain decisions and union contracts governing others.

Another major problem facing the merger of faculty unions with collegial patterns of academic governance concerns evaluating professional performance. Professional evaluation has always been based on the skills and merit of the individual. It is difficult to judge merit from observing professional behavior subjectively, but professional organizations have managed by using peer evaluation processes. Professionalism is, in many ways, an elitist concept built on professional performance and knowledge. The tradition of unionism is different because it stresses the equality of all workers and emphasizes the democratic control of the union. Unions are oriented to negotiating contracts that level the differences among individuals. Under a one-man, one-vote system, the nonelite effectively control the union, and their concerns are uppermost on the union's bargaining list. This position is not easily reconciled with judging professional performance on the basis of skills and merit. Since unions have often used seniority, not merit, as a basis for promotion, it is possible that faculty collective bargaining will encourage a procedure that violates cherished principles of professionalism. Because of all of the above conflicts, the tensions between collective bargaining and collegial processes will undoubtedly be profound.

Stages in Collective-Bargaining Process

Earlier we noted that two interpretations of academic governance were described as political and bureaucratic. Although there are distinct differences between them, the two images are not necessarily contradictory. Each one helps us to understand different phases of the collective bargaining process. Collective bargaining has three distinct stages. Stage one is unionization, the drive to elect a union. Stage two is the negotiation of the contract. These two stages are primarily political. Stage three is the administration of a contract, a largely bureaucratic process.

Unionization. Unionization is the drive to form unions in nonunion organizations. Competing unions campaign to represent the employees, and elections are held to determine the employees' choice of a bargaining agent. It is also possible to have "decertification" elections to terminate a union or displace it with another union. All of this activity proceeds under strict rules set down by the law and is highly political.

Negotiating the Contract. Once a union has been formed, the collective bargaining phase begins, and it involves negotiating a contract around a bargaining table. There are demands, threats, offers and counteroffers, and perhaps even strikes, lockouts, or arbitration. The negotiation stage is best characterized as a power struggle between employers and employees conducted within the confines of a legal framework.

The negotiation phase of collective bargaining in the industrial sector usually has four characteristics: (1) It is bilateral (between employer and employee). (2) It is essentially a power play between these two organized interest groups. (3) The least common denominator is the starting point. (4) It is adversary in tone (a "we-they" mentality).

The negotiation phase is similar in higher education. In

1967, the seven two-year campuses of the City Colleges of Chicago negotiated their first contract with the Cook County College Teachers Union, an AFT affiliate. This contract demonstrated how tough a faculty union could be, for it included reducing the course load for faculty to twelve to thirteen class contact hours per week in most departments, increasing salaries an average of $500 (in 1967 dollars!) for each faculty member, establishing a three-year tenure policy, adding $300 worth of fringe benefits per faculty member, and enlarging the role of faculty in personnel decision making. Subsequent contracts established the City Colleges of Chicago as the highest paying two-year system in the country with the single exception of the City University of New York.

According to the president of one of the colleges, the Chicago City College central administration failed to recognize the divergence of interests between employer and employee. The administration initially approached the bargaining table with a pro-union stance, assuming that if it met union demands, higher morale and an increase in productivity would result. They found, much to their chagrin, that "we lost our pants." "The lesson we learned," comments one high official, "is the meaning of *quid pro quo*. Never make a concession without exacting a price."

The political posturing and conflict processes are highly visible in the negotiation phase, as illustrated by the 1972 bargaining sessions between the CUNY central office and the Professional Staff Congress. David Newton, CUNY Vice Chancellor, commented on the content of the 62 typewritten pages of union demands (1973a, p. 3):

> Demands included [proposals for] 100 percent wage increases, for thirteen-hour work weeks for nonteaching personnel, for wholesale surrender to the bargaining agent of faculty and administration functions in academic policy and governance areas, and the like. The union's "demands" were made to the accompaniment of a press campaign that those demands were all in the cause of student welfare and concern for open admissions. In this union-created atmosphere, the administration's

counterproposal for a mere 5 percent annual salary increase (for a faculty which is already the highest paid in the country) is treated, as one might expect, with pretended outrage. Similarly, the administration's request that City University counselors, currently working only thirty hours a week, with three months paid vacation, be hired in the future to work the same hours (thirty-five per week) and months (eleven) as counselors at Rutgers and other institutions (for more money, of course, than the other pay) is attacked by the union as a step back into the Dark Ages.

Union representatives, on the other hand, criticized the administration for its "industrial warfare" approach to bargaining. Professional Staff Congress Executive Director Arnold Cantor, in reference to the fifteen months of negotiation, points out: "While parties can be in an adversary relationship and still conduct their business without rancor and venom, the CUNY administration has seen fit to employ staff and counsel who consider it necessary to demean in order to protect the interests of the administration." Ratification of the new contract in the fall of 1973 averted a strike previously authorized at the nineteen CUNY campuses. As Cantor says: "The City University administration is still in the 1930s" (Professional Staff Congress *Clarion,* May 31, 1974). It seems safe to say that there are no white hats and no black hats in the political battles over new contracts.

Administering the Contract. Once a contract is signed, the activity shifts to a more routine, bureaucratic contract administration phase. Wages and working conditions are administered as the contract provides, and grievances are filed when employees feel dissatisfied. Arbitration is often used to decide these grievances. Contract administration highlights weaknesses in the contract, and sets the stage for another round of negotiation in the next collective bargaining cycle.

As one might expect, under the first few contracts in a new collective bargaining relationship, the parties are still likely to feel the divisive effects of the bargaining election and the adversarial relations accompanying the negotiating phase. Thus, the number of grievances may be quite large. At CUNY, for example, during the first contract period (September 1969 to August 1972), the administration reported that over eight hundred Step One grievances were filed with the colleges, over five hundred Step Two grievances were filed with the Chancellor's Office, and over two hundred grievances found their way to the final arbitration step (Newton, 1973, p. 63).

Both in industry and in higher education, a major factor influencing contract administration is the language of the agreement. A legal contract requires precise and operational definitions of terms. The experience of the City Colleges of Chicago administration with its first contract provides an excellent illustration. Included in the agreement was this phrase: "During the life of this Agreement, the Board will continue its *existing policies and practices* with reference to salaries, fringe benefits and *working conditions* of faculty members which *are not specifically covered by this Agreement*" (italics added).

It was not until later that the central office realized that its hands were tied in administering the colleges. By the terms of the contract, *any* change in past practice affecting salaries, fringe benefits, and working conditions had to be negotiated. "You can well understand," commented one administrator, "that our first contract was in reality many times larger than it might first appear." Subsequent contracts have been altered to read "existing policies and *uniform* practices." Thus, only systemwide changes have to be negotiated with the union.

Because arbitration is essentially interpretation, both parties must take care to construct the agreement in such a way so as to prevent arbitration from creating new contract language. The pressure to reach agreement will inevitably result in poorly worded and vague phrases that invite "creative" arbitrators to rewrite the contract. The result can be disastrous for either or both parties.

The administration of the contract and arbitration is as important as the initial contract negotiation in forming the relationship. Contract administration first specifies role relationships and establishes channels for conflict resolution. The contract helps to rationalize organizational functioning, taking

conflict out of the political arena and routinizing it in the grievance machinery. Second, the contract may also be a means to
establish formal lines of communication and to set forth policies and rules governing personnel decision making that are both
clearer and more fair than those that existed previously. Finally,
the administration of the contract highlights misunderstandings,
ambiguous contract wording, and clumsy processes that need
streamlining—as the Chicago case vividly illustrates. Thus, contract administration helps set the stage for a new round of political negotiations to clarify and eliminate such problems.

To summarize, we have compared traditional academic
governance concepts—collegial, bureaucratic, and political—with
the more recent academic collective bargaining process. Although collective bargaining does not appear compatible with
the collegial perspective of academic governance, there is considerable doubt as to whether collegiality by itself accurately
reflects governance procedures in higher education today. The
ideas behind faculty unionization would appear to support
some of the tenets of the collegial model but not others. However, in relation to the bureaucratic and political models of
governance—images that round out the picture of how institutions of higher education are actually organized and run—collective bargaining can be seen as a natural outgrowth. When academic governance is viewed as a process of interaction between
collegial, bureaucratic, and political models, the drive toward
unionization, contract negotiation, and contract administration
all fit into the picture of higher education. Specifically, forming
the union and negotiating the contract seem to jibe most closely
with political processes, whereas the contract administration
phase is most compatible with the bureaucratic interpretation
of academic governance. Table 1 illustrates the stages of collective bargaining and identifies the governance image that meshes
with each stage.

Table 1
Stages of Collective Bargaining

	Unionization Phase	Negotiation Stage	Administration Stage

Character	1. Drive to organize unions
	2. Competition among unions
	3. Elections for certification and decertification
		1. Bilateral (employer/employee)
		2. Adversary ("we-they" mentality)
		  (a) Least common denominator
		  (b) Use of sanctions
			1. Continuing communication between the parties about contract interpretation
			2. Grievance processing by the parties
			3. Impersonal adjudication by neutral arbitrators

Results	1. One union selected as exclusive agent
	2. Contract negotiation begins
		1. Transcribed agreements with language specificity
		2. Differentiation of role relationships
		3. Contract expansion over time
			1. Rationalization of organizational processes
			  (a) Define role relationships
			  (b) Legitimize exercise of authority
			  (c) Provide dispute settlement mechanisms
			  (d) Channel and resolve conflict
			2. Highlight contract inadequacies, pointing way for new rounds of negotiation

Most Useful Governance Image	Political	Political	Bureaucratic

Causes of
Faculty Unionization

The external and internal conditions of higher education in this decade have provided fertile ground for the growth of faculty unions. As long as the number of students continued to increase every year, jobs were plentiful, salaries were rapidly rising, and institutions were expanding both their facilities and services. Now, however, the massive boom has leveled off, and job security and salary increases have become prime concerns of faculty and are contributing to widespread unionization. In the first part of this chapter, we explore why faculty members have been motivated to join unions by examining the environmental conditions that have depressed almost all institutions in the United States. Then, we look at the internal conditions, many of them governance-related, that affect various institutions and at individual faculty characteristics that help to explain the trend toward faculty collective bargaining.

In the survey sponsored by the Stanford Project on Academic Governance, college and university presidents and the faculty chairpersons of local college unions were asked to comment on ten factors influencing faculty collective bargaining across the nation. The patterns that emerged from their responses appear in Table 2. Wages, benefits, and job security are clearly rated as the most important causes of unionization by all respondents. All respondents also include fear of budget cuts, problems of teacher surplus, and the desire for increased faculty influence on governance. For the most part, people at unionized institutions—both presidents and union chairpersons—agree on the causes of unionization. However, presidents in institutions without unions have views somewhat different from those of people on union campuses. In particular, they do not believe that the need for grievance procedures, permissive legislation, the pressures of experienced union groups, or problems with faculty professionalism contribute significantly to faculty collective bargaining trends. In fact, all presidents—whether on union or nonunion campuses—sharply disagree with union chairpersons over the role of professionalism. Union chairpersons think that a drive for greater professionalism is a moderately important issue, while the presidents of the institutions give professionalism a relatively low rating.

Respondents at unionized institutions were also asked to indicate the relative importance of the causes of unionization on their campuses. Their ratings partly depend on the *type* of institution where the respondent is located. (See Table 3.) The pattern is complicated, but some general trends can be noted. Often, opinions of presidents in large unionized multiversities do not conform to those of other presidents and of their own local union heads. These presidents consistently rate all factors lower than do other presidents. The sharpest disagreements between presidents and chairpersons are also found in large multiversities.

When there is a difference of opinion between presidents in any size institution and union heads—and there almost always is—the union leaders rate the factors higher. Differences between presidents and chairpersons over professionalism as a cause of unionization are most notable in community colleges and liberal arts colleges. Faculty members in these institutions do not feel a strong sense of professional status and look to unions to help establish it. But at multiversities, both presidents and union leaders rate professionalism low; the professional

Table 2
Causes of Faculty Unionization Nationally

	External Pressure			Tenure and Job Security		Governance Issues			Strength of Unionism	Professionalism
	Desire for Higher Wages and Benefits	Fear of Budget Cuts	Fear of Teacher Surplus	Desire for Job Security	Desire for Fairer Grievance Procedures	Desire for More Influence in Campus Governance	Weakness of Existing Faculty Governance Structures	Permissive Government Legislation	Presence of Experienced Bargaining Groups	Desire for More Professional Standing
Presidents of Nonunion Institutions (N = 124)	3.3	3.0	2.8	3.3	2.5	2.7	2.3	2.0	2.3	1.7
Presidents of Union Institutions (N = 205)	3.6	3.0	2.9	3.6	3.2	3.2	2.5	2.5	2.6	1.9
Chairpersons of Unions (N = 193)	3.7	3.0	3.0	3.6	3.4	3.2	3.0	2.8	2.8	2.7

Note: The question asked was "Regardless of whether you have faculty collective bargaining on your campus, please give your opinion about the importance of the following factors for promoting it." The responses are on a four-point scale, with "1" indicating very little or no importance and "4" indicating great importance.

Table 3
Causes of Faculty Unionization on Unionized Campuses

	External Pressure			Tenure and Job Security		Governance Issues		Permissive Government Legislation	Strength of Unionism	Professionalism
	Desire for Higher Wages and Benefits	Fear of Budget Cuts	Fear of Teacher Surplus	Desire for Job Security	Desire for Fairer Grievance Procedures	Desire for More Influence in Campus Governance	Weakness of Existing Faculty Governance Structures	Permissive Government Legislation	Presence of Experienced Bargaining Groups	Desire for More Professional Standing
Multiversities (N = 12)										
Presidents (N = 8)	3.1	2.4	1.6	3.0	2.5	2.6	2.0	1.6	2.0	1.6
Chairpersons (N = 9)	3.7	2.6	2.3	3.4	3.1	2.7	2.9	2.4	2.6	1.7
Public Colleges and Universities (N = 58)										
Presidents (N = 49)	3.3	2.6	2.6	3.5	2.8	2.8	2.0	2.6	2.2	1.6
Chairpersons (N = 42)	3.6	3.0	2.5	3.6	3.4	3.2	2.7	2.9	2.5	2.3
Liberal Arts Colleges (N = 20)										
Presidents (N = 11)	3.5	3.0	2.5	3.8	3.1	3.2	2.7	1.8	1.8	1.4
Chairpersons (N = 12)	3.5	3.2	2.5	3.7	3.4	3.5	2.9	2.5	2.4	2.6
Two-Year Colleges (N = 180)										
Presidents (N = 135)	3.8	2.7	2.8	3.6	3.0	3.1	2.1	2.5	2.6	1.8
Chairpersons (N = 126)	3.7	2.6	2.4	3.5	3.6	3.3	2.9	2.3	3.0	2.8
All Institutions (N = 270)										
Presidents (N = 203)	3.6	2.7	2.7	3.6	2.9	3.0	2.1	2.4	2.4	1.7
Chairpersons (N = 189)	3.7	2.8	2.4	3.5	3.5	3.2	2.9	2.5	2.8	2.7

tradition at these institutions is already strong and is not a major factor in unionization.

From the questionnaire responses, we can form a picture of the origin of the faculty union movement in the United States. In general, the drive to form unions seems to be a protective reaction against external economic and social pressures, as well as a reflection of deep and genuine concern over internal issues of governance, tenure, and grievance procedures. Thus, we have the juxtaposition of two forces: external social pressures and internal failures of governance. These forces are affecting different campuses in different ways; coupled with the presence of strong national unions eager to gain faculty allegiance and the widespread passage of favorable union legislation, they are opening the door for dramatic growth of faculty unionism at certain campuses.

Environmental Causes

American youth are no longer attending college in numbers comparable to those in the 1960s. Among the reasons for enrollment drop-offs are the ending of the draft, the development of nontraditional off-campus degree programs, and a depressed job market for degree holders. Some institutions face actual decreases in the number of enrollees, whereas others are fortunate just to maintain a fairly stable student population. The decline in enrollment has been greatest in the so-called "emerging" state colleges, which have been severely undercut by the less expensive two-year institutions and a depressed job market for teachers (their traditional student base). The future looks even worse. A falling birthrate threatens to make the no-growth era permanent.

In addition to the slowing enrollment rate, higher education is affected adversely by the downturn in economic conditions in general. Most unionized schools are at the two-year end of the institutional spectrum. A large percentage of academics in these schools receive low salaries, are less likely to receive research support, and are more likely to teach a heavier load. As Ladd and Lipset state, "the rewards at the top dwarf those at the bottom." This lack of rewards thus constitutes a "powerful underlying factor behind the disproportionate growth of unions in the less privileged sectors of the academy" (Ladd and Lipset, 1973, p. 34).

During the early 1970s, inflation rates wiped out what appeared to be substantial across-the-board salary increases. For example, the AAUP reports that the average faculty member received a 6.4 percent increase in total compensation including fringe benefits in 1974. But the cost of living rose over 11 percent during that year. The Labor Department indicates that the cost of living rose nearly 60 percent between 1967 and 1975 and predicts it will continue to rise. Under these conditions, it is doubtful that even the most financially secure institution will be able to maintain parity between faculty salaries and inflation for very long.

Whether those who join unions are really deprived or not is immaterial. It is enough that they *perceive* themselves to be. Many community college teachers are at the top levels of teaching positions within a K-14 district. Yet, while they may be well off relative to many secondary and elementary teachers, their shifting frames of reference show them "deprived" when compared to the rest of higher education. What holds true for two-year academics may also apply to faculty at four-year and graduate institutions. For example, one Temple University union leader has noted that "even though Temple faculty members are not badly paid in comparison to faculty at other colleges and universities, their income is hardly commensurate with their own view of their status" (Katz, 1974, p. 35).

Similarly, educators who compare themselves with other professionals, such as doctors and lawyers, see themselves as deprived. The average net income for physicians in 1973 was $49,415 (*Profile of Medical Practice,* 1974), while the most common beginning salaries for corporate attorneys the same year was from $14,000 to $15,000 ("Survey of Corporate Law Department Salaries," 1973). The average faculty member received $15,459 in salary for nine months service at institutions with rank in 1973-1974. At institutions without rank (most often two-year institutions), the average faculty members lagged behind the former group, receiving $14,400 in salary. Fringe benefits added another $2110 to those in the first category and $1472 to those in the second—barely enough to place them ahead of law graduates just entering corporate practice.

In short, *rising expectations* influence the growth of unionization. This is especially true at particular types of institutions, but not at others. Confirmation of the deprivation hypothesis—whether objectively or relatively perceived—comes from ratings by presidents and union chairpersons on the causes of unionization both nationally and on their campuses. As Table 3 indicates, the factor receiving the highest rating by both presidents and chairpersons—those most directly involved—is the desire for higher wages and benefits, and that very practical economic factor is strongest at the two-year level. Because of the rapidly rising inflation rates of the 1970s, it is likely that the quest for greater economic benefits will continue to be a leading cause of faculty collective bargaining.

Inflation and recession not only reduce the real income of individual professors but also cripple the finances of institutions. As costs have risen, institutions have responded in several ways. Tuition has increased dramatically. For the first time in many years, it has become common to use precious endowment funds to meet operating costs. Foundation funds, the source of many grants in higher education, have also been hard hit. Some institutions, particularly private ones, have begun to seek new ways to continue operation. New College in Sarasota, Florida, became a branch of the University of South Florida on July 1, 1975, and other schools are exploring the possibility of leasing part of their campuses to public institutions. Antioch College dropped 33 faculty positions at its campus in Yellow Springs in 1973, and other colleges have either made similar cutbacks or are contemplating them. For some institutions, there is no alternative but to close down.

Retrenchment and State Control. As if decreasing enrollments and a sick economy have not been troublesome enough, priority shifts have taken place in state legislatures and Congress. Problems for colleges began with the student dissent of the middle and late 1960s. The result was diminished popularity of educational causes within the government and among the public in general; unfortunately, it coincided with the beginning of depressed economic conditions. The federal government dramatically cut funding programs for higher education. State appropriations leveled off as claims from other quarters increased.

Declining enrollments and exploding costs produced retrenchment and calls for accountability. New regulations and watchdog efforts by legislatures contributed to growing conflict between those managing the institutions and the faculty. Public institutions first felt the hand of state coordination during the growth period of the 1950s and 1960s. The president of Ohio State University noted in his commencement address to the class of 1973 that "As new public services are demanded, as the taxpayer revolt gains momentum, as state governments everywhere endure the crunch of too many demands and too few dollars, and as the bill of higher education continues to rise, governors and legislators are driven to the search for economies. All this has given strong impetus to the development of powerful state systems of education" (Enarson, 1973, p. 18).

Our 1974 unionization questionnaire asked the presidents in state systems to react to the statement, "System Management is increasing all the time." At community colleges, state colleges, and state universities, presidents overwhelmingly agree— 92 percent of community college presidents and 73 percent of four-year public college presidents.

Legislatures have restricted tenure and have sought to set minimum teaching loads for faculty members on state campuses. Many legislative moves have been contested in the courts. The suits are occasionally successful, as when legislative acts are judged to infringe on the constitutional authority of boards of regents; more often, however, they are not successful. Even state boards of higher education have set restrictive policies that have been subsequently upheld. The growing involvement of state agencies is paralleled by the increased desire of boards of trustees to assert control.

The pressure from legislatures, state coordinating agencies, and boards of trustees for retrenchment and accountability has accelerated the trend to adopt modern management techniques to operate colleges and universities. As Cheit states, "A new style is emerging on the campus. Unlike the old one, which sought improved quality mainly by adding income, the new one relies mainly on control, planning, evaluation, and reallocation to promote institutional strength within fiscal constraints" (1973, p. 2). The reaction to new management techniques by the faculty is highly predictable: confusion, resentment, and organized resistance.

Challenges to Job Security and Tenure. The focal point of these economic pressures and concerns eventually becomes the individual professor and his job.

It has long been assumed that tenure gives a strong measure of job security, but there is increasing concern that tenure will be undermined by institutions trying to maintain some staffing flexibility. The problem is serious: the percentage of faculty members holding tenured positions at colleges and universities rose from 47 percent in 1969 to 65 percent in 1973 (American Council on Education, 1974). The Carnegie Commission on Higher Education estimates that in the 1980s over 80 percent of full-time faculty members will have tenure if present policies continue (Carnegie Commission, 1973, p. 5). Under these circumstances, it is not surprising to find legislators, trustees, and administrators attacking tenure and to find faculty members increasingly suspicious about the real reasons that tenure is not granted. Some critics point out that, given pressures to economize, keeping down the number of tenured positions is not simply a way to maintain staffing flexibility but is actually a way to effect considerable savings, especially if a permanent revolving pool of low-paid nontenured faculty is available. In fact, younger members of the Berkeley faculty have coined a term for such a group of professors—the "sucked orange brigade." In addition, other critics worry about the impact on women and minorities. "When we examine who has tenure and who doesn't, we can see who is likely to get it—and that doesn't include native Americans, people with Spanish surnames, blacks, women, and people under 30" (Park, 1973, p. 16). Worse still, in the current buyer's market, the academic freedom of the nontenured is threatened even more than usual.

A general mistrust of authorities fuels faculty suspicions about tenure policies. Under pressure to trim budgets, administrators are more inclined than ever before to disregard faculty recommendations. In addition, many institutions have formalized the appeal process so that an instructor who is not granted tenure has no alternative except to appeal to the administration —which may be the cause of his complaint in the first place!

Lines of Defense. In the face of attacks against tenure and job security, the faculty is looking outside the walls of academia for help—to courts, professional associations, and unions. *Courts* have become increasingly involved in protecting personnel rights. Most of the cases refer to public institutions, but courts have been involved with private colleges, albeit reluctantly. Normally hesitant to interfere with the internal affairs of private institutions, courts have continued to review actions that appear excessively arbitrary. For example, in 1974 a New Jersey Court ruled that Bloomfield College had not sufficiently demonstrated that abolishing tenure and dismissing thirteen faculty members was "a measure reasonably calculated to preserve its existence as an academic institution."

The progressive extension of court authority into the internal workings of both public and private colleges and universities has stirred up a good deal of debate. Some academicians believe that intervention by external agencies into internal affairs destroys campus self-governance and undermines the essential autonomy of the professional staff. Many other observers, however, feel legal action has not gone far enough. By and large, however, courts have examined only procedural issues, normally side stepping delicate substantive issues involving peer judgment. The courts, for example, have been willing to judge when tenure review processes have been fair but have avoided judging the merits and criteria used by a tenure committee. Since court decisions are limited in their protection, threatened faculty must of necessity look elsewhere for support.

For a variety of reasons, the effectiveness of *professional associations,* such as local AAUP chapters, is severely limited: they have limited access to internal campus governance processes; they have no legal status to influence internal decisions; and in times of economic uncertainty, the sanctions open to them may have limited impact. Similarly, campus faculty associations that are not supported by collective bargaining laws are almost powerless to secure benefits for their members. For example, the faculty at the University of Scranton, a private Catholic institution, agreed in 1970 to an informal bargaining arrangement rather than organizing formally under the federal National Labor Relations Act or a Pennsylvania statute; the informal experiment appeared to be a collegial alternative to the adversary system of collective bargaining. The informality of the Scranton arrangement was its undoing, however, for when bargaining talks broke down in 1974, the administration negotiated contracts with individual faculty members. Subsequently, the faculty sought and achieved formal recognition for its bargaining representatives under federal law.

It is often possible for campus-based informal organizations to function and for unionization and collective negotiation of contracts to occur without support of a collective-bargaining statute. In the absence of legislative guidelines, however, complex disputes must be settled by the parties themselves or in the courts. Neither employer-union power politics nor judicial decision making is a good substitute for a well-written collective bargaining law, which forms the legal basis of unions.

Permissive Legislation. The success of collective bargaining depends on the legal framework. Since it has been difficult for employees in the public sector to obtain favorable legislation, collective bargaining has come to them slowly. Since 1959, when Wisconsin passed the first law, over thirty states have enacted some form of a public employee collective bargaining statute. Many of the other states are expected to do so in the near future. The federal legislation that affects private industry is permissive, but only a handful of states have similar laws covering state employees.

The first law applied specifically to postsecondary teaching personnel was the 1965 Michigan law. By mid-1975, twenty-three states had formal statutes covering employees in postsecondary institutions, twenty of which were passed or amended since 1972 (Academic Collective Bargaining Information Service, 1975). However, only five states identify college faculty explicitly as being covered. Of the twenty-seven states without enabling postsecondary legislation, twenty-three have had legislative activity in this area since 1970. At the time of this writing, it appears inevitable that a federal law might be enacted providing at least minimum standards for public employment bargaining unless the Supreme Court rules against it. Suggested minimum standards have been (1) recognition of the right to organize and engage in collective bargaining by all public employees, (2) a federal agency to administer the statute and grant exemptions to qualified state/local bargaining legislation, (3) a set of guidelines for the establishment of bargaining units and the conduct of representation elections, (4) guidelines on issues to be bargained, leaving the parties and the states to resolve debatable topics such as management rights provisions and union security devices, and (5) minimum dispute settlement requirements such as mediation and fact finding (Brown, 1974, p. 718). Such a federal law would require uniformity of essential bargaining principles, but would leave the states the discretion to handle local issues.

The importance of a supportive legal structure can be seen in the fact that most faculty unions in public higher education are located in states with "permissive" collective bargaining laws. In the Stanford survey, the presence of a permissive legal framework is regarded by both presidents and union chairpersons as a crucial influence on the growth of unions.

Stimulating Influence of Active Union. Another factor— and an important one—influencing faculty members to join unions is the growing acceptance of unions in public employment throughout the country. College and university faculties are well aware that several of the unionized CUNY campuses are among the ten top-paying institutions in the country. Community college faculty cannot fail to be impressed that unionized community colleges are regularly included among the twenty top-paying institutions in the country.

Partly because of their early successes, faculty unions in higher education are no longer a novelty. And with their growing acceptance, they are increasingly concentrating on organizing personnel in colleges and universities, particularly at less prestigious institutions. Presidents of nearly 50 percent of non-unionized two-year colleges included in the 1974 Stanford survey report their faculties to be in the advanced stages of organizing, compared to only 7 percent at nonunionized multi-versities.

On many campuses, the faculty may be hesitant to union-ize, but nonacademic personnel are not. For some time, even the elite institutions have had groups of nonfaculty personnel who have joined unions. Of the nonunionized institutions sur-veyed, 25 percent report formally elected groups either "meet-ing and conferring" or negotiating contracts with administrators on behalf of nonacademic personnel (secretaries, maintenance, and so on). As worries over job security and inflation continue, gains of unionized employees are receiving more attention from nonunion faculty on the same campus. The acceptance of unions by nonacademics, whether off-campus or on, may thus coincide with environmental pressures to sway hesitant aca-demics toward unionization.

Three national organizations are now competing for rep-resentation rights: the American Association of University Pro-fessors (AAUP), the American Federation of Teachers (AFT), and the National Education Association (NEA). Each has cer-tain attractions. As the traditional spokesman of the profes-soriate, the AAUP has only recently endorsed collective bargain-ing as a tactic to accomplish its objectives.

The NEA, while primarily the spokesman for public sec-ondary education, has committed nearly two million dollars toward organization efforts in higher education. It has won more representation elections than both of its competitors com-bined and hopes to attract more academicians by playing up its acclaimed political clout.

The AFT, the smallest and most militant of the three nationals, has also committed increased resources to unionizing higher education. One of its chief selling points is its early suc-cess in winning bargaining elections. In 1973-1974, for example, the union won eleven out of twenty elections and raised its campus membership from 26,000 to 35,000. Another strong point is the political clout of its mammoth affiliate, the 13.6

million member AFL-CIO. The AFT president, Albert Shanker, is a leading spokesman for teacher unionism and a skilled political strategist.

Prior to the bargaining activity of the 1970s, the membership of each of these organizations was strikingly different. The AAUP had its greatest membership strength in universities, the NEA in four-year colleges growing out of teacher-training schools, and the AFT in urban colleges and two-year public community colleges. Interestingly, a large percentage of professors at the most prestigious institutions were not members of any of the unions or associations. (See Ladd and Lipset, 1973, Chapter Four.) With the advent of bargaining and the growing competition to win elections, the three organizations have had to appeal to many academics not previously included among their members.

Although there has been talk of merger between the NEA and AFT—perhaps even including the AAUP—differences in philosophy will probably not allow such a move in the near future. However, philosophical clashes are diminishing. Ladd and Lipset have concluded that the tendency in contested elections for competitors to assure the faculty electorate they can do everything their rivals can do, only better, "suggests an inherent pressure toward the eventual merger of all three into one academic union" (1973, p. 106). This merger will not occur overnight, however; higher education is too diverse, bargaining too new, and the organizations too optimistic.

The organizational campaigns of the NEA, the AFT, and the AAUP are stimulating the growth of unionization in higher education. Economically hard-pressed faculty are naturally impressed with the potential pressure these national organizations can place on campus administrations through collective bargaining and on legislatures through lobbying. For example, after an in-depth study at the University of Massachusetts in 1973, Semas noted that "it is unlikely that unease would have been translated into a collective bargaining election . . . if MTA [Massachusetts Teacher Association, the state affiliate of the NEA] organizers had not come on to the campus" (p. 8). Starting with the names of ten Massachusetts faculty members, MTA organizers built an organization in less than two years that nearly won the election to be the exclusive bargaining representative of all University of Massachusetts academic employees. After its narrow defeat, it went right back to work building support for the future.

With increasingly hostile environmental pressures coming to bear on educational institutions, organizing will become easier, not harder. Unions are becoming more self-confident and are more inclined to take hard-nosed positions in the hopes of attracting supporters than ever before.

Institutional Causes

The causes of faculty unionization that originate in the world beyond the campus explain the *general* tendency toward unionization, but they do not explain why any *specific* institution unionizes or why any *specific* individual joins a union. For example, it is quite possible to have a permissive legal environment—such as that offered by the federal National Labor Relations Act—but still have no effort to form unions. This is the situation among the most elite colleges and universities, many of whom are covered by the NLRA. The sense of community present at many of these small campuses and relatively high faculty morale make it unlikely that they will abandon their professional values and traditional governance practices despite harsh economic pressures and permissive legislation. Thus, in addition to environmental conditions, institutional factors are extremely significant in the move toward unionization.

Faculties at some institutions are more likely to favor unions than others. Both the 1969 Carnegie survey and the 1971 Stanford study illustrate that support for unions is strongest at less prestigious institutions. In the Carnegie study, 68 percent of respondents at two-year colleges disagree with the statement, "Collective bargaining by faculty members has no place in a college or university." At top research and doctorate-granting institutions, 53 percent of the faculty disagree (*Governance of Higher Education*, 1973, pp. 92-93). In the more recent Stanford survey, the percentage breakdown of faculty agreement (by various types of institutions) with the statement, "The most effective way for faculty to have meaningful influence over decisions on this campus is to organize as a group and negotiate collectively," is shown in Table 4.* Overall, about 35 percent of the respondents agree with the statement.

A number of institutional characteristics correlate with interest in faculty collective bargaining. Only 30 percent of the faculty of private colleges and universities favor unions—about half the rate of local community colleges (item 2) and three fifths of the rate of publicly funded institutions at large (item 3). Private colleges and universities report less interference by outside groups (legislatures, trustees, special interest groups, and other outsiders) than public institutions, and these low interference institutions have few faculty favoring unionism (item 7).

Another cluster of characteristics is associated with fewer faculty favoring unions—a "quality" dimension, for lack of a better term. Institutions are likely to have lower pro-union sentiment if they are very selective in their choice of students (item 4), wealthy in income per student (item 6), older and well established (item 5), and have a high percentage of Ph.D. recipients among their faculty (item 9).

Some factors are clearly associated with pro-union attitudes. Public institutions have more pro-union faculty (about 49 percent) than private colleges and universities (30 percent), but significant differences occur among types of public institutions. Item 2 shows that 38 percent of the faculty in state-supported colleges and universities favor unions but that those

---

*Note that in the Stanford study the respondent had to answer questions as they pertained to his or her campus and not generally in higher education, as is true of most other surveys such as the Carnegie Commission study referred to above. We suspect that some persons might be more favorable to the general idea of unions than to having faculty unions on their own campuses. This difference may account for the discrepancies in these survey results. That pro-union sentiment has grown enormously since the 1971 Stanford study is evidenced by a spring 1975 survey by E. C. Ladd, Jr., and S. M. Lipset. Seven out of every ten faculty members they sampled say they would vote for a collective bargaining agent if an election were held on their campus (*The Chronicle of Higher Education*, Sept. 15, 1975, p. 2).

Table 4
Impact of Institutional Characteristics on Faculty Attitudes
Toward Collective Negotiations

	Percentage Who Agree Collective Negotiations Are Most Effective Way for Faculty to Influence Campus Decisions
1. *Type of Institution*	
Private Multiversity (N = 6)	27
Public Multiversity (N = 13)	28
Elite Liberal Arts (N = 25)	24
Public Comprehensive (N = 40)	35
Public Colleges (N = 16)	36
Private Liberal Arts (N = 85)	29
Community Colleges (N = 96)	55
Private Junior College (N = 19)	37
2. *Formal Control*	
State (N = 109)	38
Local (N = 44)	60
State/Local (N = 12)	57
Private (N = 135)	30
3. *Funding Source*	
Public (N = 138)	49
Church (N = 26)	29
Tuition (N = 88)	30
Dispersed (N = 48)	29
4. *Selectivity Scale*	
Very Selective (N = 78)	29
Medium (N = 80)	32
Least Selective (N = 142)	47
5. *Institutional Age*	
Old (N = 101)	28
Medium (N = 99)	34
Young (N = 100)	51
6. *Affluence:* Income/# students	
Wealthy (N = 79)	28
Medium (N = 84)	32
Poor (N = 78)	47
7. *Amount of External Influence*	
High Interference (N = 101)	48
Medium (N = 102)	36
Low Interference (N = 97)	31
8. *Highest Degree Offered by the Institution*	
Ph.D. (N = 32)	31
Master's (N = 56)	31
Bachelor's (N = 94)	31
Associate (N = 118)	50

	Percentage Who Agree Collective Negotiations Are Most Effective Way for Faculty to Influence Campus Decisions
9. *Percentage Faculty Holding Ph.D.*	
High (N = 60)	30
Medium (N = 83)	30
Low (N = 157)	46
10. *Total Number of Faculty*	
Large: 300 +	37
Medium: 75-299	37
Small: 0-75	40

in community colleges (local and state/local control) jump to nearly 60 percent. This high pro-union sentiment in community colleges is seen again in items 1 and 9. Thus, although public institutions have more pro-union faculty than private, the community colleges have more than state colleges and universities.

External influence is also associated with union sentiment. Faculty perceptions about external influence may not be accurate, but their perceptions nevertheless determine whether they will press for unionization. From a low of 31 percent pro-union faculty in institutions where they perceive little outside interference, the figure rises to 48 percent in institutions perceived as having high external influence. To some degree at least, faculty members see unionism as a defense against outside environmental pressures.

Finally, institutional size does not seem to be systematically related to union sentiments. We suspect that the many small liberal arts colleges not inclined to unionism are balanced by many small pro-union community colleges; medium and large institutions are also roughly split between public and private and low and high quality. In short, the size of an institution is little help in predicting the union attitudes of faculty.

From Table 4, a fairly clear profile emerges of the institutional features associated with faculty collective bargaining. In general, institutions are more inclined to faculty collective negotiations if (1) they are public rather than private; (2) they are community colleges rather than state colleges or universities; (3)

their faculties have fewer Ph.D.s and their admissions policies are not selective; (4) they are not wealthy in terms of income per student and are more recently established; (5) they experience more interference by outside authorities. This portrait clearly fits two-year colleges and the less prestigious state colleges—institutions where most faculty unionization has occurred.

Union Sentiment by Institutional Type. If we combine the eight types of institutions in item 1 of Table 4 into four major categories, these characteristics of union-prone schools are revealed*:

Multiversities are at the high end of the scale in relation to virtually all of the institutional characteristics. Faculty members within them are usually the best educated, as measured by percentage of doctorates, those with the highest salaries and professional esteem, and those with a good measure of autonomy. These institutions tend to be long established, to receive consistently substantial funding, and to have strong tradition of faculty participation in governance at both the departmental and institutional level. As one would expect, few have faculty unions. Of the 270 unionized institutions in the 1974 Stanford survey, only twelve could be classified as multiversities. They include the main campus of the University of Hawaii, Rutgers University, Temple University, and CUNY and SUNY.

A high percentage of the faculty is inclined toward collective bargaining at *public colleges and universities*. Such schools experienced their greatest growth during the boom times of the

---

*The Carnegie Commission on Higher Education has devised a complex system of categorizing institutions. The complete system is much too elaborate for our purposes, so we simplified it into eight, and then later to four, basic types: Multiversities: public multiversities—large, prestigious public universities; private multiversities—large, prestigious private universities. Public colleges and universities: public comprehensives—medium-sized institutions which offer the master's degree, often the doctorate; public colleges—small state colleges offering primarily the bachelor's degree (often former teachers colleges). Liberal arts colleges: elite liberal arts colleges—high-quality, high-prestige private institutions; liberal arts colleges—average liberal arts private institutions. Two-year colleges: public community colleges; private junior colleges.

1950s and 1960s, and they are most affected by the arrival of the no-growth era. Worried faculty, many of them younger and nontenured, are more likely to unionize at this level.

Few elite *liberal arts institutions* are threatened with unionization, since they, like multiversities, are high-status and high-reward institutions. However, the less prestigious liberal arts colleges, such as Hofstra University, are seriously threatened by rising costs and declining enrollments. Although most faculty members at liberal arts colleges consider themselves relatively privileged, they are more likely to fear deteriorating conditions as harassed administrators try to cope with both a no-growth era and the uncompetitive position of their schools vis-à-vis low-tuition state institutions. Unionization can be expected to increase at these institutions if their position in higher education continues to deteriorate.

Although unionism has proceeded slowly at *private junior colleges,* it has realized its greatest growth at *public community colleges*—the institutions most likely to be locally controlled and funded, to be recently established, and to be the most susceptible to pressures from the community. Their faculties are young and aggressive, many having come from elementary and secondary school teaching jobs. All of these characteristics are strongly related to faculty unionization. (See Aussieker, 1975.) Only about 15 percent of all faculty in higher education are employed in two-year institutions, yet they account for more than 30 percent of all individual union members and over 60 percent of all unionized campuses.

Weaknesses of Faculty Governance Structures. One final issue in the institutional causes of unionization remains to be discussed—whether weak academic senates have helped create conditions ripe for faculty collective bargaining. At many institutions, weak faculty governance bodies have been unable to safeguard faculty interests from the onslaught of economically related environmental pressures. The 1974 Stanford survey asked presidents of nonunionized institutions to rate the influence of their senate on several issues. The results by institutional type are in Table 5. These are the perceptions of campus presidents, who "are more euphoric about the performance

Table 5
Presidents' Perceptions of Senate Influence on Nonunionized Campuses

	Admissions Policy	Degree Requirements	Curriculum	Department Budgets	Long-Range Planning	Faculty Hiring Policies	Faculty Promotions and Tenure Policies	Faculty Working Conditions	Faculty Salaries and Fringe Benefits
Multiversities (N = 11)	2.6	3.0	3.3	1.2	3.1	2.5	3.4	1.7	2.0
Public Colleges and Universities (N = 26)	3.0	3.9	4.1	2.0	3.1	2.6	3.8	2.3	2.5
Liberal Arts Colleges (N = 50)	3.1	4.4	4.4	2.0	3.1	2.8	3.0	2.9	2.0
Two-Year Colleges (N = 22)	2.4	3.6	3.8	2.3	3.0	2.7	2.6	3.1	2.7

Note: The question asked was "How much influence does the faculty senate have on these issues, at your institution?" The respondents gave answers on a five-point scale, with "1" indicating low influence and "5" indicating high influence.

and potential of campus senates than those who are directly involved in these bodies on a daily and weekly basis," according to Hodgkinson (1974, p. 175). In any case, the influence profiles of faculty senates as perceived by presidents at all types of nonunionized institutions are striking enough to warrant inclusion here. The profiles clearly demonstrate that senates are weakest in those very areas currently of greatest concern to faculty members. The presidents report that senates are heavily involved in such academic issues as degree requirements and curriculum. Issues of faculty promotion are also strongly influenced by senates except in two-year colleges, which tend to follow the secondary school model where school administrators control personnel policy. In economic areas such as faculty salaries, department budgets, and faculty workload, senates are given far lower ratings.

Results from the 1974 Stanford survey also show that those institutions most likely to unionize are the most likely to have formed a senate recently. Under the influence of environmental pressures, a new faculty body may find its role in shared governance easily reduced. A professor active in senate affairs at Central Michigan University has noted, "We became aware that the enjoyment of many of the benefits of our hard-won battles was at the pleasure of the Board of Trustees."

Over 60 percent of senates in the Stanford samples of nonunion and unionized institutions include administrative representatives, nearly 50 percent include students, and almost a third include nonacademic staff. Since the energy of broad-based senates is necessarily dispersed to deal with campuswide problems, faculty interests cease to be a primary concern.

These weaknesses of senates in relation to faculty welfare support earlier data. In 1969, the Carnegie Commission asked faculty members to indicate the effectiveness of their senates; 60 percent of the 60,000 respondents answered "fair" or "poor" (*Governance*, 1973, pp. 98-99). In Hodgkinson's study of 688 broad-based senates, campus presidents frequently rated the influence of the senate in campus affairs as "advisory" or as having "no responsibility at all" and stressed their "possibility of access" to decision-making channels instead of their role in "shared governance" (1974, pp. 29, 136). A 1971 AAUP study of institutions with member chapters found little effective faculty participation in governance. Both chief administrative officers and chapter presidents tended to categorize faculty participation as "discussion" or "consultation." Neither could claim joint participation with the administration in decision making, much less the right to resolve issues unilaterally. This lack of effectiveness was particularly true in terms of economic and personnel issues. (See Garbarino, 1975, Chapter Three.)

Because academics are seriously concerned over economic issues and job security, many faculties are interested in organizations that can effectively represent their interests as employees. Unions, unlike senates, do not depend on the grace of the governing board and the administration in representing employee interests. The trend toward faculty collective bargaining at some institutions appears to be shaped by weak senates, as well as by concerns over job security and salary levels.

Individual Causes

Environmental pressures and institutional characteristics are not the only factors that influence faculty unionization, of course. The decision to join a union is an individual one, and some individuals are more inclined to embrace collective bargaining than others. Several individual characteristics that affect this decision are shown in Table 6.

Slightly more than one third of the respondents indicate on the 1971 Stanford survey that unionization is the best way to influence decision making on their campus. In terms of educational attainment, the least likely to endorse this position hold the highest degrees—only about 30 percent of those with professional or doctoral degrees agreed with the statement. In contrast, 57 percent of those with only a high school diploma take this position, while roughly 40 percent of those holding associate, bachelor's, and master's degrees agree.

Almost the same progression of support for the statement is evident by professional rank. The most supportive are academic faculty at two-year institutions (55 percent); the least supportive are full professors (27 percent).

Table 6
Characteristics of Faculty Urging Collective Negotiation
on Their Campuses

	Percentage
1. *Degree Earned*	
High School	57
Associate	39
Bachelor's	41
Master's	43
Professional	29
Ph.D., Ed.D.	30
2. *Rank*	
Professor	27
Associate Professor	33
Assistant Professor	36
Instructor	42
Lecturer	47
Two-Year Voc/Tech	52
Two-Year Academic	55
No Rank	38
3. *Age*	
Under 30	62
31-40	51
41-50	34
51-60	22
61 and Over	14
4. *Sex*	
Males	38
Females	31
5. *Subject Matter Area*	
Humanities	40
Natural Science	31
Social Science	36
Professional	30
Voc/Tech	44
Other	38

In terms of age, 62 percent of those under 30 support unionization on their campus. Support for campus unionization declines in a straight line progression as age increases—down to 14 percent for those over age 61.

In terms of subject-matter areas, more academicians in vocational-technical fields, in the humanities, and in the social sciences support faculty collective bargaining (44, 40, and 36 percent, respectively) than those in the natural sciences and professions (31 and 30 percent, respectively). As previously discussed, vocational-technical educators have the lowest level of academic preparation and the lowest rank within higher education, characteristics most closely related to union support. The enthusiasm for collective bargaining among humanities and social sciences faculties is best explained by Ladd and Lipset (1973). In general, their findings agree with ours on such issues as age, rank, subject matter, and so on. However, they measured a factor that we did not measure, for they link the background and political ideology of academicians to their field of study: "The differences among fields are not solely related to experience in the discipline; the fields vary in the kind of students and practitioners they attract. Thus, the 'politically relevant' social sciences, concerned with social problems, have recruited from the more liberal segment of undergraduates; whereas at the other extreme, professional fields that relate directly to the business world, such as engineering, business administration, and colleges of agriculture, draw upon the more conservative students. . . . Together, these factors contribute to the formation of distinctive subcultures" (p. 40).

Although the most liberal academicians—those attracted to the humanities and social sciences—strongly support unions, as of yet they are not actually joining unions. Instructors in vocational-technical institutions, however, do join. This difference probably exists because most liberal professors are often located at the elite institutions. The professional values they hold coupled with the rewards they receive offset the strong ideological push toward collective bargaining. "Professors at upper-tier schools, and highly achieving academics in general, are significantly cross-pressured with regard to faculty unionism: their liberalism would incline them to support it; but their objective interests and the general structure of their academic values bring them into opposition. And . . . *the latter considerations typically prove decisive*" (italics in original; Ladd and Lipset, 1973, p. 32).

Individual characteristics alone do not, therefore, explain the move toward collective bargaining. It is possible to believe in unions but refuse to join one. Alternatively, one can have a lukewarm attitude toward collective bargaining in general but be very involved in the union movement because of environmental and institutional conditions. Such a special set of circumstances describes precisely what happened in the early stages of unionization in American higher education.

Although a combination of environmental, institutional, and individual characteristics influence professors to join unions, and subtly influence the attitudes and emotions of faculty members, attitudes such as trust and satisfaction also relate to professors' desires for unionization. Respondents to the Stanford survey are considered "high trust" if they answered "yes" to three or more of the following questions dealing with trust in the administration:

(1) In general, the top administration of this institution is competent, able, and energetic.

(2) If faced with a major campus disturbance, the administration would be likely to give in to outside pressures even if the actions were unpopular with the faculty.

(3) In general, the administration has a very progressive attitude about faculty welfare in terms of salary and working conditions.

(4) Generally, the administration understands the needs of academic professionals and works hard to make this a place where academics can work productively.

(5) Communication between the faculty and administration at this institution is usually open, easy, and effective.

Intuitively, a hypothesis would be that *the higher the trust, the lower the desire for unionization.* In fact, correlations run about 0.5 between the various indicators of trust and the desire for unionization. Of those with *low trust,* 51 percent want to unionize; among those with *high trust,* about 20 percent urge collective bargaining. Simply stated, when faculty members have little confidence in their administrators, they are likely to turn to unions for help.

In a similar vein, several questions were designed to measure satisfaction with working conditions. Professors were asked to state their feelings about their salaries, the quality of their students and faculty colleagues, and the adequacy of facilities such as offices and laboratories. Correlations run about 0.4 to 0.5 between various measures of satisfaction and the desire for unionization. Again, the link is clear: *the lower the satisfaction with working conditions, the higher the desire for unionization.*

As might be expected, the levels of trust in administrators and satisfaction with working conditions vary sharply by type of institution. In the high-prestige multiversities, professors generally trust their administrators, and with good reason. Administrators are often faculty members who have the financial resources to provide good working conditions (63 percent reported high overall trust, and 77 percent reported high satisfaction).

In the public colleges and universities, the level of overall trust (60 percent) and satisfaction (58 percent) is lower, a predictable response when resources are tighter and outside pressures are stronger. Responses from the liberal arts colleges are split; the elite ones have trusting, satisfied faculty, but the average and below average schools are characterized by considerable dissatisfaction and distrust.

The two-year colleges have the biggest problems: about 49 percent of their faculty report high satisfaction and 55 percent high trust—rates that are significantly lower than at other colleges. Clearly, professors in community colleges feel the environmental pressures and the institutional constraints, and the result is quite obvious. The dissatisfactions at the two-year colleges are coupled with the greatest desire for unionization in higher education. In the 1971 survey, over 56 percent of respondents from community colleges urge collective negotiations on their campus, compared to about 25-35 percent from most other types of institutions.

Explanations of Unionism: Preservation and Enfranchisement

Faculty unions seem to appeal to two different faculty groups—those who are "preservation" oriented and those who consider themselves "deprived." The first are essentially high-status professors who, like their skilled counterparts in the industrial sector, have realized that their rights and privileges within the institution can no longer be safeguarded by tradition alone. The second—the "deprivation" group—are those who view collective bargaining as a means to gain power and benefits previously denied them. Like the semi- and unskilled workers in the industrial sector, they view collective bargaining as a means of enfranchisement. On some campuses, professors seek to preserve past gains (preservation); on others, they aspire to achieve parity with the more privileged (enfranchisement). So far, collective bargaining has primarily fulfilled the second function.

If environmental pressures continue to affect higher education adversely, the small number of preservation-oriented faculty who have turned to unions may grow. The percentage of faculty who fall into the preservation category is probably less than 10 percent of all faculty. These academicians are usually tenured faculty at institutions experiencing severe economic strains. Such strains often result in administrative action detrimental to previous patterns of faculty participation in governance and to faculty institutional rights and privileges. For example, the selection of the AAUP chapter as the faculty's bargaining agent at St. John's University in 1970, and at the University of Delaware in 1972, stemmed in part from economic concerns and in part from hostile administrative action against the faculty.

Collective bargaining has come very slowly to those institutions where faculty influence has been strong and where faculty rights have been secure. Throughout the era of faculty collective negotiations, most union defeats have occurred at private institutions. One explanation for the defeats is, of course, that these institutions were not ripe for unionization. The AAUP, in particular, has been criticized for allowing local chapters to request elections on campuses where the faculty was not sufficiently primed. By 1975, however, there were indications that the slow growth of unionization in the private sector might be a thing of the past. The union movement scored a major victory when the Boston University faculty selected a bargaining agent in the spring of that year.

As more and more tenured faculty see their economic

benefits eaten away by inflation, or as they lose power through administrative action in response to hostile environmental pressures, preservation unionism will probably become increasingly common. Such a trend is clearly indicated by the rapid expansion of the Faculty Association at the University of California, Berkeley, and the national attention it has attracted. Conflict between the Berkeley senate and the administration, primarily over budget cutbacks, resulted in a recommendation from a special Berkeley senate subcommittee in 1972 that the senate postpone affiliation with any established bargaining organization. Instead, the subcommittee suggested that a separate entity be established independent of the institutionally sponsored senate but limited to its members (1700 of the 5400 academic employees at the institution). Although the state law prohibited a faculty union, the Faculty Association became a "shadow" union—waiting for favorable legislation so that it could take action. By the summer of 1973, the Faculty Association had more than filled the minimum requirement it had set of 400 members, the largest number of dues-paying members of any faculty organization on any single University of California campus.

The chief competitor of the Faculty Association, the AFT local at Berkeley, has also aimed to fulfill the preservation function. It seeks support from the Berkeley senate ("The Academic Senate and Unionism," AFT recruitment flyer): "The AFT seeks a collective bargaining agreement with the Regents that will strengthen the senate. Through a negotiated contract, the AFT seeks to make the senate a contractually authorized body. The senate would no longer be dependent on the discretion of the administration or Regents, who now decide whether to consult it or accept its advice, or even consult it at all. . . . At the same time the AFT . . . strengthens the senate, it will advance the interests of academic employees in those areas where the senate is not an appropriate mechanism."

The second category of academicians embracing collective bargaining are the "have-nots" of the profession: those who are nontenured; those teaching at newly emerged public institutions, especially community colleges where faculty power, rights, and privileges are less than in the longer-established four-year and graduate institutions; and women, members of minority groups, and nonteaching professionals—all of whom have long faced discrimination.

For these academicians, collective bargaining, as an enfranchisement function, is a way to gain influence over governance patterns and secure greater economic and professional benefits. It is among these disadvantaged faculty members that collective bargaining has experienced its most rapid acceptance. Since the majority of academicians make up the "deprived" category, collective bargaining is most likely to be advocated as an enfranchising force by those seeking to spread unionism in higher education.

Profile of Union Advocate

By combining the major institutional and individual determinants of faculty unionization, we come up with an interesting profile of the faculty member most inclined to join a union. In general, he or she will (1) teach at a two-year community college or four-year public institution with no tradition of strong faculty participation in institutional governance; (2) have a degree short of the doctorate and be nontenured; (3) teach in the humanities or social science field; (4) be less than 40 years of age and male; (5) have a greater teaching load and lower salary than academics at four-year/graduate institutions; (6) have a record of little participation in a campus senate or similar body; (7) have low trust in the campus administration and be dissatisfied with working conditions (i.e., have low morale); (8) be conscious of the benefits of unions on other campuses and of the nonacademic level on his own campus. Admittedly, these characteristics are subjective. As external demands change, they will affect institutions and individuals differently, thereby altering the profile. For example, dramatic cutbacks in public support for higher education could change academics from union-sympathizers to union-joiners. Local conditions also have a strong influence on who votes for a union.

As a summary of all these factors, Table 7 relates external

Table 7
Factors Promoting and Hindering Unionism

	Promoting	Hindering
Environmental	Economic Crisis	Federal and State Funding Programs
	Market Conditions	
	Population Decline	High Priority for Education
	Egalitarian Revolution	Economic Stabilization
	Increased Cost of Living	Antiunion Locality
	External Controls	Restrictive Legal Climate
	Legislative Priorities	
	Standardized Management Systems	
Institutional	Large Size	Research Orientation
	Low Salaries	High Salaries
	Less than Baccalaureate Program	Graduate Level Programs
		Job Security
	High Teaching Loads	High Morale
	Low Morale and Satisfaction	Effective Senates
	Arbitrary Administration	High Peer Judgment
	Weak Senates and Faculty Committees	Effective Professionalism
Individual	Low Education	Advanced Education
	Low Rank	High Rank
	Young	Old
	Humanities or Social Science Discipline	Hard Science or Professional Field
	Liberal Ideology	Conservative Ideology
Triggering	Specific Problems on Campus	No Triggering Problems
Events	Changes in Law	No Permissive Legislation
	Help from Organized Labor	No Help from Industrial Labor
	Active Union	No Active Union
Result	Collective Bargaining	No Collective Bargaining

environment, institutional characteristics, and individual factors to each other. Not only do environmental pressures affect institutional and individual factors, but they also help to determine the pace of unionization.

We believe that these dynamic forces will accelerate and support the spread of unionization among higher education faculty members. Obviously, the factors may drastically shift at some future point. In particular, the economic situation could change quickly. While we believe that the factors listed above will continue for the foreseeable future, the rate of unionization may fluctuate considerably. There may be a slowdown when most of the fertile areas for unionization have been exhausted—the community colleges for example. Moreover, faculty resistance to unionization in prestige institutions may grow substantially as it becomes apparent that contracts are likely to be more favorable to the less prestigious sector of higher education. That is to say, there may be a professional backlash against unionization as the content of contracts becomes widely publicized. The reverse is also possible—faculty elites may find unionization less of a threat to professionalism than they once anticipated.

In spite of likely fluctuations, however, we believe that the long-term prognosis is for substantial faculty unionization. The greatest potential for future expansion lies in four-year public institutions, particularly those that are system-related. Not only do the latter contain over half of all full-time faculty, they are more likely to unionize. Garbarino (1975) notes that three times as many institutions in comprehensive systems are organized than their percentage in the total population would indicate. An added growth factor is the continuing increase in the number of campuses being included within systems of education. We note frequently in this text that centralization and collective bargaining are compatible bedfellows. As a result, collective bargaining will almost certainly be a major force in the governance of higher education.

Factors that Shape
Campus Bargaining

■■
■■

Our discussion of the causes of unions in higher education—the social, institutional, and individual factors that promote the growth and expansion of faculty unionization—now leads us to an examination of "critical determinants" of campus bargaining. What are the forces that shape the course of collective bargaining at particular institutions? These forces must be identified before the form of faculty unionization and its consequences for academic governance can be determined.

We can identify six basic issues involved in campus bargaining and ask: What institutions will be in the bargaining unit? What will be the personnel composition? Which union will represent the faculty? Will it have union "security" protection? What issues will be bargainable? What sanctions can the parties use in their struggle over the issues? These questions are largely sequential, and the solution to one can affect the next question. For example, if the bargaining unit is to represent all campuses in a complex system, a union with support on only one or two campuses will probably not win the right to be the bargaining agent. Further, if the allowable scope of bargaining is extremely wide, the allowable sanctions, such as strikes or lockouts, are

70

generally restricted. In this chapter, we will discuss each of these interrelated issues in turn.

Geographic Scope of Bargaining Unit

The first issue directly affects the other ones, as well as the outcomes of bargaining. Will the union be restricted to one campus, or will it represent an entire state system? Will the union include community colleges and senior institutions in the same unit? Will there be more than one faculty bargaining unit in the state? These questions are critical to the shape unionization assumes in higher education, and major disagreements have revolved around proposed solutions.

The unit question sometimes is resolved informally, even when the law does not provide for unionization. An example occurred in 1966, when, in the absence of a state collective bargaining law, the Chicago City College administration recognized the Cook County College Teachers Union as the exclusive representative of its full-time teaching faculty. In most cases, however, the unit question is resolved by the National Labor Relations Board (NLRB) for private institutions or by a state public employee relations board (PERB) for public institutions. Decision making in both instances is generally based on three criteria: (1) community of interest among the employees; (2) efficiency of organizational functioning; and (3) the history of representation in the industry or field (Shaw and Clark, 1971).

In the public sector, employers prefer large bargaining units because fragmentation causes serious problems. Multiple small units often produce "whipsawing," where achieving large gains from an employer in one unit then becomes a precedent for demanding equal benefits from the same employer in all other units. In addition, with several bargaining units, it is difficult to maintain uniform benefits and working conditions at various campuses. Some state laws direct administering agencies to avoid fragmentation of bargaining units. For example, the Wisconsin State Employment Labor Relations Act reads: "It is the express legislative intent that in order to foster meaningful collective bargaining, units must be structured in such a way as to *avoid excessive fragmentation whenever possible.*" (Wisc. Stat. Ann., #11.80-.97. Supp., 1973; italics added.)

Because most private colleges or universities are composed of a single campus, geographic extent is usually not a problem for these institutions. As a general rule, however, the NLRB has decided that professional schools (such as law and medicine) which seek separate representation should not be lumped together with the rest of the university because their faculties have different interests—not the least of which is higher levels of pay. Although state PERBs prefer large multicampus units, they differ on whether to separate colleges within a university. For example, the Pennsylvania PERB separated the law, medical, and dental schools at Temple University in 1972, whereas in the same year, the Michigan board ruled that the medical faculty at Wayne State University be included with the total university faculty.

In studying various institutions, the Stanford project illustrates that decisions about the geographic extent of bargaining units extend along a continuum and points out some of the problems caused by units of different sizes.

Single Campus Unit Determinations. At Hofstra University and at Central Michigan, the unit determinations by the NLRB and the Michigan PERB were limited to a single campus. (The Hofstra unit does not include the law school, and Central Michigan has no professional schools.) Because it conforms to the preexisting organizational structure, a single campus unit creates no special problems.

Horizontal Multicampus. The administration and the AAUP bargaining agent agreed and the New Jersey PERB concurred that the bargaining unit for Rutgers University should include all faculty members on all three campuses—Camden, Newark, and New Brunswick. This determination provides an example of a horizontal multicampus unit since all three components of the institution are similar.

In the case of a horizontal multicampus, union support from only one or two campuses within a system makes it foolhardy to try to win an election over all the campuses. The obvious union strategy is to first achieve a campus-by-campus determination, and then to try to gain control over the whole system gradually. The six-campus New Jersey State College system illustrates such a strategy. Originally, the New Jersey Public Employment Commission decided on a campus-by-campus unit determination, only to have an NEA affiliate win elections on all six campuses and then negotiate for a uniform systemwide contract as a coalition. In 1973, the commission reversed its prior determination and formed a systemwide unit. With horizontal multicampuses, it is important to keep in mind that *winning union elections is easy where the units and the diversity of interests among employees are small. Conversely, where units are large and include many employees, only experienced powerful unions with wide bases of support are likely to win.*

Vertical Multicampus. The bargaining unit for the City University of New York (CUNY), which includes two-year institutions as well as four-year, graduate, and professional schools, is an example of a vertical multicampus unit. Although the extent of this unit was not contested by the parties and was accepted by the New York PERB, its structure has been a source of friction.

The City University has operated as a system since 1926 and has included community colleges since 1955, but considerable diversity has remained among its member institutions. Beginning with the first contract negotiated in 1969, the CUNY union adhered to a now-familiar philosophy: *in large complex systems with units having differing working conditions, unions usually demand parity in benefits and workload throughout the system.* When the second contract was signed in the fall of 1973, economic parity had been substantially achieved: community college, four-year college, and university professors were equalized.

One highly placed official in the CUNY central office states that the administration "gave up the ship" by agreeing to parity for the community colleges. This official argues that homogenization in benefits and workload is inevitable where vertical-unit bargaining occurs since "the union cannot exist by recognition of individual merit." His viewpoint is contested by the faculty union (Professional Staff Congress), which strongly believes in parity. One union official writes: "What the PSC has achieved for community college personnel is a commitment to the equal treatment and professional recognition of every segment of the University staff, whether in two-year or four-year colleges. This principle will be applied in future negotiations in order to attain equality and equity for those CUNY staff members who still receive unfair treatment from the University administration" (Professional Staff Congress/CUNY *Clarion*, September 10, 1973).

The CUNY case illustrates an important consequence of large bargaining units—*a strong tendency toward institutional homogenization, toward "leveling" the distinctions between institutions and their professors.* The general trend of that leveling is clear—salaries and benefits are leveled "up" to the highest side, but qualifications and work standards are leveled "down" to the lowest common denominator. Although the CUNY union worked hard to equalize salaries for the community college professors, they did not support a move to require doctorates in the community colleges as well as in the four-year institutions and universities. The leveling process seems to work only on one side of the equation! As one rather embittered university professor said in an interview: "My degree is a hard-won Ph.D. in Economics, ten years at Princeton including bachelor's, master's, and doctorate degrees. My publication record is good, and I teach a full load. And under the union contract a community college teacher with a 'cheap' master's, one year beyond his bachelor's, from any two-bit teacher's college, will get approximately the same pay and benefits. In my opinion the outcome of the union contract is disgustingly unprofessional, even antiprofessional." The opposite opinion is expressed by community college faculty, who claim that they received less than their fair share of faculty benefits in the past relative to the work they performed.

The difficulty with evaluating the impact of leveling stems from conflicting values placed on community college teaching versus senior college teaching and research and on the importance of advanced training and education. Whether leveling is good or bad, it certainly is easy to see that it is a natural consequence of large bargaining units.

In contrast to the example of CUNY, there was disagreement from the start as to the geographic extent of the State University of New York (SUNY) unit. The community colleges were automatically excluded from the bargaining unit because of their relationships to local districts; this decision left a total of twenty-six campuses, ranging from four university centers to six two-year agricultural and technical colleges, in the unit. The State University Federation of Teachers (SUFT), an AFT organization, petitioned for a campus-by-campus determination, because SUFT support was localized, not systemwide. All other union groups preferred a single SUNY professional unit.

The New York PERB ruled in 1969 that the geographic extent of the SUNY unit would be systemwide. This decision, upheld by the State Supreme Court, prompted much criticism. One SUNY faculty member says: "SUNY was one University in many respects, but the terms and conditions of employment on one campus were often vastly different from the terms and conditions on another, and no one who looked carefully at SUNY could envision a single set of terms and conditions emerging in the near future from the new collective bargaining relationship" (Doh, 1974, p. 27).

Because of differences between campuses within SUNY, a few union officials believe the union should negotiate a *master contract* and then allow each campus to bargain over local conditions in a *secondary* contract. Most administrators in the SUNY central office disagree. As one person puts it: "A master contract-secondary contract arrangement creates *centers of conflict* at each campus because it proliferates bargaining. In addition, when disagreements and questions arise, they have to be settled at the central office anyway. Thus, we get the worst of both worlds, and the inevitable result is complication of both the bargaining and contract administration process. Centralized bargaining helps to keep tension and conflict on local campuses at a minimum. In collective bargaining, somebody has to be the bastard. With centralized bargaining, the enemy becomes the central administration, not the local campus president."

Although there has been much criticism of the all-encompassing SUNY unit, it has also been recognized that a large bargaining unit has a unifying effect on a fragmented system: "From the perspective of the employee, the single-unit designation has done more than any SUNY effort since formation of the conglomerate in 1948 to open lines of communication, one campus to another, and between local campuses and the central administration. Collective bargaining has resulted in communication, however much painful sometimes, and the vastly increased flow of information and opinion will be a unifying force in SUNY" (Doh, 1974, pp. 38-39).

The benefits of coordinating services and preventing bargaining fragmentation are appealing to some state officials. In addition, the unifying effect of centralized unions may be gaining the favor of both administrators and union chiefs.

A third example of a vertical multicampus is the unit determination in Hawaii, the largest one made to date. The state collective bargaining law declares that the higher education unit shall consist of "faculty of the University of Hawaii and the community colleges." Thus, the geographic extent of the unit can be classified as a statewide-vertical multicampus. It illustrates a serious implication of large units in general and vertical multicampus units in particular: *complex units create serious tensions between campuses and professors with different statuses, and can result in sacrificing the needs and desires of high status professionals to gain benefits for the "disadvantaged" majorities in the union.*

In the first certification election in 1972, no union received a majority, and a run-off was held between the AAUP-senate alliance and the AFT affiliate. In the second election, the AFT affiliate won by a vote of 995 to 805, primarily because the more militant community college faculty overwhelmed the main campus vote. On the main campus, the AAUP-senate alliance was the choice of the majority, 672 to 549. The Hilo campus, however, favored the AFT affiliate by a vote of 83 to 52, while the community colleges heavily supported the AFT affiliate 352 to 62 (see Seidman and others, 1974). As we will discuss in Chapter Five, this split between the main campus and the community colleges led to union favoritism toward the community colleges, a contract with no tenure provisions, a fight over management prerogatives, and the ouster of the AFT union. The complex, multileveled bargaining unit created many problems, not the least of which was conflict between the "elites" at the Honolulu campus and the "regulars" in the community colleges.

As these three examples show, no *one* geographic form is appropriate for all bargaining units. A variety of alternatives are open to the NLRB or state PERBs. Where multicampus systems exist, however, the tendency to date is to have multicampus unit determinations. The Stanford questionnaire responses of union chairpersons indicate that over 75 percent of unionized public college and university campuses are part of multicampus units. This percentage is not surprising, considering the recent trend toward centralization. Within the past decade, the number of multicampus institutions has increased several-fold; and, as we have noted, centralization promotes unionization. Interestingly, a majority of community college union chairpersons reports a single-campus unit. The desire to preserve local district control of community colleges is apparently stronger than recognizing ties to a public education system. CUNY and Hawaii are exceptions because they include community colleges with four-year institutions.

Several other conclusions about the geographic composition of bargaining units came out of the Stanford project research. A negotiation problem peculiar to public higher education is pinpointing the identity of the employer. This problem is complicated by large unit determinations because many issues, such as funding a negotiated wage increase, must ultimately be resolved by state officials. At CUNY, the union finds itself negotiating in three arenas: "Initially, we make the contact with our board of trustees. . . . Since a substantial portion of our funds still comes from the City of New York, we also talk with the city administration. In addition, many aspects of our contract require a working relation with New York State" (Zeller, 1972, p. 102).

At SUNY, negotiation is carried on between the union

and the Office of Employee Relations, a state agency responsible to the governor, even though one might have expected that bargaining would be between the union and the Chancellor's office, the SUNY Board of Trustees, or the Board of Regents that oversees educational development in the state. Asked if the nuances of academia are often lost on state officials at the expense of SUNY, an official in the Chancellor's office reported that state officials depend heavily on members of the Chancellor's staff and that the rapport with the administration during bargaining has been good to date. All these examples, however, point out an inescapable conclusion: *large complex bargaining units and direct state involvement with bargaining tend to drive administrative power upward since both union and administration seek to equalize power parallel to one another.* This tendency is potentially threatening to the traditional decentralized concept of shared governance as manifested in campus, senates, and councils.

Personnel Composition of Bargaining Unit

An integral part of the geographic extent issue is the personnel composition of the unit. When collective bargaining first began in higher education, some campus administrations tried to persuade administering agencies to exempt faculty from bargaining units. The argument was (and sometimes still is) that the faculty are essentially a part of college management because they serve on committees, participate in policy formulation through representative bodies, and help in personnel decision making. The contention was that they were supervisors, not employees. The opposing argument is that even where faculty do exercise supervisory prerogatives, they are still employees. Unlike other professionals, they do not set fees nor do they have much governance control in most institutions.

The issue is now moot because most laws and rulings include faculty in the bargaining units. Administering agencies in the public sector endorse the rationale first announced by the NLRB in its 1971 C. W. Post decision: "We are of the view that the policy making and quasi-supervisory authority which adheres to full-time faculty status but is exercised by them only as a group does not make them supervisors. . . . we find that full-time university faculty members qualify in every respect as professional employees and are therefore entitled to all the benefits of collective bargaining if they so choose."

Presently, the problem centers on which faculty members to include in the unit—teaching faculty, nonteaching academics (librarians, registrars), part-time academics, teaching assistants, department chairpersons, and/or nonacademic employees.

Teaching Faculty Versus Nonteaching Professionals. Should the unit be limited to teaching faculty or broadly defined to include all academic employees? Either way, the impact can be far-reaching. Although a broad-based unit reduces the employer's chances of being whipsawed by several units of academic employees, it is likely to increase tension within the unit. In addition, faculty membership differentials and status distinctions may be curtailed or eliminated under the pressure of union majority rule. Let us examine a case in point.

At SUNY, the New York PERB ruled in 1969 that one broad-based unit should include all 16,000 professional employees—teaching faculty as well as nonteaching academics (librarians, counselors, registrars, and so on). Although this ruling meant that the administration did not have to face pressure from many small units, it did create tension within the union amid charges of "leveling." Initially, the 3500 nonteaching professionals (NTPs) were the most deprived members of the unit. They had no job guarantee, low wages, long working commitments, and were subject to dismissal with no appeal. The SUNY faculty union (United University Professors, or UUP) worked hard for the NTPs, achieving what one commentator terms "extraordinary" results in securing a system of personnel administration equal to that of the teaching faculty (Garbarino, 1975, p. 246). But those results were not enough. By the summer of 1973, many in the NTP group were thoroughly dissatisfied with the union leadership. They found a ready ally in the Civil Service Employees Association (CSEA) that represents most of the nonprofessional employees at SUNY. Although CSEA petitioned to decertify UUP as the bargaining agent for nonteaching professionals, the challenge was defeated, and the United University Professors continues to represent both teaching faculty and nonteaching professionals.

The above example illustrates a particular problem for unions: The more diverse the membership, the harder it is to satisfy the needs of every component. It is generally said that under normal circumstances it is more difficult to negotiate with one's own side than with the opposition. A diverse union membership forces the leadership to spend an inordinate amount of time maintaining internal stability.

Part Time Versus Full Time. Should part-time academic personnel be included in a unit with full-time employees? The NLRB decided in 1973 that, contrary to earlier private sector rulings, part-timers should *not* be in the unit with full-timers.* Up to this time, the NLRB has not established guidelines for part-time faculty, preferring to proceed on a case-by-case course of decisions (see Finkin, 1974b). Since the rulings could foster fragmentation and a consequent proliferation of bargaining groups, the consequences may be extensive.

When part-time academicians are included in the bargaining unit, as at CUNY, the problems are obvious. Initially, the Board of Higher Education was the only party arguing for one unit to represent all academic employees in the CUNY system. The position of the Board was based on the understandable desire to avoid whipsawing by multiple units representing faculty and on its perception that the administrative and educational practices of the system dictated one unit. The New York PERB disagreed. In upholding its decision to split the faculty into two groups, the PERB concluded that "The faculty-rank-status personnel are at the heart of the university. It might be compromising to their independence and to the very stability of the university for nontenured instructional personnel [mostly

---

*The board decided at the same time that law professors should have a chance to vote against collective bargaining even if the rest of the university faculty votes for it. Under the same rationale, presumably other professional school faculties may be allowed the same option. Although no precedent has been set for public institutions, state PERBs tend to follow the lead of the more experienced NLRB.

part-time], in numbers almost equal to that of faculty-rank-status personnel to be included in the unit." Several years later, however, the "impossible" happened: the unions representing full-time faculty and part-time faculty combined. Completely reversing its previous position, the CUNY Board opposed the single union. Through a special election, City University faculty members overwhelmingly approved a single unit, a union in which traditional tenure-eligible classroom teachers were a definite minority.

The part-time faculty component of the union, however, has not fared well. Union leadership has been reluctant to endorse part-time employment, calling the use of part-time faculty "an economic policy, not an educational policy." The interests of part-timers were subordinated to those of the full-time faculty during the protracted 1973 contract negotiations— a fact apparently not lost on the administration. Israel Kugler, whose AFT union had represented part-time faculty prior to the merger, and who opposed ratification of the 1973 agreement, openly accused the administration of trying to destroy the union by promoting dissension within the ranks.

Why did the union not fight harder for the part-timers? To an extent, that question can be answered by considering their involvement in the union. In the democratic environment of a union, the majority is usually "deprived" in relation to the elite status groups. Since that majority can control the union, it follows that the most deprived control the union's objectives. At CUNY, however, part-time faculty represent about 5 percent of the union membership even though they are a large employment group. The lesson is that failure to join the union can keep control out of the hands of the disadvantaged.

Department Chairpersons. Another thorny question is whether department chairpersons should be included in the unit. As with part-timers, there is no pattern discernible in the public sector, but the NLRB has determined for the private sector that chairpersons are generally not supervisors and that they should be included in the bargaining unit unless the administration can offer substantial reasons to the contrary.

Again, events at CUNY provide a vivid example. Department chairpersons are included in the bargaining unit, primarily because they are elected by department members and not appointed by the administration. As a result, they face an identity crisis of major proportions—they are not sure whether they are administrative supervisors, faculty agents, or union shop stewards. In Chapter Seven, we explore the plight of the department chairperson in detail.

Data from our research point out several developing patterns, and Table 8 outlines the composition of faculty bargaining units at the seven case study institutions. Unit composition changes over time; despite initial limits restricting unionization to specified employees, there are constant pressures to change—to include or throw out part-timers, to welcome or push out student personnel experts. Moreover, the initial determination sometimes sidesteps tough issues, allowing the election and contract negotiations to continue without composition issues being resolved completely. At Hofstra, for example, the union and the administration were still contesting the inclusion of certain groups as late as 1974, after the contract had been signed and two years after the initial determinations had been made.

Table 8

Personnel Composition of Bargaining Unit at Seven Case Study Institutions
(April 1974)

	Teaching Faculty	Nonteaching Professionals	Department Chairpersons	Teaching Assistants	Part-time Academic Personnel
Central Michigan University	yes	yes[1]	yes	no	no
Chicago City College	yes	no	yes	no	no
City University of New York	yes	yes	yes	no	yes[2]
Hofstra University	yes	no	no	no	yes[2]
Rutgers University	yes	yes	yes	yes[3]	no
State University of New York	yes	yes	yes	no	yes[2]
University of Hawaii	yes	yes	yes	no	yes[2]

[1]Considered members of the teaching faculty.
[2]Primarily teaching.
[3]Coverage limited by contract.

From Table 8, it is obvious that units were broad in our case study institutions and that most contained personnel other than teaching faculty. The pattern of broad personnel inclusion is also evident in findings from the 1974 Stanford survey. For example, nearly 90 percent of all bargaining units include non-teaching professionals such as counselors, librarians, and registrars. Lesser numbers include part-time academicians, department chairpersons, and teaching assistants. *From the trend toward multicampus bargaining units and the inclusion of professionals besides teaching faculty, we conclude that the comprehensive bargaining unit has become a characteristic of collective bargaining in higher education.*

Bargaining Agent

As noted in Chapter Three, one factor promoting the growth of collective bargaining is the presence of experienced bargaining groups. Since the different philosophies and objectives of the AAUP, NEA, and AFT have been described in detail elsewhere (see Lussier, 1974b; Garbarino, 1975, Chapter Four) and are generally well known, we will not review them here. Suffice it to say that the AAUP has only recently endorsed collective bargaining as another means of securing its goals, though a number of its members disfavor it and hope to minimize its use. Both the NEA and the AFT have eagerly embraced the industrial model of collective bargaining. In addition to these organizations, a few faculties at single-campus private institutions and professional schools have opted for independent representation, usually a stepchild of the traditional governance structure. We know of no institutions that have selected a state civil service employee association to be their representative.

We contend that despite rhetoric to the contrary, *the different bargaining agents are becoming more alike in their operational goals and that their tactics and strategies will also grow to resemble each other.* For example, as the group many people consider a "different" union, the AAUP does not differ radically from other unions when it is elected to power.

The ability of the AAUP to be an effective bargaining

force is hampered by a number of forces. For one thing, during the first few years of faculty unionization, the AAUP had neither the desire nor the funds to mount effective campaigns on many campuses. Although its membership is large, even today it lacks the financial resources of its competitors; thus, it is somewhat handicapped in financing organizational campaigns and in servicing its chapters when they are elected as faculty bargaining agents. Further, its membership is heavily concentrated in four-year, prestigious institutions—schools whose faculty will probably be among the last to unionize. The association attracts few members from community colleges, from the relatively new four-year public institutions, and from the less visible private colleges and universities. In order to compete in unionization campaigns, the AAUP has recently broadened its membership base to encompass any professional employee included in a collective bargaining unit, yet this step has compounded a long-standing fear among traditional AAUP members that nonteaching professionals may come to control AAUP bargaining units.

Its history of lukewarm commitment to bargaining has cost the AAUP support. When some faculty first considered collective bargaining at Central Michigan University, they tried to interest the local AAUP chapter in the idea. Because this tactic proved fruitless, they then switched allegiance to the NEA. With NEA assistance, the CMU Faculty Association became the collective bargaining representative. A similar story can be told about the stirrings of faculty collective bargaining at CUNY and SUNY.

In recent years, the AAUP has strengthened its interest in collective bargaining and lobbying, but it has lost the support of some of its more traditional members. In 1974, the AAUP general secretary stated that the AAUP must become more involved in lobbying for state and federal funds, both alone and in alliance with other organizations. He emphasized that although these new union-like activities are important, collective bargaining is not necessarily "the wave of the future." Nevertheless, the growing commitment of the AAUP to bargaining and lobbying may jeopardize its chances to continue as philosophic spokesman for the profession.

Even as the AAUP has been shifting its stance, other forces have served to narrow the differences between unions. Spreading conflict across the higher education spectrum tends to drive wedges between administrators and faculty and to build bonds between the different unions. In addition, the gains one group of faculty achieves from collective bargaining are apt to influence faculties at other institutions even though they may be represented by different unions. As an administrator at Hofstra has commented, many Hofstra faculty members have their eyes on the accomplishments of the Professional Staff Congress at CUNY and hope to realize the same gains through their AAUP representation—even though Hofstra is a totally different institution from CUNY with limited resources.

The increasing number of large, all-encompassing bargaining units also makes it difficult to maintain philosophic differences, for prospective unions must appeal to a wide range of academic personnel in order to win and maintain bargaining agent status. At SUNY, the Senate Professional Association (SPA) was an outgrowth of the faculty senate. Initially, the SPA had planned to take a nonlabor union stance toward bargaining, but the association turned out to be little different from other unions (Doh, 1974, p. 37): "Experience—including such distasteful concerns as the workings of the grievance machinery, obvious adversary management-employee relationships, and pressures from members for kinds of improvement typical of cohesive bargaining demands—forced the SPA leadership, and much of the SPA membership, to realize that SPA's performance had not been really very much different from a 'union' performance, the kind of performance one would have expected from SUFT [an AFT union]. Whatever the distinction between SPA and SUFT might have been in campaign rhetoric, it did not materialize as SPA proceeded with the work of representing the 15,000 professionals."

Bargaining in multicampus systems is a formal and adversarial game played for high stakes. As a result, experts from outside the system assume a significant role. Further, large bargaining units in multicampus systems intensify the need for those broad-based unions to affiliate with statewide and national organizations. Failure to do so weakens their ability to apply pressure on the employer—who may be the state legislature. Thus, both the Professional Staff Congress at CUNY and the United University Professors at SUNY have multiple affiliations at the local and statewide levels. As Dr. Belle Zeller of the Professional Staff Congress said in an interview: "We have to have the muscle to safeguard higher education—to help management. Everything isn't always decided on its merit. Anyone who has ever had anything to do with lobbying knows this." As a result of the merger of the AFT and NEA in New York, the Professional Staff Congress can boast of an impressive list of affiliations: American Federation of Teachers (AFL-CIO Local 2334), National Education Association, New York City Central Labor Council, New York State AFL-CIO, and New York State United Teachers. Union leadership does not hesitate to point out that when it appears before city officials and the state legislatures, it speaks with a loud voice.

Although differences between unions appear to be narrowing, some groups resist the trend. Single-campus unions work hard to protect their independence and maintain characteristics distinct from unions affiliated with national organizations. Take, for example, faculty members at Central Michigan. They knew that without the financial support and the expertise of an outside source, they could not mount an effective unionization campaign. One faculty member describes the assistance of the NEA as follows (Hepler, 1971, p. 106): "The state and national organization sent representatives to the campus from Lansing, Detroit, and even Washington to speak in favor of [NEA] as a bargaining agent and to answer questions. These campus visitors seemed well informed on organizational tactics and recruitment, the labor laws, and labor vocabulary. One [NEA] board member said at the time that the organization had poured over $8,000 into the CMU election. It was clear that every effort was being made to see that [NEA] would not be defeated on the local campus." Subsequently, however, the Central Michigan Faculty Association has not allowed outsiders to take control, and both union and administration have pushed off-campus personnel into the background. As a result, bargaining has an informal, personal tone with some members of the bargaining team being long-standing friends. The localized character of bargaining at this single-campus public institution has helped to keep traditional bargaining rhetoric at a minimum and to focus discussion on honest—and often deep—philosophical differences.

In the long run, a number of factors blur the philosophic differences between competing organizations: the gradual shift in the stance of the AAUP, the growing rift between administrators and faculty that cements bonds between faculty groups, the common economic pressures that lead to similar salary demands, the pressure toward parity in large bargaining units, and the drive toward national affiliations and union mergers.

The similarity of contracts negotiated by the various unions demonstrates that the identity of the bargaining agent has little influence on the outcomes of campus bargaining. Goodwin and Andes (1974) no longer use the identity of the bargaining agent as a criterion in contract analysis. Major contract differences can be more easily explained by local issues and by state laws than by who the agent is. In fact, *bargaining agents influence a standardization across campus lines that directly threatens institutional diversity.* This disturbing issue will be examined in the last chapter.

Union Security Agreements

It is critical to understand the nature of union "security" agreements because, in large part, they affect the strength of a union and its ability to act. Union security agreements are the means by which free riders are eliminated; in other words, they ensure that those who enjoy the collective benefits of the union pay for them. Such agreements take several forms:

(1) A *closed shop* requires that an employee belong to the union prior to employment and remain a member after being hired. In most cases, the closed shop is now illegal.

(2) A *union shop* requires that an employee join the union within a specified time after employment. Over 60 percent of industrial contracts contain union shop provisions.

(3) *Maintenance of membership* requires that once an employee

joins a union, he remain a member as a condition of employment. There is no requirement that he join a union, although maintenance of membership stipulations are often in
tandem with the union shop.

(4) An *agency shop* requires that an employee, whether or not
he belongs to the union, pay fees equal to the union initia-
tion fee, periodic dues, and general assessments.

(5) A *fair share agreement* requires that in lieu of union membership employees pay the union a pro rata share of bargaining costs as a condition of employment. The fair share agreement, unlike the agency shop, only includes costs incurred
by the union in bargaining on behalf of employees.

Although bargainable under the National Labor Relations
Act and although there is increasing pressure on states to permit
them, union security provisions are not allowed by most states.
In fact, a number of states have "right-to-work laws" that make
such employment requirements illegal. Limited union security,
however, is sometimes allowed in the form of "dues checkoff"
—the deduction of union dues from the employee's wages. The
benefits of a dues checkoff work two ways: the union does not
have to play the role of bill collector, and the employer knows
the strength of the union. A study in 1974 showed that about
60 percent of contracts in higher education contain a form of
dues checkoff provisions (National Center for the Study of Collective Bargaining in Higher Education, *Newsletter,* March-April
1975).

There are several arguments in favor of union security
agreements. Not only do they require employees to pay their
fair share of collective bargaining costs, they also stabilize the
collective bargaining process. Since union security agreements
make it difficult for rival organizations to unseat an incumbent
union, the union leaders can focus on the issues rather than on
membership roles and the bank balance. As one CUNY administrator notes: "Once the union becomes stable and stops worry-
ing about its membership it doesn't have to always play the
'tough-guy' role, looking over its shoulder to impress an audi-
ence to have to win over. Instead it can begin to be concerned
with some of the common issues which determine our very

existence." Further, not only do paying members decide what is to be demanded in negotiation, they also ratify the contracts. Without security devices, the union may be controlled by a minority of employees, for it is possible that only a few will join.

Of course, there are also strong arguments against union security provisions: (1) Employees have a right *not* to join unions or be forced to support their programs (the philosophy behind state right-to-work laws). (2) Public sector employees argue that their Constitutional right to free speech is infringed upon if their employers agree to devices like the union or agency shop because funds obtained from them can be used to finance political programs and candidates they do not support. Additionally, since all union security devices are inducements to union membership, they allegedly violate public employees' First Amendment right to freedom of association.* (3) It may be difficult to enforce union security agreements where employees refuse to obey them. Discharges may violate tenure policies and civil service laws. (4) By curtailing opportunities to challenge incumbent unions, union security agreements allow stagnation to occur. Unions can grow old, "fat," and nonresponsive to their members. (5) Union security agreements enable unions to amass funds that can be spent in lobbying, increasing the chances of disproportionate political power accruing to unions. (6) The absence of union security agreements in higher education enables faculty who prefer to devote their limited time and funds to other activities, such as a professional association or senate, to do so. Forcing everyone to support the union will help destroy traditional faculty professional associations and campus governing structures.

The example of Central Michigan illustrates the arguments for and against union security agreements. The union, bowing to collegiality, allowed nonunion members to vote in contract ratification elections. In 1974, however, the union changed its mind and successfully added a hybrid agency shop

---

*For a particularly insightful discussion of the legal complexities surrounding union security devices in the public sector, see Blair (1975).

provision to the new contract, compelling all employees to pay dues. (The catch is that the *union,* in order to enforce payment, must resort to civil legal procedures outside the institution. Unlike what happens with the usual agency shop provision, the burden of enforcement is thrust upon the union itself. When the union exercised the provision against an unwilling faculty member, she promptly countersued the union.) The idea of compulsory payment did not sit well with a majority of the Central Michigan faculty, especially when the union decided to let only union members (30 percent of the total faculty) vote in the contract ratification election. Feeling the union had gone too far, a majority of the faculty petitioned for a new certification election. The election petition was rejected on a technicality, leaving the Faculty Association in power for three more years— time enough to muster new forces to thwart any challenge. The events at Central Michigan indicate that a minority union is well advised to tread lightly where union security agreements are concerned.

The absence of union security agreements substantially weakens unions, and professors are not likely to join a poorly supported union. Membership in faculty unions at the seven case study institutions varies, but the costs of doing business remain high, especially where unions maintain off-campus affiliations (see Table 9). Responses to the Stanford unionization questionnaire reveal national membership patterns; about half of the unions in higher education have a membership of less than 75 percent of those eligible, and thirty percent of these have memberships between 31 and 50 percent. Low membership rates reflect not only faculty apathy and the lack of union security agreements, but they also reflect that holding membership in more than one group is costly. The AAUP estimates that when its competitors are chosen as bargaining agents, its membership declines about 43 percent (Lussier, 1974a, p. 9). Since union security agreements force faculty to shift economic allegiances, their ratification would hasten the decline of multiple memberships.

Few unions in higher education have been able to secure security devices such as the agency shop. Except for the dues

Table 9
Membership Rates and Dues at Seven Case Study Institutions
(January 1974)

	Approximate Membership Rates (% Unit Total)	Annual Membership Dues
Central Michigan University	30% of 590	$135
City Colleges of Chicago	85% of 1300	8/10 of 1% of gross salary
City University of New York	50% of 16,500 (60% of 10,000 FT)	$186[1]
Hofstra University	55% of 400 (65% of 300 FT)	$20 to $80 dependent on rank
Rutgers University	60% of 3000	$48 local dues; $12-$36 national dues (optional)
State University of New York	32% of 16,000	1% of gross salary to $200
University of Hawaii	Less than 50% of 2400	$102[2]

[1]Those earning less than $15,000 a year receive a $27 rebate. This measure is designed to benefit the part-time component of the union.

[2]Hawaii law specifies that everyone in a bargaining unit must pay a service fee equivalent to the reasonable cost to the union of negotiating and administering the contract. In effect, a Hawaii union has automatic agency shop status.

checkoff, less than 10 percent of the contracts in 1974 contained any form of union security provisions. A hostile legal environment, suspicion from many sectors of higher education, and the weakness of unions have prevented their negotiation.

If union security agreements do become negotiable items, unions will find it difficult to win them at the bargaining table. One CUNY official comments, "When the Taylor Law is amended to allow agency shops, it will be a very costly item for the union to buy."

Bargainable Issues

What will the parties bargain over? The answer is as interesting as it is complex. Many factors determine the scope of negotiation: philosophy of the bargaining agent, strength of the union, needs of the members, institutional characteristics. Further, a Rutgers administrator says, "I have come to believe that the antiquity of the institution may have a good deal to do with what is bargainable and what is not." At the head of the list of influential factors is the legal framework within which bargaining takes place.

The law strongly determines what issues are bargainable. For many years, for example, union contracts at campuses within the Massachusetts State College System never mentioned economic subjects. An observer might have concluded that faculties in this system were more concerned about professional issues and avoided the typical union topics of wages and fringe benefits. The fact is that the *law* expressly excluded economic matters from the scope of bargaining until an amendment changed the ruling in 1973.

Before 1959, the National Labor Relations Act (NLRA) was the only legal statute governing the scope of bargaining, stating that "bargaining shall be over wages, hours, and other terms and conditions of employment. . . ." From this one sentence, the NLRB has determined over the years that two kinds of issues are bargainable. First, there are *mandatory subjects of bargaining,* matters covered by the phrase "wages, hours, and other terms and conditions of employment." Such issues are primarily economic, and must be negotiated if one party desires to do so. Second, there are *permissive subjects of bargaining,* matters not expressed by the phrase quoted above but not illegal. The parties may bargain over these issues only if both sides wish to do so. Internal union affairs, the selection of administrators, and the goals of the organization belong in this category. It is illegal to use economic weapons to compel the other side to bargain over these issues. However, increasingly state PERBs are following NLRB practice in declaring that the impact of permissive subjects on terms and conditions of employment must be negotiated. This decision has special significance for retrenchment decision making. For example, while an administration may not have to bargain over the right to curtail a program, it may be forced to bargain over the impact such termination will have on employees affected. Generally, the longer the list of permissible topics management agrees to discuss and the longer the list of mandatory topics, the less freedom employers have to make unilateral changes.

In industry, the mandatory list is usually short: wages, hours, working conditions. Only craft agreements negotiated by skilled workers are apt to have a wider scope of bargaining. Historically, skilled workers have played a major role in organizational policy formulation and administration. In higher education, faculties have demanded a wide scope of bargaining because they also have actively participated in governance at their institutions. Accordingly, a faculty union may seek to bargain over matters such as personnel decision making, the role of the senate in campus affairs, and other governance issues. Because of the limited bargaining experience at private colleges (the only ones covered by the act), what is *mandatory* and what is *permissive* under the NLRA is indefinite. The mandatory-permissive dichotomy will probably continue, for the National Labor Relations Board is likely to treat educational employees no differently from other employees.

In the public sector, several arguments are advanced against a broad scope of bargaining for faculty. Public employment is viewed as essentially different from industry employment, and thus some people feel that bargaining should be restricted to a few issues.* They argue, first of all, that bargaining cannot be allowed to remake policies established by local and state governments, such as civil service policies for public employees. This argument has kept many states from adopting any collective bargaining legislation.

Second, they point out that some governmental levels lack the authority to bargain over particular issues. For example, a tax increase may be needed to pay for negotiated wage improvements, but state laws may prevent a community college district from increasing those taxes. A jurisdictional dispute between governmental levels would be likely to erupt.

Third, they argue that in order to keep disproportionate political power from unions, public sector collective bargaining must be carefully regulated. For example, consider this sce-

---

*For a thorough analysis of the differences between the public and private sectors and recommendations on constructing a legal framework compatible with the characteristics of higher education, see Gee (1973). Also, see Rehmus (1969) for a discussion of the constraints on local governments in bargaining with public employees.

nario: Through political clout, a multicampus union with extensive off-campus affiliations influences the election or appointment of pro-union personnel to boards and commissions of higher education; the union bargains and wins; and the union then lobbies in the legislature to fund the fruits of bargaining. This circle of activity would result in the presence of the union on the *employer's* side of the bargaining table.

Fourth, they reason that a broad scope of public employee bargaining would provide little incentive to public employers to keep costs down through tough bargaining. The result would be ever-increasing costs of performing public services being passed on to the state legislature and eventually to the taxpayer.

For all of these reasons, some concerned parties have tried to severely restrict negotiable issues by proposing laws with "management rights" clauses. For example, in early 1975, the public collective bargaining law was painfully working its way through the California legislature, and the various parties were jockeying over the issues. The Chancellor of the California University and College System, in a memo to his staffs, proposed a legislative fight to ensure strong "management rights" and a narrow scope of bargaining. After reading his memo, one wonders what would be left to bargain over:

> In the California State University and Colleges, the scope of bargaining shall not include any areas of shared governance or management including but not limited to matters of classification and reclassification; merit principles; direction of employees; establishment and determination of student and employee qualifications, standards for work or leave (excluding earned vacation); the nature and content of programs, curriculum and examinations; degree and course requirements; organizational structure and selection and direction of personnel for employment and leave purposes; promotion, transfer, assignment, reassignment, retention, and permanent status of employees in positions; creation, modification or discontinuance of the universities, colleges, schools or departments; functions, programs and efficiency of the

institution; class size, grading standards, methods of instruction; student affairs and conduct, allocation of resources, standards of service of the institution; utilization of technology; determination of methods, means, and personnel by which the institution's operations are to be conducted; peer evaluation; standards of professional responsibility; academic freedom standards; and academic senates and faculty councils.

In 1975, half of the states with collective bargaining legislation for public college employees had restrictive clauses on the scope of bargaining.

Another attempt to restrict bargaining comes from the venerable protector of the faculty, the AAUP. Some of its chapters have endorsed "dual-track" bargaining, which confines union negotiations to one set of issues (wages, working conditions, and fringe benefits), leaving senates and departments to control another set (curriculum, governance, promotion, and professional criteria). The hope—shared by many academicians —is that unions will not encroach on traditional areas of professional judgment, peer evaluation, and academic decision making. Paradoxically, on many campuses, unions are assisting faculties to *gain* governance power (the enfranchisement function) through bargaining. An AAUP official agrees that the dual-track approach could work against the AAUP principle of shared governance in much the same way as do the NLRA "mandatory-permissive" dichotomy and state exemptions of "management rights" from bargaining. He suggests that a *flexible* dual-track approach would be best. Under this concept, governance issues would be bargainable at the discretion of the union. Acknowledging that such an approach is unlikely in future laws, this official concludes that when the AAUP is forced to choose between a wide or narrow scope of bargaining, the best bet is to opt for a wide scope. In so doing, the AAUP would at least be consistent with its fundamental principle of shared governance. In Chapter Six, we will explore the dual-track approach in its most workable setting.

Despite the arguments and laws designed to restrict the scope of issues, some leading experts in the collective bargaining field agree that the scope of issues should be broad, including such traditional faculty concerns as governance, curriculum, and administrative practices. Wollett (1971) writes, "Such [issue-restricting] laws, which encourage or require public employers to avoid problems rather than deal with them, are mischievous because they produce strife and frustration rather than understanding and peaceful accommodation of conflicts between government and its employees. In the public sector, as well as the private, what is bargained about, as well as what the terms of the bargain are, should be a function of the bargaining process" (p. 182).

Strong unions can act to modify laws restricting the scope of bargaining through powerful legislative lobbying. More likely, university administrators may find that strong unions can work their way despite prohibitions in the law. Undoubtedly, cases will arise in which management, and not the union, wants to include a contract provision covering an excluded subject— for example, a clause to protect a particular policy or practice from outside assault.

An administrator at Central Michigan University told us that the administration wanted bargaining sessions to include discussion of issues that were not mandatory topics of bargaining. The goal in expanding the issues was to promote understanding and rapport between the union and the administration. As a single-campus public institution with local bargaining, CMU is a setting conducive to far-ranging, philosophical discussion. Such discussion is less likely to occur in larger systems of higher education where adversarial relations, huge national unions, heavily bureaucratized central administrations, and overt power politics all converge on the bargaining table.

The previous arguments have presented two sides to the bargaining quandary—a restricted scope and a broad one. A third view states that what is negotiable ought to depend in part on the *sanctions* each party can legally employ against the other. For example, if the law allows employees the right to strike, then the scope of bargaining ought to be curtailed. Conversely, if the sanctions are limited, then broad bargaining should be permitted (see Bok and Dunlop, 1970, p. 327). In Hawaii, the law permits strikes, but the scope of bargaining consequently is limited. In general, however, the "strong sanction/narrow scope" thesis is rarely put into practice.

Creeping Expansion of Collective Bargaining Contracts

Despite arguments against a broad bargaining scope, the issues covered in collective bargaining contracts are steadily expanding. After three years of analyzing contracts negotiated in higher education, a team of researchers at West Virginia University reported: "Current contracts [1973] are significantly longer and contain a wider range of items. Early contracts tended to focus more on economic benefits and some working conditions. The 1973 contracts have far more items in the area of governance and academic affairs" (Andes, 1974, p. 10).

This expansion of bargained issues appears to follow three levels: The first level is confined to economic issues such as wages and fringe benefits. The second level adds issues of personnel decision making such as reappointment, promotion, tenure, and grievance procedures. The third level adds bargaining over governance structures and processes.

Progressively longer and more encompassing contracts result partly from external economic and social pressures, from stronger unions, and from the deepening relationship between the parties. Equally potent are the forces exerted by the contractual process and by the character and functioning of the union. The five major thrusts toward more encompassing contracts are summarized as follows: (1) language specificity, (2) grievance pressures, (3) shifts from traditional governance operations to the union, (4) contract interpretation, and (5) hard bargaining at the table.

First, contracts expand because both parties—union and administration—find that contract wording often results in unexpected problems that later need renegotiating. Usually the process is a combination of compromises. At Chicago City College, the administration discovered to its horror that it had agreed to negotiate *any* policy change on working conditions with the union. Later, the contract was renegotiated to read any "uniform, systemwide" policy, thus allowing local campuses the discretion to meet unique needs. In short, contracts expand to meet the need for language clarification and specificity, as well as a need to plan for unexpected consequences that later emerge (contingency planning).

Second, contracts can expand without a single provision being altered, through constant grievance appeals that subtly change the administration of the contract. Traditionally, unions use the grievance/arbitration provisions to gain what they could not win at the bargaining table. Arbitrators who are not thoroughly familiar with the contract, the positions of the parties, and campus traditions are susceptible to this familiar tactic.

Third, contracts expand because activities that previously came under the domain of traditional senates, departments, and other governance processes are inadequately handled and the faculty shifts to the union for better results. This process occurs particularly in those institutions where campus governance is already weak. Even where bargaining is adopted for limited purposes and coexists with traditional governance mechanisms, a breakdown in the latter will work to expand the scope of union activities. At Rider College, a four-year private college in New Jersey, the first contract specifically exempted the tenure process from coverage. But after only several months under the contract, some candidates for tenure were seeking the assistance of the AAUP grievance officer in advising their departments how to write up recommendations. As one union official notes, "This indicates a movement from peer judgment to peer support in the personnel area" (Byrnes, 1975, p. 45).

Fourth, contracts expand to account for PERB interpretations and court rulings that have occurred between contracts. These interpretive decisions can substantially alter the contracts and extend bargaining far beyond what the parties originally intended. For example, collective bargaining legislation determines that the scope of bargaining will include wages, hours, and other terms of employment. To the untutored observer, the phrasing of these issues probably seems clear enough, particularly as it applies to the economic rewards of work. But, like the National Labor Relations Board, state PERBs have had the difficult task of applying the law to diverse conditions. The result is often a complex series of rulings which, taken together, may expand the scope of bargaining.

Table 10 illustrates that in New York many issues are considered mandatory topics of bargaining and must be negotiated as conditions of employment if one party desires to do

Table 10
Subjects of Negotiations in New York State
Under the Taylor Law (Through 1974)

Mandatory	Permissive
1. *Designations by PERB*	
Arbitration as last step of disciplinary proceedings against tenured teachers	Agency shop
Change in conference hours	Budget cuts and resultant economically motivated decision to reduce work force
Compulsory retirement	
*Department rules and regulations	*Call in off-duty personnel precluding reassignment of on-duty personnel
*Discipline and discharge	
*Dismissal of probationary employee, decision and procedures for accomplishment	*Composition of committees to evaluate faculty
*Establishment of labor-management and joint safety committees	Demand that each student have specific number of contact periods with teaching specialists
*Exclusivity of representation	
*Extra work outside regular hours of duty	*Demand for greater role in the formulation of policy relating to student guidance in high schools
*Impact of employer's decision to abolish positions claimed to exist by employee organization	Demand that supervisor be of a specified rank or grade
Impact of modification of class size	*Demand for union to have greater role in making decisions relating to development of curriculum, the evaluation of principals, the assignment of paraprofessionals, and other educational matters
Impact of professional development plan that would constitute a basis for an annual evaluation and for reappointment	
Impact on unit members of reduction in work force	Demand that work force not be reduced except by attrition or disciplinary charge for cause
Job duties of unit employees	*Elimination of jobs
Length of work year	*Employer intercession to obtain work from other employers at extra compensation
Manpower requirements when related to safety	
*Paid leave	*Equipping of police car with shotgun
*Paid time off for union activities	*Filling of vacancies within 30 days
*Parity (to extent demand for reopener and for subsequent negotiation)	Initial employment qualifications
	Insistence upon consideration by a fact

Table 10 (continued)

Mandatory	Permissive
Parking fees at work locations controlled by employer	finder of nonmandatory subjects of negotiation
Procedures for evaluating probationary or untenured teachers	Maintenance of membership
*Procedures relating to layoff	*Numerical limitations on class size
*Promotional procedures for unit employees	Overall policies and mission of government
*Reallocation of job grades	*Parity
Reimbursement for job-related personal property damage	*Pistol permits
Reimbursement of tuition for graduate courses	*Political activities
*Retirement for eligible employees	*Promotion and filling vacancies in competitive class
Sabbatical leave	Promotional policy for job titles not within the negotiating unit
*Seniority	Residency requirements
Special salary increment in last year of service before retirement	*Retirement and social security benefits for ineligible employees
*Time to process grievance without loss of pay	Seminar or conference designed to enrich the professional staff at which attendance is not compulsory
Tours of duty, except that employer may unilaterally determine the number of employees it requires to be on duty at specified periods of time	
*Unpaid leave of absence for union activity	
Wages and hours	
*Workload	
*Work schedules	
*Zipper clause	
2. *Designations by Court*	
Cash payment for accumulated unused sick leave	
Incentive pay plan	
Medical, dental, and life insurance benefit payments by employer to a union administered welfare fund	
Sick leave bank	

*Cases decided in 1974

Source: *New York State Public Employment Relations Board News,* March 1975.

so. The list includes such seemingly disparate issues as grievance arbitration, conference hours, impact of modification of class size, parking fees, and reimbursement of tuition for graduate work. Other subjects have been classified as nonmandatory;

both sides have to agree to include them in contracts. Note that many of the subjects on both the mandatory and the permissive lists were added in 1974. As time passes, then, it is quite likely that some items once thought to be outside the scope of bargaining entirely may become bargainable on a mandatory basis! In fact, there is evidence that state labor boards and courts become progressively more lenient in interpreting the language of a collective bargaining statute, thus accommodating the continuous union push for more inclusive contracts (see Kay, 1973).

PERB rulings and court interpretations, of course, can also overrule the claim of the union to a larger role. CUNY provides a recent and important illustration. The Professional Staff Congress demanded in 1972 that the new contract bar students from participating on personnel and budget committees. The Board of Higher Education refused to negotiate, claiming the choice of evaluators is a management prerogative. The union disagreed, arguing that student membership on these committees falls under the scope of bargaining as a condition of employment. In 1974, the New York PERB ruled against the union in a split decision with both majority and minority opinions claiming to support collegiality. The majority held that the faculty are both employees and policy makers and that student evaluation of faculty is a policy question involving many members of the community. "It would be a perversion of collective negotiations to impose it as a technique for resolving such disputes and thus disenfranchising other interested groups." In short, said PERB, the faculty may sit on both sides of the bargaining table, but that their union may not. The dissent defined collegiality as *professional* collegiality and said only faculty could evaluate professional competence.

Acknowledging that the majority's position was an accurate reflection of the industrial world, the dissenting member argued that the uniqueness of higher education requires a different ruling. Unlike industrial employees, faculty members as professionals have long exercised great control over evaluation of their peers. The minority member would thus not categorize faculty evaluation as a prerogative of management, but as a "basic condition of employment" in higher education. Specifically, the PERB ruling does not affect other procedures of faculty evaluation which are mandatory subjects for union-employer negotiation nor does it prevent the union and the board from voluntarily negotiating over student participation. It does declare that student participation on personnel and budget committees continues as long as the employer wishes it. If the employer were to unilaterally terminate student participation, the union would be unable to do anything about it. As one authority notes, the broad distinction drawn by the majority between matters of union concern and matters reserved to traditional faculty governance practice "is simply unworkable and hinders the parties from achieving a satisfactory combination of bargaining and governance" (Finkin, 1974a, p. 241). In effect, the New York PERB places higher education in the same mold as other types of public employment despite obvious differences. In this particular case, then, the more typical pattern of "contract expansion by judicial decision" was reversed.

Fifth, contracts tend to expand because of enlarged demands at each new bargaining session. Because a union is responsible to its membership and must confer benefits to justify membership dues, it can never afford to rest on its laurels. This is particularly true where the membership is under no compulsion to join the union or pay dues in lieu of membership. A long-term contract may diminish the importance of the union in the eyes of its constituency. To counteract that attitude, the union may make a concerted effort to develop a comprehensive list of demands for the next negotiating session, or it may actively press grievances under the current contract. In addition, weak and/or new unions must be aggressive in order to grow. For these reasons, the collective bargaining process has often been characterized as a never-ending quest for "more."

In sum, expectations of union members, internal union politics, and the democratic method of selecting union leaders all contribute to contract expansion at each successive bargaining session. Eventually the result may be "jurisdictional extension" by the union that ultimately challenges management prerogatives, particularly if economic benefits are not forthcoming. In the public sector, legislatures, taxpayers, and students are becoming sensitive to educational costs, creating even more aggressive unions.

If the pattern of ever-expanding contracts continues for educational institutions, then dual-track bargaining may be an unrealistic approach unless countervailing forces stop the expansion. The power and influence of the union may grow at the expense of both traditional academic forums, such as senates and councils, and powerful administrative groups. In any case, it is particularly important not to conclude too much about collective bargaining from the first few contracts because contracts change and expand rapidly under a variety of pressures as bargaining progresses.

Use of Sanctions

In private industry, economic weapons—such as the employer's lockout and the employees' strike and slow-down—have been regarded as central to successful bargaining. The assumption is that these weapons are necessary to compel the parties to bargain seriously. In the public sector, the availability of economic weapons is controversial and unresolved. Few states allow public employee strikes; when they do, strikes are usually permitted in nonessential services and only after mediation and fact finding by third parties have failed to break deadlocks. The limitations and prohibitions against strikes stem from concerns that public employee strikes inconvenience and endanger the public by disrupting essential services; that they are often aimed at an immediate employer who cannot resolve the issue since his hands are tied by the legislature; that they cannot be countered by lockouts since public employers cannot deny essential services to the public; and that they contribute to disproportionate power accruing to unionized groups (see Wellington and Winter, 1969 and 1970).

Without economic weaponry, however, there may be no compulsion to bargain in good faith. Employee unions can exaggerate their demands and wait for binding arbitration to split the difference; or, if impasse procedures are weak, unions may resort to a strike despite the strike prohibition. Illegal strikes in the public sector have increased markedly in recent years. A weak union could cause collective bargaining for public employees to become, as one commentator says, "collective begging."

Although we do not have much experience to go by yet, strikes by professors in higher education have traditionally been considered ineffective. Although their skills are considered essential to the society, the short-term loss of services lacks the acute, life-and-death impact of strikes by police, firemen, or hospital staffs. Moreover, the loss of academic services poses no substantial public inconvenience compared to the loss of services by transportation workers, garbage collectors, or public school teachers. Certainly, the critical actors on the academic stage are not mortally wounded by strikes; since administrators' salaries increase in ratio to faculty pay increases, the benefits may be worth the inconvenience. Ironically, trustees and legislators may see a faculty strike as a convenient way to save some badly needed funds to balance precarious budgets. And students, who make up the lost time with the help of sympathetic faculty, may relish the holiday. The traditional argument is that the only people really hurt by a faculty strike are those who lose pay—the professors themselves.

Although strikes by professors are assumed to be ineffective, if not counterproductive, this assumption may not always be true. Few administrators are permitted the privilege of retaliating by unilaterally closing down the campus, and few have been effective in dealing with faculty strikes. At Chicago City College, the faculty has repeatedly used strikes to win its demands. Of course, striking professors at a community college may have more impact on a community than professors at a four-year private institution. Community college instructors do not perform the same custodial function as elementary and secondary teachers, but their students are under more time and economic pressures than those at liberal arts institutions. Thus, students may press both sides for a settlement; in fact, students were a key force in strikes at City Colleges of Chicago.

At four-year and graduate institutions, a strike may be a more potent weapon than it seems at first glance. Presumably, administrators at these institutions are as much interested in preserving a collegial environment as are professors. A strike could devastate the aura of collegiality. More than any other aspect of bargaining, a strike portrays the contrasts between administrators as employers and faculty as employees. The Professional Staff Congress at CUNY threatened to strike during contract talks in 1973, but an agreement was quickly reached. As one union leader notes, "Although it is highly possible that the university could have withstood a walkout without too much disruption, past experience with public school teachers' strikes has shown educators that it is often years before the bitterness created by such action is erased." In addition, if faculty members strike, service employees may refuse to cross the picket lines, virtually shutting down campus operations. Perhaps a faculty strike could have its greatest impact if such sympathetic action were to result.

Whether successful or not, academicians will strike if they feel it is necessary to do so. Of the respondents in the 1969 Carnegie Commission sample of 60,028 faculty members, 45 percent acknowledged that a faculty strike might be legitimate under some circumstances. This percentage was similar for both public and private institutions of all types. In his study of the Pennsylvania State system, Lozier (1974) finds that faculty attitudes toward striking correlate strongly with the official position of the AAUP, NEA, and AFT. As expected, the most sympathetic are AFT members, and the least sympathetic are AAUP members. Faculty usually choose union chairpersons who will endorse a strike. Faculty union chairpersons overwhelmingly supported striking in the 1974 Stanford survey, with over 80 percent agreeing that "the strike is a legitimate tactic for faculties to use in bargaining." Only 16 percent of presidents of unionized schools concurred, and a bare 12 percent of the presidents' sample at nonunionized schools agreed with the statement.

Continued prohibition of strikes in the public sector may force unions to use other tactics and sanctions. The most effective procedure is to lobby the legislature directly for benefits, a tactic which intensifies the disproportionate power that strike bans were meant to reduce (see Burton and Krider, 1970). For example, the Professional Staff Congress at CUNY is especially aware of the lobby weapon. In justifying a dues increase in

1974, the union treasurer noted the importance of expensive national affiliations to PSC (over $100 of per capita union dues goes to affiliates off-campus): "PSC, in order to do the job for which it exists, must have considerable 'clout,' both political and professional—in Washington, Albany, and City Hall—which only the state and national teacher organizations and organized labor can give us" ("The Case for a Dues Increase," Professional Staff Congress *Clarion*, October 18, 1973).

Other alternatives to the strike are *mediation, fact finding*, and *arbitration* to resolve contract negotiation disagreements. Third-party intervention is favored in contract negotiations over public services, especially when a strike might imperil the health and safety of the public; many states now provide for such intervention. Nationally, the NLRA states that when a strike or lockout threatens to "imperil the national health or safety," the President of the United States may proclaim an 80-day "cooling off" period during which mediation and fact finding occur.

The strike and lockout are economic weapons equally expensive to both management and labor. As a result, arbitration is preferred to the right to strike in both public and private sectors. Arbitration has long been used to settle grievances under ongoing contracts. Currently, many disputes over the negotiation of new contracts are also being settled by arbitration. Contract term arbitration may actually reduce campus conflict by channeling it into outside agencies—the "conflict channeling and resolving" function mentioned in Chapter Two. The majority of state laws governing public employees now contain arbitration provisions either to settle grievance disputes under an existing contract or to settle interest disputes regarding the negotiation of new contracts, or both. A few states have adopted innovative legislation in this area, a topic we will discuss in Chapter Seven.

Respondents to the Stanford survey were asked to agree or disagree with the statement, "I prefer binding arbitration as a strategy for settling disputes." Of the union chairpersons, 81 percent agree, but only about 25 percent of the presidents agree. Presidents appear to be more wary of arbitration than

Table 11
Factors Shaping Bargaining and Their Implications

	Implications	Comments
1. Bargaining Unit		
(a) Geographic Scope	Horizontal or vertical multicampus units increase centralization, standardize personnel practices, improve systemwide communication and coordination, and decrease bargaining conflict on system campuses in comparison to single-campus units. Vertical multicampus units increase state control, institutional "leveling," and interinstitutional conflict.	The nature of the unit is a critical determinant of bargaining impact on personnel decision making and campus governance.
(b) Personnel Scope	The broader the personnel composition of the unit (nonteaching personnel, part-time faculty, and so on, besides teaching faculty), the more internal conflict and "leveling" of status distinctions among personnel. If department chairpersons are included, new layers of middle management are developed. If part-time faculty and nonteaching personnel are included, faculty rights are extended to them.	The general precedent is for large units: 75 percent of public colleges are in multicampus units, and 90 percent of all units include others besides teaching faculty.
2. Bargaining Agent	AAUP affiliation may retard enlarging the scope of bargaining and may preserve status differentials among academicians. AFT, NEA, or other employee organization affiliations may stimulate a trade-union approach to bargaining by promoting the enlargement of the bargaining scope to personnel and governance issues and by using economic weaponry to influence management. An independent agency is most likely to preserve campus traditions and to be a "company union." Generally weak, with limited resources to effect bargaining, it is unlikely to win elections in multicampus systems.	The identity of the agent is less critical than might be expected from organizational statements because a number of factors force unions to act alike: economic difficulties affect all institutions; faculties have common needs; large units force agents to broaden their appeal; collective bargaining laws and rulings limit new patterns; and collective bargaining as a decision process forces common behavior regardless of affiliation.

(continued on next page)

Table 11 (*continued*)

	Implications	Comments
3. Union Security Agreements	*Dues check-off:* very common in higher education contracts. Convenient for unions; provides valuable information about union strength to management; does not compromise faculty autonomy. *Union shop:* very rare in higher education because of restrictive legislation and fear of building up strong unions at the expense of faculty autonomy. *Agency shop:* fewer than 10 percent of contracts in higher education contain an agency shop provision. As laws increasingly allow bargaining over an agency shop, more such provisions will appear since they are more compatible with higher education than other provisions. *Service fee:* a few state laws require all bargaining unit members to pay a service fee for services rendered. Like the agency shop, a service fee provision is less threatening to faculty autonomy since it does not require union membership.	Aside from dues check-off, union security agreements are often legally taboo. However, the agency shop is gradually gaining acceptance and will become a major topic of bargaining. Although security agreements produce much stronger unions, it is less certain they will broaden representation of faculty interests, since many faculty will pay fees but not get involved in union affairs.
4. Scope of Bargaining		
(a) Factors limiting scope	Restrictive legislation PERB rulings Contract agreements Traditional faculty governance processes	A significant determinant of bargaining impact on personnel decisions and governance.
(b) Factors broadening scope	Permissive legislation PERB rulings Militant union membership Collective bargaining as a decision process Weak governance mechanisms Complexity of line-drawing Trade-offs at bargaining table	

(*continued on next page*)

(c) Results of strong restraints	The stronger the restraints the less likely unions will threaten traditional practices of personnel decision making and governance in higher education. At the same time, unions will be least likely to widen the role of disenfranchised faculties in governance decisions.
(d) Results of weak restraints	The weaker the restraints on the scope of bargaining and the stronger the drive of faculty and union leadership to win benefits, the more likely the scope of bargaining will enlarge with each successive bargaining session.
5. Sanctions (Strike, Slow-Down, Lock-Out, and so on)	Often limited or prohibited by law, and generally considered ineffective because few faculty believe in striking; their use has greatest impact on students and less impact on the general public or the institution. Alternative settlement devices (mediation, conciliation, fact finding, voluntary or mandatory arbitration) may place final decision making in the hands of an external third party and may detract from serious bargaining. Experience with collective bargaining in industry and education illustrates a natural tendency for the range of bargaining to expand with successive contract negotiations regardless of restrictions. Most new public collective bargaining legislation provides for peaceful settlement of contract disputes through alternatives to strikes. Strikes may be more potent in higher education than supposed—if faculty are willing to use them and sympathizers refuse to cross picket lines; lasting bitterness is the likely outcome.

union officials, presumably because they fear loss of control to outside agencies. Nevertheless, arbitration is expected to take its place along with strikes, lobbying, and lockouts as weapons in the collective bargaining struggle.

The determinants that shape campus bargaining and the implications of each issue discussed in this chapter are summarized in Table 11.

We believe that the least influential determinant in bargaining outcomes is the identity of the bargaining agent. Although the use of sanctions may appear unlikely to exert influence over bargaining, the use of economic weaponry may be more powerful than is commonly supposed. In descending order of importance, the most influential determinants appear to be the unit determination, the scope of bargaining, and the presence or absence of union security agreements. Now that we have reviewed those forces that shape campus collective bargaining, we can begin a detailed examination of the consequences bargaining has for academic governance.

Consequences for Personnel Decisions

■■
■■

Having examined academic governance patterns and unionization—including why faculty join unions and what shapes the
nature of campus bargaining—our discussion now focuses on the
consequences of faculty collective bargaining. In this chapter, we
begin with the personnel issues of job security, grievance procedures, and tenure—issues with immediate, personal impact on
faculty members; in other words, the policies and practices that
link the individual to the institution.

Union Goals

Initially, a union seeks to be recognized at an institution
as the exclusive representative for faculty on personnel issues.
Once unions are established as the primary spokesmen on these
issues, they then press for other personnel gains: contractualizing personnel policies, protecting job security and tenure, and
preventing tenure quotas.

Contractualizing Personnel Policy. Unions argue that faculty control of personnel issues is secure only when trustees
grant authority to the faculty through a written formal con-

tract. Unlike trustee-granted privileges that can be taken away easily, contracts are backed up by the courts. Thus, personnel policies covered by a contract cannot unilaterally be modified by trustees or administrators. Collective bargaining, notes the NEA, offers the best chance to safeguard and expand due process in personnel decision making because, "Mutual agreement on such procedures can be reached at the bargaining table —the only areas where the power of the staff and that of the administration are equalized" (NEA, 1974).

Promoting Job Security and Protecting Tenure. As long as faculty members are concerned with job security, unions will strive to secure broad guarantees. The result will be an ever-widening application of grievance processes and neutral, third-party arbitration as the final step. One commentator concludes: "Grievance machinery offers the long-term potential to resolve abuses of the faculty evaluative process once academics become familiarized with the grievance machinery; many disagreements will be settled at the informal stages. Properly administered, it will highlight weaknesses in the evaluative process which can be corrected and will encourage thorough justification of appointment and evaluation decisions. All of this may be an improvement over academic grievance systems which have not been effective in my experience" (McHugh, 1973, p. 58).

In addition to formalizing grievance processes, unions try to protect job security by strengthening the tenure system. Although some unions at first seemed willing to compromise on tenure to attain other goals, a few outstanding instances have determined emphatically that unions will support tenure. A case in point is the overwhelming rejection of the first contract negotiated by a faculty union at the University of Hawaii. Controversy raged over the apparent willingness of the Hawaii Federation of College Teachers (HFCT), an AFT affiliate, to compromise tenure to secure a larger wage package for community college instructors; most of its backing came from the six community colleges. When the first contract talks began in 1973, the HFCT faced a tough adversary, for the Board of Regents was unyielding at the bargaining table.

When the proposed contract reached the faculty in

November 1973, criticism centered on two features: (1) The contract recognized a new type of nontenured employment— the five-year renewable contract. Many faculty saw this as a sellout to administrators eager to reduce the number of faculty. One line of the proposed contract even seemed to imply the possibility of quotas: "A decision to recommend or to grant a tenured or extended appointment *may be based upon other institutional considerations in addition to the faculty Employee's competence*" (italics added). (2) The contract approved the use of administration-appointed committees in personnel decision making. Faculty representation on the committees was left to the discretion of department chairpersons or high level administrators. As one AAUP commentator told us, "One looks in vain for reference to the faculties' prime responsibility for matters of faculty status. A 'potential' committee at the department level is wholly inadequate."

Coupled with an unsatisfactory salary package, these encroachments on faculty prerogatives and traditions raised a storm of protest. The professors on the main campus, fearful of being sold out by the union to the needs of the outlying community colleges, mounted a strong campaign against the contract.

Hawaii law provides that *all* members of a bargaining unit may vote on a contract, not just union members. When the voting was over, the faculty overwhelmingly rejected the proposal, 1301 to 279. Not only had the contract been defeated, but the status of the HFCT as bargaining agent was questioned and the national AFT organization was shaken to its foundation. Shortly thereafter, a decertification election was held, the HFCT was voted out, a NEA/AAUP coalition was voted in, and tenure was vividly etched in everyone's mind as an issue not to be compromised by unions!

Preventing Quotas. Widespread publicity combined with the militant stance of unions kept many institutions from seriously considering tenure quotas for academic employees in the early 1970s. Perhaps the toughest battle was waged at the City University of New York by the Professional Staff Congress during the 1973-1974 school year. In October 1973, the New York

City Board of Higher Education adopted a controversial restrictive policy imposing "mathematical guidelines" on tenure conferral. Continuing attacks by the Professional Staff Congress,
combined with a change in Board membership, resulted in rein-
statement of the old policy. Belle Zeller, president of the union,
hailed the rejection of the tenure quota as "a turning point in
the history of faculty unionism." She went on, "What we have
proved here is that a strong union can overcome these attacks
and protect its members against an erosion of their rights." Zeller's dramatic comments emphasize that fights over quotas are
central to the efforts of any union to maintain faculty job
security.

Progress Toward Union Goals

How far have unions come in achieving their goals in personnel decision areas? Ongoing research in the forms of contract
analysis and questionnaires to various campuses helps to answer
this question.

Professors Harold I. Goodwin and John O. Andes of West
Virginia University have been analyzing faculty union contracts
for the last several years. Their analysis gives a rough idea of the
progress of unions toward their goals. Tables 12 and 13 provide
information about the content of union contracts throughout
the United States. Before examining the figures closely, however, it is important to realize that contract analysis has a number of serious limitations. First of all, knowing that certain
items appear in contracts does not help us to understand much
about their *substance*. Even if the substance of contractual provisions can be determined, how individuals will behave in relation to those provisions is an unknown consideration. Second,
knowing the *affiliation* of the bargaining agent does not tell us
much about the substance of contracts because the positions
taken by local chapters at the bargaining table depend more on
individual campus conditions and on the desires of the local
membership than on the national postures of the AAUP, NEA,
and AFT. Third, certain provisions may appear rarely, partly
because of a legally *constricted scope of bargaining*. Statutory

Table 12
Contract Provisions in Relation to Personnel Issues by Year

| | Percentage of Contracts Covering Issue | | |
	1971 (N = 46)	1972 (N = 101)	1973 (N = 131)
Personnel Policy	85%	80%	95%
Grievance Procedures	91	91	92
Appointment	78	100	82
Reappointment	78	100	82
Dismissal	70	79	76
Nonreappointment	70	79	75
Personnel Evaluation Procedure	57	75	66
Promotion Policy	80	60	53
Staff Reduction	15	39	50
Tenure	50	40	49
Individual Contracts	0	0	27
Professional Awards, Merit Pay	9	6	11
Tenure Review Committee	0	0	11
Evaluation Committee	0	0	9

Source: Andes, 1974.

Table 13
1973 Contract Provisions in Relation to Personnel Issues
by Type of Institution

| | Percentage of Contracts Covering Issue | | |
	Universities (N = 21)	4-Year Colleges (N = 21)	2-Year Colleges (N = 98)
Personnel Policy	100%	95%	95%
Grievance Procedure	92	95	91
Appointment	83	95	80
Reappointment	75	95	80
Dismissal	83	86	72
Nonreappointment	67	86	73
Personnel Evaluation Procedure	42	67	69
Promotion Policy	50	67	51
Staff Reduction	33	57	51
Tenure	67	71	42
Individual Contracts	17	29	24
Professional Awards, Merit Pay	50	14	5
Tenure Review Committee	0	14	11
Evaluation Committee	0	14	9

Source: Andes, 1974.

provisions and rulings of administrative agencies may severely limit or prohibit negotiation of contract terms related to personnel decision making. Fourth, weak unions coupled with inexperienced bargainers on both sides may also contribute to relatively *constricted contract coverage.* Most unions in higher education have negotiated only one or two contracts, and they have not yet had the time to expand the negotiable issues. The absence of an arbitration provision, for example, may indicate that the union was not able to win this point at its first, or even second, negotiation session—not that the faculty abhors the thought of third-party adjudication.

Despite these reservations, contract analysis can help us to understand the objectives of unions in relation to personnel decisions. Table 12 shows that almost every union has negotiated a grievance procedure for satisfying individual claims against the institution. Such grievance procedures provide methods of channeling conflict and resolving difficulties in the political process of governance. In addition, the bulk of the contracts deal with the central issues of hiring and firing: appointment, reappointment, nonreappointment and dismissal. These key items in union contracts help ensure job security.

Beyond these basic items, the contracts vary considerably, with few contracts containing the same procedures. Over a period of several years, several issues have decreased in importance while others have increased. For example, the number of contracts with promotion policies and personnel evaluation policies has actually decreased slightly between 1971 and 1973. During the same period, provisions for staff reduction, individual contracts, merit pay awards, and evaluation committees have increased. These last few items were almost nonexistent in the early contracts.

The variations over time can probably be explained by two factors. First, the worsening economic situation of the last several years has caused administrators to consider staff reduction as a financial expediency. Second, the composition of unionized schools has shifted slightly with more four-year colleges and universities turning to collective bargaining. Therefore, issues once neglected in contracts at two-year colleges are now receiving attention in the contracts of four-year institutions, especially in the areas of merit pay, individual contracts, and formal committees. Traditionally, these issues have been the concerns of senior institutions.

Table 13 details the contract provisions in different types of institutions. On the basic issues—grievance, appointment, and dismissal procedures—the various institutions do not differ significantly. All the contracts include these "gut issues," regardless of the institutional type. On other issues, however, interesting differences reflect the varying professional worlds of the various academic institutions.

From analyses of contract provisions, some basic trends about personnel decision making can be noted. First, almost all contracts include sections on the basic issues of grievance procedure, appointment, and dismissal. On the items concerned with the professional aspects of tenure, merit pay, and review processes, however, unions have not made much headway. Finally, contracts at universities and at other types of colleges show some significant differences in relation to professional items, probably a factor of differing traditions of professionalism in the various institutions.

Another indicator of the effect faculty unions have on personnel matters is the questionnaire data obtained from the Stanford Project on Academic Governance. Respondents were asked to rate union influence on many issues and to contrast unions with academic senates. Table 14 contains the influence ratings on personnel issues that campus presidents and union chairpersons gave senates and unions, where senates and unions coexist and where each exists alone. It is important to remember, of course, that only the *perceptions* of presidents and chairpersons are recorded and that perceptions may or may not be accurate reflections of reality. With this limitation in mind, the following generalizations can be made about the questionnaire results.

First, both unions and senates were rated only low to moderate in relation to faculty personnel decision making at all institutional types. Presumably, the low ratings show that the respondents felt there were other significant influences on per-

Table 14
Influence of Senates and Unions on Personnel Decisions

		Multiversities		Public Colleges		Liberal Arts Colleges		Two-Year Colleges	
		Senate	Union	Senate	Union	Senate	Union	Senate	Union
Both Senate and Union									
Faculty	Presidents	1.9	1.5	2.6	2.5	2.6	1.9	2.5	2.4
Hiring	Chairpersons	2.0	2.0	1.5	2.9	1.9	2.6	2.0	3.0
Faculty	Presidents	3.4	2.4	3.1	3.0	3.2	2.9	2.8	3.4
Promotion	Chairpersons	3.0	3.4	2.5	3.8	3.4	3.6	2.4	3.8
Senate Only									
Faculty	Presidents	2.5		2.6		2.8		2.6	
Hiring									
Faculty	Presidents	3.2		3.8		3.0		2.6	
Promotion									
Union Only*									
Faculty	Presidents								2.7
Hiring	Chairpersons								2.6
Faculty	Presidents								3.2
Promotion	Chairpersons								3.1

*Because few institutions, with the exception of two-year colleges, have unions but no senates, only two-year institutions are included here.

Note: The question asked was "How much influence does the faculty collective bargaining unit and senate have on these issues, at your institution?" Respondents gave answers on a five-point scale, with "1" indicating low influence and "5" indicating high influence.

sonnel processes—such as the departmental faculties and the administration. Certainly, unions and senates were involved in these decisions, but they were not dominant according to the ratings.

Second, senates are generally *weakest* at two-year colleges. This is an expected result, since administrators usually assume an authoritarian role in faculty matters at these institutions. Unions, on the other hand, are generally *strongest* at two-year institutions. Because no strong senate tradition exists to compete with, it is easier for these unions to demand control over faculty personnel issues.

Third, in nearly every instance, both senates and unions are perceived to have more influence over faculty promotion and tenure issues than over faculty hiring. Presumably, administrators and departments still retain a major role in hiring activities.

Fourth, according to the presidents where unions and senates coexist, senates have more influence over faculty personnel issues. Union chairpersons, on the other hand, consistently see unions outperforming senates. This difference of opinion is not really surprising!

Finally, senates existing alone are not rated any higher than when they coexist with unions. Unions existing alone at two-year institutions earn about the same influence ratings from presidents and chairpersons. Unions are slightly more influential than senates on two-year campuses.

These findings suggest that unions rival or surpass senates in affecting faculty personnel decision making. Especially at two-year institutions where faculty influence traditionally has been limited, unions have moved into an effective position. In a short time, they have taken an equal place alongside senates, and are now virtually as powerful as senates in promotion, tenure, and hiring matters. It must be emphasized, however, that neither senates nor unions appear to be dominant in relation to these issues. They are only two groups on a stage of actors that includes administrators, departmental peers, and trustees. The next sections evaluate in more detail the positive and negative impacts of unionism on the complex personnel process.

Positive Consequences: Faculty Rights

Will unionism have a healthy impact on personnel decision making? That is a tough question, but for some colleges the answer is clearly "yes."

Some institutions have never provided for strong faculty involvement in personnel processes and have tended to run roughshod over faculty rights. Interference by legislatures, trustees, and administrators has prevented some colleges from letting professors be involved in personnel procedures. This is especially true in community colleges, for these faculties have often not developed a sense of professional cohesiveness and lack the deep-rooted understandings of professional obligations.

The differences between colleges are clearly shown in the results of the Stanford Project on Academic Governance. From the several questions on personnel practices in the Phase One (1971) questionnaire, those dealing with the amount of departmental autonomy to *select and hire* and to *promote* faculty are particularly important. We assumed that the most professional institutions would show high departmental autonomy on these issues because the department is the disciplinary home of academic experts who should have the greatest influence over personnel decisions. Additional questions dealt with professional evaluation, asking who evaluated work performance and on what criteria. From the answers to those questions, a composite "peer evaluation" score for each institution was constructed. Basically the score is a measure of how much of the evaluation is done by faculty colleagues as opposed to administrators, trustees, and other noncolleagues. We assumed that if the score were higher for faculty colleagues than for the other groups, it would indicate a more traditional professional stance.

The results of these questions, shown in Table 15, are dramatic, with enormous differences between various types of institutions. On the *faculty selection* issue, high departmental autonomy varies from 83 percent in the elite private universities to 8 percent in private junior colleges. On the *promotion* question, the results are not as sharply divided, but the variation from high autonomy (49 percent) to low (8 percent) is still

Table 15
Faculty Perceptions of Locus of Personnel Decisions by Type of Institution
(1971)

	Average Percent of Faculty Reporting Department Has High Autonomy in Faculty Hiring and Selection	Average Percent of Faculty Reporting Department Has High Autonomy on Promotions	Average Percent of Faculty Reporting Evaluation Done by Faculty Peers
Private Multiversities (N = 6)	76	49	64
Public Multiversities (N = 13)	83	43	46
Elite Liberal Arts Colleges (N = 25)	66	39	58
Public Comprehensives (N = 40)	65	30	29
Public Colleges (N = 16)	64	26	44
Private Liberal Arts Colleges (N = 85)	36	13	25
Community Colleges (N = 96)	44	18	23
Private Junior Colleges (N = 19)	21	8	9

large. On the *peer evaluation* question, the divisions are similar. In private multiversities (the major private institutions), high departmental autonomy measures 64 percent. By contrast, the community colleges and private junior colleges have scores of 23 percent and 9 percent, respectively. Whether due to external interference, administrative arbitrariness, or lack of a professional tradition, the professional personnel processes as measured by these questions appear crippled in many institutions. Because the institutions seem to fall into distinct professional worlds, faculty unionization can be expected to affect them differently.

It is our belief that *the most positive aspects of faculty unionism will be (1) to expand professional processes to those institutions where faculty essentially have been disenfranchised for years, and (2) to extend rights beyond the tenured teaching faculty.* Through collective action protected by law, these faculties may be able to gain many professional rights that have been

denied them. Of all the positive features of unionism, this one is the most important.

One specific example of how unions can bolster professional processes where they are lacking comes from the City Colleges of Chicago. In 1966, control over the community college system passed from the Chicago Board of Education to a special College Board. As in most secondary schools, personnel decision making was in the hands of the administration until that time. Faculty members were granted tenure on the basis of competitive examination and review by the Board of Education. The new College Board was developing its by-laws about the same time as the Cook County College Teachers Union started bargaining on behalf of the faculty. Beginning with the first contract in 1967, the department peer group progressively has acquired an increasingly substantial role in personnel decision making. Departments establish the appropriate procedures and evaluation criteria for initial employment, renewal of contracts, and tenure conferral. Extensive due process safeguards are included throughout the three-year probationary period for new employees. Union and administrative officials agree that few serious disputes over personnel decision making have occurred. As one administrator notes, there was—and continues to be—"a mutuality of interest in getting the best possible." With the Chicago City Colleges as an example, it is possible that collective bargaining may bring a blend of peer judgment and due process to institutions where they are missing.

Although the major benefit of unionism will be protecting faculty rights at institutions with little professional tradition, other benefits will affect all types of institutions. Unions always seek to win extensive "due process" rights for members of the bargaining unit, who may be full-time faculty, nonteaching professionals, part-time faculty, and teaching assistants. As a result, due process rights are extended beyond the full-time teaching faculty who benefit from existing due process procedures. Due process is a complicated concept that can be divided into two categories: substantive and procedural. *Substantive* due process seeks to guarantee that convincing reasons exist for whatever decision is reached. As a National Education Association (1974) position paper describes it:

Substantive due process means that the reasons for an adverse action must not be arbitrary or capricious; that they must be relevant to the competence of the individual to adequately perform the responsibilities and functions of his position; that they must not either directly or by their effect deny the individual the right to exercise any rights under the Constitution or laws of the United States, nor be a retaliation for such exercise. Furthermore, the reasons given must be the genuine reasons, not a subterfuge disguising other, unconstitutional intentions; and finally, they must be sufficient to warrant the action taken.

By contrast, *procedural* due process refers to the method for carrying out the decision process. For example, the NEA (1974) lists these procedural safeguards:

Procedural due process means that there must be available procedural safeguards to ensure that any adverse action can be dealt with fairly and equitably so that the individual affected has every opportunity to face his accusers, respond to the charges and refute the evidence against him. Included in these procedures must be the following:

1. That appropriate reasons and timely notice will be given before any adverse action is taken.

2. That it will be the burden of the institution to substantiate its charges and justify its actions through the presentation of proper, relevant, and sufficient evidence.

3. That the individual adversely affected will have an opportunity for a hearing in which he and his representatives will be enabled to hear and see all the evidence, cross-examine any person giving evidence against him, and present his own evidence to refute the charges against him.

4. That this hearing will be open or closed at the discretion of the individual.

5. That the individual will have the right to be represented by counsel of his own choosing.

6. That the hearing agency will render a decision based solely on the unrefuted evidence produced at the hearing.

7. That the individual will have the right to

appeal its decision to binding arbitration by a neutral third party (such as the American Arbitration Association).

Unions have stressed procedural due process, leaving the substantive content of the decision to departmental faculties. As they struggle for more job security, however, unions are more likely to move into substantive issues.

Union emphasis on due process has resulted in a tightening up and regularization of procedures and an elimination of informality. One question on the Stanford Governance Questionnaire raised this issue: "Where it occurs, faculty collective bargaining will result in greater specificity of employment rules." Over 90 percent of all respondents agree with the statement. And it does not matter whether the respondent is a union official, a college president, or from what kind of institution.

In many ways, the systemization of personnel procedures is beneficial. For example, unionization can help protect faculty from inconsistent and vague administrative decisions resulting from external economic pressures. A drastic cut in state appropriations for a public institution or a dramatic incline in the income of a private college can panic trustees and administrators into making arbitrary personnel decisions. Faculty trust is accordingly reduced and conflict arises. For instance, the administration at Bloomfield College recently abolished tenure and dismissed a number of tenured faculty. In rapid-fire order, the faculty unionized with the AAUP, then the college was censured by the AAUP and taken to court. The trial court ruled that Bloomfield had no adequate grounds to dismiss the faculty. In mid-1974, the college asked to be placed in court receivership.

The advantage of bargaining over personnel issues is to establish procedures before crises develop. Administrators as well as faculty may be the beneficiaries of formal personnel procedures. As an administrator at Hofstra University puts it, contractual procedure "minimizes occasions for conflict by impersonalizing the relationship between faculty and administrators" on economic and personnel issues.

Not everyone agrees with such a positive interpretation, of course. The 1974 Stanford survey asked people to agree or disagree with this statement: "Faculty collective bargaining will result in more equitable personnel decision making (for example, who gets tenure, who is laid off, who is promoted)." The most sharply contradicting answers in the entire survey resulted. Presidents generally disagree (nonunion school presidents = 62 percent disagreement; unionized school presidents = 43 percent disagreement). By contrast, the faculty chairpersons agree, by 94 percent. We received a similar response pattern to the statement: "Faculty collective bargaining will help safeguard faculty rights and academic freedom." Whether unionism will help or hinder faculty professional rights is certainly debatable!

Negative Consequences: Academic Professionalism

An important aspect of unionism vis-à-vis personnel processes is its impact on traditional concepts of professionalism. Union leaders feel that one cause of faculty unionism is a concern for increasing professionalism. Campus presidents, however, play down this factor. The issue demands close examination, for it is a potential trouble spot when unions come to the campus.

Professionalism, Subjective Criteria, and Peer Evaluation. Before examining the consequences of faculty unionization, we need to ask questions about some of the current patterns of academic professionalism. What are the professional characteristics of colleges and universities that make their personnel decision processes different from most organizations? What procedures have academic organizations evolved to evaluate faculty performance on educational tasks that are inherently subjective? Are there major differences in professional evaluation methods in various types of educational institutions? From the answers to these questions, it is possible to predict how unionization might affect academic professionalism.

Most organizations know what they are doing. Business firms are supplying needed goods and services as a way of making a profit, government bureaus have tasks specified by law, hospitals are trying to overcome illness, prisons are in the business of "rehabilitation." By contrast, colleges and universities have vague, ambiguous objectives. What are the goals of a college or university? The list of possibilities is long and hard to refute: teaching, research, service to the local community, administration of scientific installations, housing for students and faculty, support of the arts, solving social problems. When goals are finally specified in concrete terms and put into operation, disagreement promptly results; thus, the problem is not only that academic goals are unclear, they are also highly contested.

Two important characteristics of academic institutions play an important part in academic goals. First, like schools, hospitals, and welfare agencies, academic organizations are "people-processing" institutions that serve clients—the students. Second, because they serve clients with disparate, complicated needs, "people-processing" organizations frequently have no one "best" way of doing things. A company manufacturing steel or plastics develops a specific technology that can be divided into steps and routinized; unskilled, semiskilled, and white-collar workers can be employed without relying heavily on professional expertise. By contrast, academic institutions are dealing with the minds, bodies, and spirits of student clients. Not only is it difficult to serve clients, but it also is difficult to evaluate accomplishments and to demonstrate even short-term successes. If, at times, colleges and universities do not know *what* they are doing, they often do not know *how* to do it either.

How does an organization work when its goals are unclear and contested, its service is directed to clients, and its technology is nonroutine? Most organizations solve the problem by hiring expertly trained professionals—whether doctors and nurses, social workers, teachers, or professors. Instead of subdividing the task into a routine, assembly-line process, professional work tends to encapsulate a wide range of skills into a single professional employee.

When the task is vague and complex, and when a client is being served by a professional with esoteric knowledge, then performance standards are, to a large degree, inherently subjective. It is important to emphasize that no matter how often tasks are specified, objectives listed, or performance criteria catalogued, the subtleties of the academic task will never be completely eliminated. Managerial techniques such as "system theories," "curriculum objectives," and "outcome specification" cannot simplify the complexities of the professor's work. Like the job of the artist or statesman, the academic job is not easily quantifiable, measurable, or subject to minute supervision. Under these circumstances—vague goals, client service, professional tasks, and subjective criteria—it is extremely difficult to evaluate work behavior. How can performance be judged in order to make personnel decisions such as promotions and granting tenure?

Evaluation is indeed difficult, but not impossible. In fact, professional organizations such as colleges, law firms, and hospitals have developed peer evaluation procedures that do work. Most professionals demand that their colleagues, trained and inculcated with the values of both the profession and the institution, evaluate each others' work; like other professionals, academics tend to reject the evaluations of nonexperts. As the Rutgers University Senate noted in its 1969 "Policy on Academic Promotions":

> It is exceedingly difficult to measure and judge the various areas of activity. Judgment in these matters can be made only by qualified colleagues. It is for that reason that recommendations for promotion are initiated at the department level, considered by committees on appointments and promotions within each college, passed upon by appropriate deans, considered by the senior staff members in each field in all divisions of the University, and reviewed by the Provost and the President. By this process, it is hoped that all significant information with respect to the services and accomplishments a faculty member is rendering within his department, within his college, within his scholarly field, and within the University will be brought out and compared with the services and

accomplishments of other colleagues having the same or similar duties.

Such subjective judgment by persons competent to evaluate duties, responsibilities, services, and accomplishments will protect the interest of the professor himself, the department, the college, the University, and the students better than any objective rating that could be devised.

Union Threats to the Peer Evaluation Process. The above description of professionalized work and peer evaluation is the traditional picture of academic personnel decision making. The crux of the matter is: What impact will unionism have? Unions have many goals, but during a financial crisis, the prime goals are job security and gaining economic benefits. These goals pose a dilemma for academic professionalism because they are complicated by the faculty's traditional responsibility to evaluate professional competence and performance.

Will unions dilute faculty quality by providing legal and procedural barriers behind which incompetency can hide, or can unions preserve quality even as they protect job security? Can unions shelter academics from arbitrary administrative meddling in personnel decisions, or will unions tie up the system so that effective administration is impossible? These questions are crucial, for the push toward unionization has seriously challenged professional patterns of personnel decision making.

Earlier, we concluded that the most important positive outcome of faculty unionism will be the extension of faculty rights and governance opportunities to institutions that lacked such professional procedures. Now we offer another opinion. *The major negative consequence of faculty unionism may be a protectionist, job-security orientation that could thwart personnel policies so that incompetency is protected and seniority, not merit, becomes the main decision-making criterion.*

The fear of protectionism does not apply only to academics involved in unionism, for today the charge of professional irresponsibility is also leveled at other occupations. Doctors are often accused of defending each other's incompetence rather than responding to their patients' needs; teachers are often blamed for ignoring students as they protect each other from the public's cry for educational accountability; lawyers are often suspected of leniency when they examine their colleagues' professional conduct; and college administrators often charge that departmental academicians pass the buck on hard personnel decisions.

We strongly support traditional notions of academic professionalism. We believe that subjective performance criteria can be successfully used for peer evaluation of faculty members; that merit can be judged and should replace seniority as the basis of tenure and promotion; that incompetence can be identified and dealt with; that students as the principal clients should be involved in personnel decisions; and that our institutions, students, and publics deserve the best, quality-oriented faculties. We fear that in their quest for job security, faculty unions do not always share these basic beliefs and may undercut them. The next few pages examine some of the trends that worry us.

Promotion and Tenure by Default. In their efforts to expand due process, unions seek to protect their members by insisting that employment evaluation be based on *specific criteria.* This is well illustrated by experience at four-year colleges. In his study of four-year college contracts containing tenure provisions, Mortimer (1975) found over 40 percent specified the categories of evidence to be used in reaching tenure decisions. Unfortunately, specific criteria are difficult to establish in education. Traditionally, the profession has compensated for the difficulty by depending on a complex, subtle, peer evaluation process much akin to a jury system. Unions, however, have pushed in the other direction, demanding detailed and specific criteria. Because such criteria are not easily developed, the ones that are suggested and used are often challenged if they actually result in a faculty member's dismissal—student evaluation of teaching being a case in point.

Evaluation based on objective criteria is the first part of a two-step process demanded by unions. The second, still largely unachieved, is for *appropriate reasons* to be given for nonreappointment or dismissal based on "proper, relevant, and sufficient evidence." In the view of most unions, there is no difference between nonreappointment and dismissal in terms of sub-stantive due process procedures.

An administrative official at Rutgers told us that the per-plexities surrounding the quest for convincing evidence are par-ticularly troublesome to administrators. The dilemma stems from administrative reluctance to interfere in peer judgment processes at lower levels for fear of incurring charges of med-dling with academic judgment. Yet, if administrators wait until the lower levels of decision making have all been completed, they appear to be acting arbitrarily in reversing earlier decisions, even if they believe those decisions are not justified or may not stand up if legally contested.

One way out of the dilemma is for administrators to insist that all faculty be evaluated much earlier in the probation-ary period—well before a tenure decision arises. This is precisely the position advocated by one union official at CUNY as an example of "responsible management." Proponents of peer judgment point out, however, that a shorter probationary peri-od would prevent departments from doing thorough evalua-tions, militate against "late bloomers," and add fuel to union charges of a cheap labor policy by junior faculty's being put through the "revolving door." Further, a thorough search for objective data in a short time may constitute a violation of a nontenured staff member's academic freedom.

Specificity of reasons (or lack of them) creates special problems for both unions and administrations where minorities and women are involved. One administrator complained to us that most of the reasons and evidence produced to support ten-ure denials to members of minority groups are often not objec-tive enough to stand up in court. Yet, an official of the AAUP union at Rutgers notes that the subjectivity inherent in the eval-uation process has made it most difficult for the union to prove discrimination in grievance cases! (Laity, 1973, p. 59.)

Unions are under pressure from the more disenfranchised of their memberships to enlarge the scope of contractualized personnel procedures. During the two years of the first contract at SUNY, for example, 55 percent of the grievance appeals came from the nonteaching professionals and nontenured faculty (Satryb, 1974, p. 4). Another 22 percent were class action grievances filed by the union. Only 23 percent of the grievance appeals came from associate or full professors. Most of the grievances were concerned with job security.

The inadequacy of noncontractualized procedures also motivates unions to press for contract expansion. Again, SUNY furnishes a good example. The Satryb study shows that many grievants sought to challenge nonprocedural issues relating to "personality conflicts with administrators or substantive judgments of colleagues sitting on personnel committees" (Satryb, 1974, p. 3). Satryb concludes that it is imperative for campuses to establish effective parallel mechanisms, which faculty will support, for the relief and redress of noncontractual employee grievances. Failure to do so will increase the pressure on unions to expand contractual provisions. Since most campuses have paid little attention to these matters in the past and may be slow to respond to them in the future, it is quite likely that the discretionary power of senates and departments over personnel issues will be further eroded at the bargaining table.

An unrestricted grievance system that ends in binding arbitration and that is based on overly specific criteria could result in a process we call "tenure by default." The logic of tenure by default produces this pattern: (1) The union maintains it is the burden of the institution to prove incompetency—not the burden of the faculty member to prove competency. (2) The union rejects the subtle peer evaluation process and demands concrete, specific criteria. (3) When specific criteria and evidence relating to them are presented, the union challenges them as irrelevant, inaccurate, or biased. (4) When it is the burden of the institution and when specific criteria and evidence are unavailable or challenged, then the faculty member goes unevaluated by default and the institution is unable to make a substantial case for dismissal. The union has, by default, ensured job security.

If the default option were reversed so that the *individual* had to prove competence, then we believe the demand of the union for hard, specific criteria would be dropped, and that the traditional peer evaluation process would be more readily accepted. For example, as long as the default option favors the individual, faculty members will resist student evaluation and colleague observation of classroom teaching. If, on the other hand, the failure to prove competence resulted in dismissal, we suspect unions would be open to more evaluation by both students and faculty colleagues, not less.

So far, tenure by default has not become a serious problem, particularly at the four-year and graduate levels. Peer review is still strongly defended by many unions in higher education. In fact, it is possible that faculty power over personnel decision making will be compromised to a greater degree by unilateral administrative action than by union contracts. However, at two-year institutions and some four-year colleges, there is much less commitment to the discretionary power of peers to render what is, in effect, a decision about job security. Thus, tenure by default provisions are increasingly likely to appear in union contracts at many of these institutions. Whether tenure by default will become common where unions exist is a topic for future research.* However, there do seem to be trends in this direction.

In discussing this controversial issue we must emphasize both sides of the issue, for in the past evaluation procedures have been unclear, arbitrary, and in many cases indefensible. In short, the older unprofessional procedure of "nonrenewals by default" and by administrative arbitrariness was all too common. Unions have every right, even an obligation, to fight against such processes. Nevertheless, the opposite extreme of "promotion and tenure by default" is equally unprofessional. Somewhere between the two extremes must be a compromise that protects the individual against unreasonable and arbitrary procedures while simultaneously protecting the institution and

---

*Among others who are studying this aspect of faculty bargaining and who have shared some of their preliminary findings with us are Kenneth P. Mortimer, professor of Education and Research Associate at Pennsylvania State University; David Leslie, assistant professor of Education at the University of Virginia; and Thomas Mannix, acting director of the National Center for the Study of Collective Bargaining in Higher Education at Bernard Baruch College/CUNY.

its students against personnel decisions that occur by default. Both responsible unions and administrators will have to build the framework for a workable compromise. This compromise must necessarily include tightening up procedures and creating specific criteria. The compromise must also allow for the unmeasurables and the nonquantifiables that are the essence of academic work and for which peer evaluation remains the major judging process.

Burgeoning Bureaucratization. Another problem may result in personnel decisions occurring by default—bureaucratization. Union concern with procedural due process per se is not necessarily a threat to peer group decision making. Fair procedures, including the right to appeal, are accepted as innate to the process of peer judgment. The problem comes with a proliferation of procedural rules, resulting in technical violations and in frustrated buck-passing. Extensive evaluation processes and cumbersome procedures threaten to smother department chairpersons in paperwork and details. Even more frustrating is the nagging suspicion that all of the evidence produced is still not objective enough to thwart many grievances. Job security pressures, grievance threats, and possibilities of court cases for affirmative action may result in what one administrator calls "avoiding painful judgments subject to challenge."

An overwhelming amount of time is involved in grievance processing. A union official estimates that it takes over 20 hours to process a single grievance in the City Colleges of Chicago. Time required to iron out grievances and to administer contractual evaluation processes might deter faculty members from serving on committees and as department chairpersons. Should this occur, then obviously the concept of shared governance and peer evaluation will be compromised accordingly.

The growth of bureaucratic red tape is already hampering faculty effectiveness. For example, a union official at one of the CUNY campuses remarked in an interview that the elaborate evaluation procedures specified in their contract could not be applied effectively to large departments. The department chairperson of a large department agreed, noting that technical errors in carrying out all of the contractually required procedures are inevitable. Thus, it is likely that grievances will be filed and won because procedural technicalities are violated. Another department chairperson complained that formalized faculty evaluation procedures have created a "super-suspicious" faculty and "huge amounts of paperwork over trivia" for department chairpersons.

Asked to comment on these criticisms, a top union official agrees that the procedures need revision but strongly defends them because they guarantee that department chairpersons will carry out fair faculty evaluation. Asked if the mandated procedures strangle peer judgment and result in buck-passing, the official notes that in the past many departments had been derelict in their responsibilities and that administrators had allowed them to get away with it. "One of the outstanding aspects of the first contracts," notes the union official, "were the provisions on evaluation and procedural due process. Technical violations were common at first and some departments got caught. But by the second contract technical violations were reduced to a minimum."

There is also an economic factor involved in such elaborate procedures. Grievance processing and arbitration alone are expensive without even considering possible court costs. The Executive Director of the Professional Staff Congress at CUNY estimates that his union spends $45,000 per academic year just for central office salaries to process grievances that do not go to arbitration. Since it is standard practice for each side to bear half the cost of arbitration, the union must also pay $3,000 for arbitrating each grievance. The CUNY administration encounters a much larger cost involving administrative salaries, one half the cost of arbitration, legal expenses, and released time allowed faculty for grievance processing. Thus, increasing economic costs may also stimulate a tendency to "avoid painful judgments," particularly at institutions suffering severe financial strain. Hard-pressed institutions may find it easier to surrender to default personnel procedures rather than to spend scarce money to fight them.

Students and Evaluation. Another aspect of academic professionalism that may be affected negatively by unionization is student evaluation of the teaching faculty. Although student evaluation has been a contested topic even on campuses without faculty unions, there is some evidence that unions are hostile to student participation in governance, especially in relation to faculty personnel issues. Two examples support student claims that unions would like to exclude them from personnel decision making. At CUNY, although the Professional Staff Congress supports student evaluation of probationary faculty, it does not believe students should have a direct role in faculty hiring and promotion. In fact, it tried to make the role of students on personnel and budget committees a mandatory bargaining issue as a condition of employment, but the New York Employment Relations Board would not concede to this demand.

In another case, the faculty at Salem State College in Massachusetts rejected a contract in 1974 which provided for student participation in faculty hiring, promotion, and tenure decisions. A typical faculty reaction to proposed inclusion of students in faculty personnel decisions is the comment in a memorandum circulated prior to the contract rejection at Salem State: "Can you completely erase from your mind that kid sitting in your class who may have the deciding vote on your promotion and tenure?"

The wisdom of student evaluation of teaching is a hotly debated issue. Nevertheless, we believe that systematic, careful, and prolonged student evaluation can be helpful, and union resistance to the idea seems shortsighted. The client's needs are important and the client's voice should be heard.

Future Problems and Union Cooperation. Many institutions are now faced with the necessity of eliminating programs as a result of economic pressures and declining student populations. For example, the New York Board of Regents recently released enrollment projections showing a sharp downturn in the 1980s. By 1990, the Board estimates that full-time undergraduate enrollment in New York will be 21.4 percent below the 1973 level. The implications for CUNY and SUNY should be to begin planning for those contingencies now. Are the unions ready to cooperate? Insofar as planning involves establishing quotas for academicians achieving tenure, the answer is clearly no. Professional Staff Congress president Belle Zeller

responded to a quota threat at CUNY (PSC/CUNY *Clarion,*
October 18, 1973):

> The argument that quotas are required to
> give the institution "flexibility" is a false argu-
> ment. It is simply not true that you need tenure
> quotas to assure against the retention of teachers
> for students who do not exist or for courses that
> do not exist or for classes that do not exist. We al-
> ready have all the flexibility we need to drop
> courses that are no longer considered relevant and
> to adopt other courses and indeed whole curricula
> that are more relevant. We already have all the
> "flexibility" we need to assure that all our staff
> members are working—and working hard.

But if the development of new courses or other curriculum changes does not solve the problem, then what? Union concern with job security implies that administrators will not find
it easy to reduce staffing. Assuming administrators can present a
convincing case, they will still have to move according to objective criteria established at the bargaining table. In 1971, 15 percent of the contracts had items relating to staff reduction; in
1973, 50 percent of the contracts had such items. (See Table
12.) As pressures to adapt to declining enrollments increase, this
percentage is likely to continue climbing.

Proposals of the National Education Association pertaining to Reduction of Force (RIF) provide ample illustration of
the restraints unions seek to place on administrative discretion.
Among other features, the NEA supports institutional retraining
to help displaced staff members qualify for openings in other
divisions or departments, and it supports continued payment of
from one half to three fourths of the displaced person's salary
during retraining. The result, in the words of one administrator,
is that "You can't fire anyone with tenure until you've re-
trained them" (Winkler, 1975, p. 3). Obviously, union response
to these complex problems is to shift the burden to the administration.

In sum, while realizing that union goals for personnel
decisions can result in positive consequences on some campuses,

we must acknowledge that there are possible negative consequences as well. In relation to job security, tenure, and economic benefits in general, it appears that unions are making progress in serving faculties during these times of an uncertain economic environment. On campuses where there has been a tradition of faculty participation in governance, such gains may not appear significant. Where faculty senates are weak, however, or where administrators have systematically excluded faculty from personnel decision making, unions have contributed a measure of security and guarantees of due process that should be among the rights of faculty members.

Unfortunately, in the process of securing and protecting faculty rights, unions sometimes run headlong into traditional patterns of academic professionalism. If job security and tenure can be secured only by compromising performance standards and evaluation procedures, then unions pose a serious threat to the values of higher education. Unions must be able to incorporate procedures for peer and student evaluation in their demands for objective evaluation criteria. They must be able to cooperate with administrations in working toward realistic solutions to problems of declining enrollments. If they cannot serve to protect professionalism at the same time as they strive to expand contract provisions, then they may be damaging irrevocably the cherished ideals of higher education.

6

Consequences for Academic Senates

Along with academic departments, faculty senates are considered to be the heart of collegial processes in colleges and universities. They exemplify the oft-asserted claim that the faculty *is* the university. As traditionally conceived, senates are where faculty and administrators meet as educational professionals to deliberate on matters of shared concern. Although senates function as decision-making bodies, their powers are largely advisory. Administrators usually are included in the membership, and more broadly based senates often involve students, alumni, and staff. In one sense, then, senates are the forums for the deliberations of the academic community.

This idealistic vision is challenged, however, by critics who charge that senates act more like "company unions"—that is, like the employee organizations in industry that are so heavily influenced by management thinking that they seldom revolt even against unpopular decisions. Company unions have a reputation for being manipulable by managements who retain ultimate authority, and many faculties have an uncomfortable feeling that senates now share this reputation. Faculty representative bodies, for example, have little control over budgetary allocations at a time when economic considerations dominate campus decision making. Without this power, senates are relegated to the outer fringes of decision making.

As the leading alternative to the senate, unions may substantially affect the faculty's power over institutional policy formulation. Some observers believe that collective bargaining may emerge as the *protector* of traditional academic governance procedures. Yale law professor Ralph S. Brown, Jr. notes: "An administration and a bargaining representative who were of like minds on principles of shared power could contract . . . to withdraw all sorts of academic issues from unilateral control of either administration or bargaining representative, and to reserve them for prescribed internal procedures with full faculty participation. In this way, ideals of academic government could become the third-party beneficiaries of collective bargaining agreements that might otherwise threaten them" (Brown, 1969, pp. 1078-1079).

Others, however, fear that collective bargaining is a threat to senates and to collegial practices. Former president William B. Boyd of Central Michigan University warned his faculty of the consequences of unions on governance: "Increasingly, matters that ought to be reserved for the deliberation of faculties are transferred from the floor of the Senate to a table-top pounded by adversaries engaged in something less than reasoned debate. Educational policy thus becomes the product of negotiation rather than of deliberation. The exaggerated demands and counterclaims common to the bargaining process make a mockery out of scrupulous respect for truth and seem entirely alien to the scholarly processes" (Speech, September 8, 1969, p. 6).

Whether unions will affect senates by strengthening or weakening them is a moot question but somewhat difficult to answer. It is our opinion that the importance of senates has been overstressed in the literature on academic governance. Frankly, it is very doubtful that senates at most institutions deal effectively with substantive matters. The critical issues are generally handled by the *faculty* at the departmental level (curriculum, student relations, faculty hiring, firing, and promoting), or by the *administration* at higher levels (budgets, overall staffing, physical plant, long-range planning). The average academic senate, we suspect, deals with relatively minor issues and readily responds to administrative rather than faculty leadership. For example, the Stanford survey revealed that presidents and union chairpersons felt senates addressed a limited number of issues, and they rated them fairly low in influence. (Data for these ratings are shown in Chapter Three and later in this chapter.) In light of these reported senate weaknesses, unions may not pose a life-or-death threat to the academic governance process. In fact, they are apt to have a much more crucial impact on other areas, such as personnel decision making.

These reservations apply particularly to unionized institutions—community colleges, less prestigious state colleges, and weaker liberal arts institutions. To restate an earlier argument, *because these institutions rarely have had effective faculty governance, it is difficult to determine how much unions have affected the process.* At the bulk of these institutions—about 65 percent according to our survey—senates were formed in the last decade, which has allowed them little time to establish a strong faculty voice. Under these circumstances, we can relate the effects of unions on *weak* senates, but we cannot predict what may happen to healthier senates in institutions with a long history of faculty governance. Therefore, we are cautious about projecting our conclusions beyond the class of institutions where unionization has occurred. The consequences may be entirely different at prestigious colleges and universities if they turn to faculty collective bargaining.

Senates as Unions: An Unlikely Possibility

Will weak senates move toward collective bargaining in order to be more effective? On some campuses, when the need for more faculty power is felt, the first thought is to label the senate a union and proceed to negotiate a contract. Because senates depend on administrative financial support and because administrators are often senators, such a conversion is usually not possible under collective bargaining statutes that outlaw company unions. The NLRA states that it is an unfair labor practice for an employer "to dominate or interfere with the formation or administration of any labor organization or contribute financial or other support to it."

Where senates assume the role of a surrogate union without divesting themselves of administrative support or membership, they are open to challenge as company unions. For example, in 1974 at the 21-campus Pennsylvania State University system, the NEA union filed an unfair labor practice suit against the administration, charging that the University Faculty Senate had assumed the guise of a union when faced by collective bargaining groups. At the hearings, the union tried to show that the sudden proliferation of senate committees dealing with traditional union concerns such as grievances, salaries, and fringe benefits could be traced to the president's desire to undercut the union. The union demanded that the administration withdraw financial support to the senate, disband the senate, or confine the senate to academic issues.*

In its defense, the university administration accused the NEA of bolstering its own campaign against its chief competitor, the AAUP, by challenging shared governance. By cutting back the activities of the senate, the union could then attempt to fill the vacuum by being elected the bargaining agent for the university. To counter the union, the administration argued that

---

*Two NLRB rulings appear to support the union position. In June 1975, the National Labor Relations Board declared that the Northeastern University Faculty Senate is not a labor organization under federal law. The Board noted that the Faculty Senate functions as a group of advisory committees and makes recommendations to the president that are quite different from bargaining demands made by a union. The board also rejected the contention of the university that the faculty handbook was a contract and thus barred an election for a bargaining agent under federal law. This ruling supports an earlier declaration by an NLRB hearing examiner that the Argonne National Laboratory Senate was not a labor organization and therefore could not communicate with administrators over employment conditions. As a result of his ruling, the Argonne Senate was left with the option of either limiting its activities to strictly professional issues or converting into a union. If these NLRB rulings set a precedent for state PERBs, the role of academic senates in American higher education will be substantially challenged when they confront unions.

the senate had always been involved in broad policy formulation regarding academic programs and that present financial pressures had increased senate concern with economic issues. Our conclusion is that *most senate attempts to usurp traditional union functions will probably be challenged successfully, particularly if the senate has not previously or consistently dealt with economic issues and working conditions.*

The best way, of course, to avoid challenges to senates is to protect them through enabling legislation. Then, their destiny would not be determined by PERBs that tend to follow the example of industry. A prime example is the 1974 Montana higher education bargaining act; it provides that collective bargaining shall not interfere "with the right of the faculty senate or similar representative bodies of faculty, or the committees thereof from consulting with and advising any unit administration concerning matters of policy." It seems unlikely that senates will often be singled out for such protection, however, because they are not universally endorsed by faculty. Even if they were, faculty members—who would be the ones to benefit from such legislation—make up only a tiny percentage of public employees and could rarely muster the political clout to obtain favorable legislation.

Under most collective bargaining statutes, a senate that wished to convert into a full-fledged union would first have to disband and then either reform into an independent organization or sponsor an independent satellite group that overlaps senate membership. These options may not be feasible. A senate that includes supervising employees such as administrators cannot function as a union nor create one with overlapping membership. In public systems, the tendency toward large, all-encompassing units eliminates the opportunity for faculty on a single campus to win representation with a senate-based union. The expertise and money required for successful bargaining is so costly that affiliation with an outside agency would probably be necessary. Of the more than 300 unionized schools included in the 1974 Stanford survey, fewer than 30 had independent bargaining agents and most of these were special purpose institutions such as law schools with small faculties.

The ability of a senate to sponsor a viable union that wins elections depends on several factors. First, the personnel composition of the bargaining unit is critical, because if a bargaining unit includes a large number of academicians who were excluded from the senate, they will organize against a senate-based union and detract from its chances of success. Second, the strength of the senate is important. A recently formed or a weak senate will probably not attract many followers to the independent union it sponsors. Finally, senate-based unions face competition from other bargaining agents who have the resources to campaign for members and fight recalcitrance and delays at the bargaining table. Senate-based unions without outside affiliation are sadly underfinanced and understaffed.

To be successful, independent organizations would probably adopt the characteristics of a union. Of course, even a senate that performs the functions normally reserved to a union will be ultimately tested by its success in meeting employee needs. Serious liabilities are inherent and may be insurmountable. Since the senate functions outside a legal framework, it lacks the legal backing to challenge the administration. In addition, since fiscal problems predominate today, experiments based on "shared governance" principles are unlikely to be successful, especially in institutions with weak faculty senates. Therefore, the basic conclusion is that *national trends and general conditions indicate that on many campuses senates will not be successful in assuming the role of unions.*

Union-Only and Senate-Only Campuses

Can collective bargaining create a tradition of faculty governance at institutions where it has not previously existed? When there is no union, can a senate assume union functions? Although unions most often coexist with senates, the Stanford survey showed that several unions existed without a senate. We were curious to know whether, in such situations, unions would take over functions usually reserved for senates. We also contrasted these union-only situations with senate-only situations.

Table 16 compares the influence ratings of unions and

Table 16

Union-Only and Senate-Only Influence in Community Colleges

	Admissions Policy	Degree Requirements	Curriculum	Department Budgets	Long-Range Planning	Faculty Hiring Policies	Faculty Promotion and Tenure Policies	Faculty Working Conditions	Faculty Salaries and Fringe Benefits
Union, according to Presidents of Unionized Institutions without Senates (N = 54)	1.3	1.9	2.1	2.1	2.0	2.7	3.3	3.8	4.6
Union, according to Chairpersons of Unionized Institutions without Senates (N = 33)	1.4	2.0	2.4	2.1	2.2	2.6	3.2	3.7	4.2
Senate, according to Presidents of Nonunionized Institutions with Senates (N = 22)	2.4	3.6	3.8	2.3	3.0	2.7	2.6	3.1	2.7

Note: The question asked was "How much influence does the faculty collective bargaining unit and senate have on these issues, at your institution?" Respondents gave answers on a five-point scale, with "1" indicating low influence and "5" indicating high influence.

senates at institutions where they exist by themselves. In order
to simplify the picture, only data from community colleges is
given, for these are the institutions where the union-only pattern seems to occur most often. Unions are most likely to influence economic issues, such as faculty salaries, working conditions, faculty promotions, and tenure policies. Both presidents
and union chairpersons agree that faculty unions on their campuses have little control over strictly academic issues, such as
degree requirements, curricula and admissions policies. In contrast, senates existing alone are rated higher on almost all of
these academic issues and relatively weak in economic areas.
The only significant overlap between unions and senates are faculty working conditions. Because the ratings are based on
respondents' opinions, they may have built-in biases, with presidents likely to overrate senates and union chairpersons likely to
overrate unions. Even taking this precaution into account, the
data indicate that senates and unions have not poached in each
other's territory.

If unions eventually become influential in areas that traditionally have been the province of senates, will they then
assume a senate-like character? Experience in the Massachusetts
state system suggests they will not.

The state college system did not have a well-developed
senate structure before collective bargaining arrived, and many
faculty and administrators felt that unionization would encourage faculty participation in governance. When faculties at the
eleven colleges began to organize, many key administrators
looked favorably on bargaining. Until 1974, the law prohibited
bargaining over economic issues, a fact that may have elicited
the positive administrative attitudes.

The union accepted five conditions laid down by the
administration: (1) governance machinery would exist independent of the union; (2) participation in governance would be
extended to all faculty in the bargaining unit whether or not
they were union members; (3) the governance system would be
advisory with all authority remaining with the Board of
Trustees; (4) governance would be tripartite, representing administration, faculty, and students; (5) faculty would retain sole

control over matters directly related to them (see Walters, 1973). Thus, although the union agreed to share some of its authority, it also acquired a formal role in the governance system. Further, without union concurrence, the Massachusetts system probably never would have been set up; without continuing union support, it probably could not continue to exist.

One administrator who favored union participation in governance was Donald E. Walters, deputy director of the Massachusetts system. When we asked in an interview whether he was as optimistic in 1974 as he had been earlier, Walters admitted that he had lost a certain amount of enthusiasm. First, he noted that the Massachusetts law had been changed to allow economic bargaining, thus giving unions the right to bargain over both governance and economic issues. Second, other conditions than the law were undermining collegiality, such as the lack of student involvement in tripartite governance—even though that is understandable in a commuter school. Moreover, faculty union leaders had provoked conflict, and the faculty had not totally committed itself to the new governance mechanisms, particularly in relation to student participation in faculty personnel decisions. Walters emphasized that he still believed that unionism could promote collegiality "as long as we are willing to experiment with it."

The Massachusetts experience is unique because until 1974 the unions could bargain only over governance-related items. Yet it shows that when a union did become involved in governance, it stressed the inherent conflict between administrations and faculty and sought to secure gains through political influence. Garbarino (1973, p. 6) compares senates and unions:

> The union is likely to have a different attitude toward the administration, one more independent and probably more adversary in tone. No administrators will be found among the membership, the agenda of the organization's concerns is likely to be different and to be more responsive to the discontents of relatively smaller aggrieved sectors of the constituency. Leadership style and attitude will be more oriented to the membership and

less to the academic establishment both within the faculty and within the administration. If the institution is large and the union active, professional nonfaculty leadership may be employed to handle the day-to-day affairs on a continuous basis. . . . The union will tend to monopolize the representative function, challenging the legitimacy of any consultative mechanisms such as administrative committees whose membership has not been selected [by] and is not accountable to the union.

The conclusion we reach is that even without competition, neither unions nor senates appear to usurp each other's normal role. When unionism is still new to a campus, senates and unions have distinct styles of action, addressed to different issues. A trend is evident, however, that as unions mature, they may challenge traditional senate prerogatives—the "creeping expansionism" of union control.

Coexistence: Senate and Union Influence

When a campus has both a senate and a union, what areas do each influence? Further, what are the factors that promote or diminish conflict between unions and senates?

The 1974 Stanford survey asked people on unionized campuses to rate union and senate influence in relation to a broad spectrum of issues. Table 17 shows the responses of presidents and union chairpersons and indicates that: (1) The ratings of presidents and union chairpersons are basically similar, although presidents tend to rate senates higher and chairpersons tend to rate unions higher. (2) Senates at two-year and four-year institutions have essentially the same influence patterns, with senate influence increasing slightly in four-year institutions. (3) Unions also have similar influence patterns in two- and four-year institutions, with union influence over economic issues increasing slightly in two-year colleges. (4) Unions outperform senates at both types of institutions in influencing economic issues, particularly faculty salaries and working conditions. (5) Senates retain influence over academic issues at both

Table 17
Influence of Coexisting Senates and Unions

	Admissions Policy	Degree Requirements	Curriculum	Department Budgets	Long-Range Planning	Faculty Hiring Policies	Faculty Promotion and Tenure Policies	Faculty Working Conditions	Faculty Salaries and Fringe Benefits
Four-Year and Graduate Institutions									
Presidents (N = 59)									
Senates	2.9	3.9	4.2	1.9	3.2	2.5	3.1	2.2	1.5
Unions	1.3	1.5	1.7	1.6	1.9	2.3	2.9	2.8	4.1
Union Chairpersons (N = 56)									
Senates	2.5	3.7	3.8	1.5	2.6	1.8	2.7	1.6	1.3
Unions	1.4	1.5	1.8	1.4	2.4	2.7	3.7	3.7	4.7
Two-Year Institutions									
Presidents (N = 70)									
Senates	2.8	3.7	3.8	2.3	3.2	2.5	2.7	2.5	2.0
Unions	1.2	1.6	1.6	1.7	1.6	2.3	3.3	4.2	4.7
Union Chairpersons (N = 78)									
Senates	2.2	3.3	3.6	1.7	2.7	1.9	2.4	1.9	1.7
Unions	1.6	1.8	2.2	2.0	2.6	3.1	3.9	4.1	4.6

types of institutions. (6) Senates and unions share influence over personnel issues such as faculty hiring, promotion, and tenure policy. (7) Whether they exist alone or together, neither senates nor unions influence department budgets. (8) Unions have little influence over long-range planning; senates have some. (9) Little difference is evident on all these issues between single campus unions and multicampus unions (data not shown in Table 17).

Both presidents and chairpersons react as the dual-track model of governance predicts. That is, senates have their greatest influence in academic areas, while economic matters are the province of unions. Where the lines of demarcation are unclear, such as in faculty working conditions and long-range planning, unions and senates share influence to certain degrees.

The survey data showing the separate areas of senate and union influence can be checked against the content of contracts as analyzed by John Andes (1974). His data show that the contracts essentially deal with "working conditions." With each passing year, however, more contracts are containing more items that were once the province of senates, such as teaching load, class size, selection of administrators, and matters related to faculty by-laws and policies. The scope of union concerns is steadily expanding.

Dual-track bargaining assumes that there are two mutually exclusive areas of influence for senates and unions. However, one flaw appears in this model, for there is one large area of *overlapping* concern. At one end of the continuum, economic issues are under union jurisdiction, and unions recognize the adversary posture between administration and faculty. With their legal backing and their legal right to economic information, unions undoubtedly have more power to gain economic benefits than senates do. On the other hand, senates, with jurisdiction over academic issues such as curricula and degree requirements, recognize the need for a professional forum to resolve these academic matters. Between the two poles is a grey area where unions and senates share influence over department budgets, hiring policies, faculty promotion and tenure policies, faculty working conditions (student-teacher ratio, class load) and long-range planning. In most cases, the dual-track approach leaves procedural issues to the union but allows the senate to determine policy affecting substantive decisions, with academic departments actually responsible for the decisions.

Threats to Dual-Track Bargaining

If the areas of senate and union influence would remain stable, then dual-track bargaining would be a reality. Many factors, however, contribute to a breakdown of the dual track and encourage unions to expand into senate territory.

Collective bargaining is a political process. In order to maintain membership support, union leaders press to expand the scope of bargaining. Who is to decide which issues belong to the senate or to the union? Over a period of time, the dilemma of drawing fine lines between issues suggests that the dual-track system is likely to become unstable.

Prognostications abound about the future of senates in the face of union encroachments. Some are unclear, some are hopeful, but most are pessimistic. A joint commission of AAHE and NEA states: "While we support a division of issues between a bargaining agency and an academic senate when both are well established on a campus, we recognize that any such demarcation is likely to be unstable over time. The record of collective bargaining in industrial settings reveals a steady expansion of union concern. . . . A parallel series of developments may take place in higher education" (*Faculty Participation in Academic Governance*, 1967, p. 65).

Similarly, the opinions of presidents and chairpersons in our survey predict a bleak future for senates. We asked people to agree or disagree with this statement: "Where it occurs, faculty collective bargaining will undermine the influence of faculty senate or other established decision bodies." The presidents overwhelmingly agree—74 percent of presidents at nonunion colleges and 69 percent of presidents at unionized colleges. By contrast, only 36 percent of the union chairpersons agree with the statement.

Does this mean that senates are doomed in the face of

union pressure? Not necessarily, because *most unionized campuses initially had a weak tradition of faculty participation in governance.* It is no surprise, then, to find that unions have undercut senates, for the senates were impotent to begin with. In addition, forces other than unionism threaten senates—especially institutional growth, centralization, and powerful economic pressures. When unions and senates coexist, the health or weakness of the senate depends on many variables other than faculty unionization. One of these variables is the conflict in values between various academic groups.

Value Conflicts. Our society has felt the impacts of cultural differences in many areas, including our educational institutions. These differences have created an expected conflict on campuses about the proper mission of the academic profession. President Edward J. Bloustein of Rutgers concludes that collegiality is disappearing under the onslaught, but he does not blame unionism. Instead he believes unionism is a symptom, a result, of a deeper problem: "What has happened is that our faculties and our student bodies and our boards of governors have now discovered that their interests are adverse on occasion and that there is no single common overriding interest which can or should unite them on all issues" (Bloustein, 1973, p. 191).

Budget cuts and declining enrollments force latent differences between campus constituencies out into the open and undermine the spirit of cooperative decision making. At the SUNY College of Arts and Science at Geneseo, institutional researchers uncovered dramatic evidence in 1975 of faculty, administration, and student conflict over institutional goals and practices. Faced with the growing unmarketability of a purely liberal arts program, over 70 percent of the enrolled students and over 50 percent of the administrative group sampled favored including substantial field work and intern-like experiences in undergraduate academic programs. In marked contrast, less than 30 percent of the faculty sampled endorsed this idea, preferring traditional classroom instruction. Likewise, a strong majority of the students (84 percent) and administrators (67 percent) endorsed student evaluation of faculty members, whereas two thirds of the faculty group opposed it (SUNY College of Arts and Science at Geneseo, 1975). We believe such fundamental differences are becoming common on all campuses as the external economic and political climate worsens—and dual tracking is becoming more and more difficult. The breakdown in value consensus is particularly threatening to the continued health of academic senates, for in many ways senates represent the traditional professional viewpoints that are being challenged.

Recall that the leadership of a union is chosen democratically by the membership and that leaders must satisfy the membership in order to stay in power. Even if senate and union membership overlap perfectly, internal procedures of each may produce different leaders with different objectives. Those who join the union will probably be the most aggrieved—the junior faculty, the untenured, the part-timers. If the aggrieved faculty dominates the union and the well-placed senior faculty controls the senate, extreme environmental pressure may cause pitched battles between the two. Certainly a senate composed of a small number of elites will have difficulty keeping a broad-based union from threatening its jurisdiction. Consequently, many senates can be expected to broaden their composition and assert their independence from the administration. Unions, for their part, will seek to get union sympathizers into positions of authority within the senate. In this situation, the real loser may be the administration. As one commentator notes, "Management becomes the little white ball in a continuous union-senate game of ping-pong" (Williams, 1973, p. 54).

Administrative Support of Senates. The role of administrative leaders is another variable influencing the future of dual-track bargaining. Woodrow Wilson once likened democracy to living tissue: it must be carefully protected and nourished to thrive. Senates possessing little legal authority are extremely fragile and, like a democratic government, they depend on individuals willing to work on their behalf. If administrators refuse to recognize faculty discontent with ineffective senates, unions can quickly replace them. If administrators attempt to defeat a faculty union by negotiating with the senate on union matters, they are essentially promoting unionization. Too often administrators pay lip service to the senate while condemning the union

—forgetting that both are creations of the faculty. As a result, unions grow more militant, senates become weaker, and faculties are torn by conflict. Administrators can support senates by not allowing union contracts to spread into areas of governance. They can insist that the right of the senate to control academic issues be kept separate from the right of the union to bargain over economic issues.

Clarifying proper roles is a critical administrative task made difficult by the multiple, overlapping decision-making bodies on a campus. It is not unusual for a single campus to have most of the following: (1) department, school, and division committees; (2) faculty senate; (3) student senate; (4) broad-based senate; (5) faculty union (sometimes more than one representing academic employees); and (6) administrative council. Drawing the boundaries for the spheres of influence of each organization can be mind-boggling. Nevertheless, because of its unique position of authority on campus, the administration should take the lead in establishing a workable governance scheme.

The Legal Context. A major factor determining the future of senates, and hence their role in dual-track bargaining, is the legal situation. Even a politically astute administration will have a hard time altering the effects of an all-encompassing unit determination or a court decision upholding union involvement in governance. For example, the NLRA and most state laws outlaw company unions and establish the union as the exclusive employee representative. A charge of company unionism by a competing union may challenge continued administrative support of the faculty senate, as in the Northeastern University decision. Once a union is voted in, it may force the administration to consider it the exclusive employee representative and thus curtail the jurisdiction of senate and department committees. Where the scope of bargaining is unclear—as it often is—the administration may be hesitant to communicate with the senate simply because a mistake could trigger the filing of an unfair labor practice charge. In effect, the legal framework may confine the jurisdiction of the senate to academic matters and inhibit its communication with administrators on other issues.

Where there are few restrictions on mandatory subjects of

bargaining, the law invites unions to move continually into new areas indirectly related to economic concerns. Some laws restrict the union by establishing "management prerogatives," activities essential to management control over which the union may not bargain. The management prerogatives approach, however, is limited because (1) it is at odds with shared governance, and (2) it may be rendered ineffective by unions that bargain about issues irrespective of the law.

Administrative rulings by the NLRB or by state PERBs become part of the legal context. Although decisions interpreting the law in relation to given situations do not yet form a distinct pattern, such judgments can play a critical role in shaping bargaining activities on a particular campus. Administrative rulings pertaining to the scope of bargaining may determine the fate of senates and unions. For example, in 1975, a district NLRB official ruled that the AAUP union as a labor organization at St. John's University could not force the administration to bargain over the faculty's role in the selection of administrators or over incorporation into the contract of the AAUP Statement on Government of Colleges and Universities. The university *may* bargain over these issues, he said, but they are not mandatory subjects of negotiation. In this case, the complaint filed by the university was dismissed because the official ruled the AAUP had not forced the university to bargain over the contested matters, which were included in the new agreement. The university did not appeal the ruling since its general position was upheld. It will be interesting to see what happens in future negotiations at St. John's.

Another legal question revolves around writing governance matters into the contract. Even where governance is not a mandatory subject of bargaining, an administration may agree to bargain about it. Opinions about writing governance into the contract are divided: it may strengthen formerly weak academic processes, or it may subject governance provisions to future negotiation. Both sides of the argument seem plausible, and the trends are likely to be determined by local conditions on individual campuses.

Faculty Apathy. The increase in union power at the

expense of the senates can be blamed partially on unsupportive administrators and on laws that arm the unions with legal weapons. But much of the responsibility for ineffective senates must be laid at the feet of the faculty themselves. Do they care if the senates fail? Of the 1969 Carnegie Commission survey of 60,028 faculty members at 303 representative institutions, 43 percent of the respondents reported below average participation in institutional government (see *Governance*, 1973, pp. 100-101). Demands of teaching and research to satisfy the requirements for tenure probably preclude prolonged active participation by many junior faculty in campus governance, whereas many tenured faculty members may find more satisfaction in their professional activities than in campus politics. For whatever reason, lack of participation may account for why only 18 percent of faculty in the Carnegie study reported having significant influence over institutional policy formulation. Confirming the Carnegie findings, the 1971 Stanford survey found that only 21 percent of the faculty said they participated frequently in academic decision making; 51 percent of the faculty were not involved.

Time and again, the people interviewed in our case studies reported that senates were ineffective because faculty were not active participants. For example, the broad-based senate at Hunter College had difficulty getting a quorum to conduct meetings.

Interestingly enough, the same reluctance to participate also characterizes unions. At Central Michigan, for example, only 30 percent of the eligible faculty had joined the union prior to the 1974 contract negotiations. Thus, 70 percent of the faculty were content to allow 30 percent to determine governance matters. When agency shops are written into the law, they may compel faculty involvement; still, many may choose simply to pay their dues and not participate.

If faculty do not become involved in both senate and union affairs, the ominous predictions about the demise of faculty governance may come true. Combined with the other factors undermining dual-track bargaining, faculty apathy may strike the final blow to traditional academic governance.

Having discussed the possibilities of senates becoming unions, the influence of senates and unions when they exist alone and together, and the future of dual-track bargaining, we now turn to case studies that demonstrate the impact of collective bargaining on senates. There are two basic institutional arrangements: (1) One union represents one campus, and there is a local campus senate; or (2) one union represents an entire educational system, and there is usually both a local and a systemwide senate.

Single Campus Unions and Senates

Over half of the respondents to the Stanford survey report that their union represents only the local campus. About one third of these respondents are at four-year colleges, and the rest are either at two-year private or locally controlled community colleges. How have unions affected senates on these campuses? Few senates have disappeared because of unions, but their future is clouded. Our survey showed that only union chairpersons at two-year institutions believe the union has positively affected their senate, and the majority of union chairpersons at four-year schools believe unions have had little impact at all. Conversely, a majority of presidents at both four-year and two-year institutions believe senate influence has decreased as a result of unionization. (See Table 18.)

As we mentioned in the previous section, the tradition of effective faculty participation in governance is crucial to maintaining viable dual-track bargaining. Unions may be threatening to senates on single-unit campuses because these recently established senates are still insecure. More than half of the four-year institutions and 72 percent of the two-year institutions reported that their senates were less than nine years old. When faculties express an interest in unionization, then, they may be saying that they lack confidence in existing organizations; unions offer the hope of gaining previously denied participation in governance.

The experience of Central Michigan University illustrates the tension between unions and senates on single campuses. In

Table 18
Impact of Unions on Senates

| | | Percentage Reporting Influence of Senate | | |
		Increased	About Same	Decreased
Single Campus Unions				
Four-Year In-	Presidents (N = 17)	6	35	59
stitutions	Chairpersons (N = 24)	21	50	29
Two-Year In-	Presidents (N = 51)	16	29	55
stitutions	Chairpersons (N = 49)	45	27	29
Total	Presidents (N = 68)	13	31	56
	Chairpersons (N = 73)	37	34	29
Multicampus Unions				
Four-Year In-	Presidents (N = 41)	17	42	42
stitutions	Chairpersons (N = 32)	9	44	47
Two-Year In-	Presidents (N = 22)	14	27	59
stitutions	Chairpersons (N = 34)	21	32	47
Total	Presidents (N = 63)	16	37	48
	Chairpersons (N = 66)	15	38	47

1969, Central Michigan became one of the first four-year institutions in the country to have a faculty union. Several unique factors help to account for campus unionization: 24 percent of the faculty had been at the institution only one or two years; 35 percent of the faculty were full or associate professors; and, in a state where unionism dominates public education, about 20 percent of the faculty were in the education division. In addition, the recently formed senate included faculty, administrators, and students—a combination less likely to respond to faculty desires than a faculty-only composition. The first contract was primarily limited to financial issues and received an overwhelming vote of approval in the ratification election.

By 1973, Central Michigan was optimistic that a union and a senate could coexist, mostly because of the decision of the union to confine its jurisdiction to wages, fringe benefits, and matters directly related to working conditions. It did not bargain over academic issues or evaluation methods, and personnel issues were limited to grievance procedures.

There were problems, to be sure. The Faculty Association was accused of splitting the faculty and the administration and destroying collegiality. The administration was criticized for being top-heavy, for being remote from the faculty, and for making arbitrary decisions. On the whole, however, the union, senate, and administration seemed to have succeeded at dual-track governance.

By late 1973, the dual approach began to break down in the face of stringent economic policies. The administration talked to the senate about the ramifications of retrenchment, but it refused to discuss the matter with the union. Through senate action, the administration then instituted new policies on faculty workload, teaching evaluation, and teaching effectiveness. As a result, the Faculty Association filed an unfair labor practice against the university in relation to the effectiveness policy, which included students as evaluators.

Adding to the conflict was the ongoing, laborious contract renegotiations, with personnel issues heading the list of concerns. The Faculty Association bargained hard for expanded job security. An equally tough bargaining stance by the administration kept the union from contractualizing issues of promotion and tenure. The university did agree, however, not to change personnel policies unilaterally during the life of the agreement. Changes could be instituted only through using the same machinery by which the policies were originally established.

During this period, the weaknesses of the young senate became more evident. First, since the senate included students and administrators, it was not a faculty body. Yet the leader of the senate in 1974 (who was also a union member) criticized those who urged removal of the administrative contingent. He argued that it would be counterproductive to force administrators out because so much of the information needed by the senate comes from the administration. He also argued that a university needs a widely representative deliberative body if the spirit of community is to prevail. Second, the senate was powerless to solicit budgetary facts, and thus it was prevented from making informed decisions in a time of funding cutbacks. Third, the senate could only recommend policies to the president, who then carried them to the trustees without direct faculty input. The president controlled the communication channels, creating

"an uneasy, suspicious atmosphere" concerning the motives of
the administration. Finally, the senators were viewed as apathetic and "simply unversed about governance." The senate was
criticized for dealing with relatively unimportant matters and
for wasting time haggling over procedure and personnel. As a
result, members were easily coopted by the administration.

   Is criticism of the senate a sign that academic values and
consensus are deteriorating at Central Michigan University?
"I'm troubled," said the senate chairman. "I see no reason for
conflict between senate and union as long as the union stays out
of academic areas. I pay my dues and I expect the union to be
my vigorous representative in *economic* areas." But he went on
to observe that the university had grown from a small school to
a multicampus university serving 14,000 students, many of
whom are academically weak. "The result is a new breed of faculty and a changed reward system, one that generates an appeal
for the greater economic benefits promoted by unions." The
way to get recognition now at Central Michigan, he noted, is
"to be a politician, to look upon the administration as anti-
academic. It is this element which is heavily represented in the
union." Many union members we interviewed labeled the senate
a tool of the administration and freely admitted that one way
for the union to gain the cooperation of the senate is simply to
take it over. Indeed, there was a good deal of membership overlap, particularly among the leadership, at the time of our campus visit.

   Coupled with growing state pressures for retrenchment,
the conflict among the faculty at Central Michigan could upset
the precarious coexistence of the union and senate. The president of the university told us, "If the dual-track concept can't
exist at Central Michigan, I don't know where it can." But
almost in the same breath, he admitted, "I'm gloomy about the
outcome."

Systemwide Unions and Senates

   How will multicampus unions affect senates? One obvious response to that question is that not every campus senate
within a system will be affected similarly, for campuses are

usually quite diverse. This is particularly true in systems such as
SUNY and CUNY. On campuses with little faculty involvement
in governance, a multicampus union might fight to obtain governance rights. On other campuses where the faculty has long
held governance power, a multicampus union contract might
safeguard that tradition. The status of local senates may thus be
varyingly affected. Experience under the first contract at
SUNY, a vertical multicampus system, suggests that where traditional structures were firmly established prior to unionization,
as at the four SUNY University Centers, they are less threatened. However, where traditional structures have always been
weak—as at the two-year specialized institutions of SUNY—
collective bargaining may rapidly become the primary governance mechanism for the faculty (see Doh and Johnson, 1974).
The only accurate way to assess the impact of a systemwide
union contract on faculty governance at a particular campus is
to study that institution.

As Table 18 shows, presidents and chairpersons generally
are pessimistic about the effect of multicampus unions on senates. About half of all respondents say unions have decreased
senate influence. Compared to the single campus situation, this
rate is slightly less for presidents but nearly double for union
chairpersons. Another third of the respondents say unions have
made little difference; only about 15 percent said unionism had
helped. The reason presidents at two-year campuses express
negative attitudes is probably due to their fear that unions
would encroach on their wide open field of presidential power.

As with single campus senates and unions, an important
factor in the decline of senate influence in multicampus systems
is the lack of a strong tradition of faculty participation in governance. Of the senates at four-year multicampuses and two-
year schools, 67 and 70 percent, respectively, were established
less than nine years ago. More significantly, administrative centralization and multicampus bargaining pose a double threat to
campus senates, for they remove decision making on critical
issues from the individual campuses. Not surprisingly, the Stanford survey shows that 70 percent of presidents and 50 percent
of union chairpersons at campuses covered by systemwide con-

tracts agree that collective bargaining will undermine the influence of the senate. The following case studies help to clarify how centralization and unionization combine to threaten senates.

   Hunter College: A Multicampus Situation. Founded in 1870 as a normal school for women, Hunter College was placed under the New York Board of Education in 1926. Hunter remained an elitist institution until the late 1960s, when social changes dramatically altered the character of the student body, and the instructional programs were revised to serve minority groups and community college transfers.

   Faculty governance at Hunter is complicated, because not only is there a union but also a broad-based senate and a faculty-only body. Although faculty members form a majority in the broad-based senate, administrators and students make up a sizeable contingent. Charles Sherover, the 1974 senate president, characterizes the body as an "umbrella organization"—one that seeks to engender and broaden community participation in governance. Some faculty members doubt that the senate successfully represents faculty. Students comment that the senate has difficulty getting a quorum, considers petty issues, and is characterized by in-fighting.

   The faculty representative body, the Faculty Delegate Assembly (FDA), has no official role in governance, but Hunter President Jacqueline Wexler views it as a strong faculty lobby. As the "voice of the faculty," the FDA maintains ties with the CUNY University Senate, a university-wide faculty representative body. Because of its limited power and because of pressures from the CUNY central administration, one faculty member calls the FDA a "holding action" with a bleak future. Further weakening faculty involvement in governance, says another faculty member, is President Wexler's tendency to play one representative body off against another.

   How do these organizations relate to the union? Apparently, the local chapter of the Professional Staff Congress at Hunter strikes no fear in either the Hunter Senate or the Faculty Delegate Assembly. The local union often seems to cooperate more with the local campus bodies than with the central union.

Most of those interviewed about governance at Hunter sharply criticize the CUNY central office. A high administrative official says: "The central office is removed physically, emotionally, and intellectually from the colleges. Administrative centralization is a more significant threat in its effects than collective bargaining. The union is a minor nuisance, but the central office is a major problem. We are second-guessed at every turn; there are all sorts of university-wide forums: student senate, faculty senate, bargaining unit, and central administration. In short, the destiny of Hunter is now in the hands of the Chancellor and his staff."

The college gets its share of criticism, too; both the system administrators and the central union have had problems with the Hunter campus. Both groups have complained about the elitist tendencies of Hunter and several other senior colleges in the system. A CUNY administrator denies that centralization has drained power from the campuses, suggesting instead that the college presidents have "unused" power—they have failed to use it and instead look to the central office for problem solving.

One central union official notes that the presidents failed to take a stand on tenure quotas and did not properly administer the recruitment and probationary period of faculty members. While acknowledging the unclaimed and ill-defined zone between union business and campus senate affairs, that same official says the union needs to expand into governance issues because the "local campus senate is a tool of the president." The impression we gained from conversations with union officials is that local campus senates are not the direct target of the union. Instead, the Professional Staff Congress is more concerned with the central administration and, to a lesser extent, with the university-wide senate.

To summarize, the Hunter case study demonstrates a new dimension of the senate/union relationship. On a campus that is part of a huge system, local senate power is subject to attacks from many directions: the local union, the local administration, the system administration, the system senate, and the system union. The major problems emanate from the policies of the central administration and the systemwide contract negotiated with the Professional Staff Congress. If personnel and budget matters continue to command greater attention from both the union and the central office, local campus senates will find that they have little authority to deliberate over substantive matters. *In short, centralized, systemwide union contracts reinforce a trend already begun by centralized administrative networks—a steady decrease in the decision-making power of local campuses.*

City University of New York. Having discussed a single campus union and senate, and a multicampus union and a local campus senate, we now need to examine a multicampus union and a university-wide senate. There is little doubt that collegiality and shared governance as traditionally conceived are very limited in such a situation, yet multicampus senates do provide channels for faculties at various campuses to influence decision making at the board level. How will unions affect the limited role of systemwide faculty bodies? CUNY provides a pertinent example.

The CUNY University Faculty Senate, an all-faculty representative body, is handicapped by traditions of faculty autonomy on local campuses and by the reluctance of centralized administrators to share their authority. Nevertheless, the senate does have two important functions. It selects members to serve on Board of Higher Education committees, and its Executive Committee is a convenient sounding board for the Chancellor's Office. Thus, although it is essentially advisory, it has channels of communication that the union does not have. The executive director of the University Senate feels that it has almost no legislative, executive, or judicial powers, but that it does have the power of persuasion—and the New York Board of Education seems inclined to listen.

The systemwide union, the Professional Staff Congress, regards the University Senate as the purest form of company union. Even a member of the CUNY central office admitted that the University Senate is "on the horns of a dilemma." It was formed at the same time faculty collective bargaining began, and it looks like an administrative creation to deflect unionization. A union spokesperson notes that independence for the University Senate is unrealistic because its staff is paid by the central administration. The ultimate conflict of interest, according to one interviewee, is the goal of some of the University Senate leaders to become future administrators.

The image of the University Faculty Senate was not helped when the Chancellor said the senate supported his controversial "mathematical guidelines" policy on tenure in 1973. The policy was vigorously—and successfully—opposed by the union. Although the senate later denied that it had endorsed the controversial proposal, that body was portrayed as the handmaiden of the central administration, whereas the union was pictured as the heroic champion of the faculty. *At CUNY the trend is toward decreased senate influence at the system level. Given the traditional weaknesses of systemwide senates, the paramount importance of economic issues at the system level, and the strength of unions in economic matters, we suspect that this trend will become a national one.*

To summarize, it appears that the future of academic senates is questionable for many reasons—not just because faculty collective bargaining has posed a new challenge. It is unlikely that senates, especially weak ones, will become unions as a way to increase their influence. In the early stages, at least, senates and unions seem to share responsibilities in a dual-track approach: unions are concerned with economic matters, and senates retain influence over academic issues. Generally, they share influence over personnel decisions and have little input on departmental budgets.

As the bargaining continues past the initial stages, however, unions begin to pose threats to senates. Where faculty senates seem to be most vulnerable, the tradition of faculty participation in governance usually has been weak. Other variables that affect the future of senates include value conflicts between different campus groups, the stance taken by administrators, the legal context that determines which issues will be bargainable, and faculty apathy.

At a single campus, the prospects for effective dual-track bargaining of senate and union are reasonably optimistic, but faculty bodies will probably face a difficult struggle in relation to multicampus unions. Much will depend on the variables mentioned above, the specific traditions and environmental pressures of individual campuses, and the extent to which faculty and administrators invest their time in establishing or preserving faculty authority over academic matters.

7

Consequences for Campus Administration

Faculty unionism is one of many problems administrators must face in managing institutions that are rapidly changing under the onslaught of environmental pressures. Many administrators perceive collective bargaining as a threat to their management power and fear that campus polarization will make effective decision making virtually impossible. Paradoxically, evidence from the Stanford project shows that faculty collective bargaining actually affords greater—not less—power to certain administrative components.

In an interview, a university president expressed concern that the rise of faculty unions signals the impending collapse of administrative authority in colleges and universities. For the last decade, he says, campus constituencies have gradually organized into formalized power blocs: first, blue collar workers; then students; then faculty; and now, office staff and middle management seeking a part in governance. As a result, power has shifted away from the board and administration and has become dispersed among competing groups. We have reached, this president feels, a state of paralysis with political veto groups canceling each other out and thus halting effective decision making.

Many campus officials say that the power drain to unionized groups comes at a particularly bad time—when the problems of administrators are proliferating. As one commentator notes, "The college administration, especially in state-supported systems, must walk the tightrope between legislators and state officials (super-managers) and the college faculty (employees) while balancing the interests of students (consumers) against the needs of an increasingly specialized and technocratic society" (Olsen, 1974, p. 363). Such problems alone would create fears of diminished authority, but the union movement magnifies them.

On the Stanford questionnaire, a substantial percentage of administrators at public colleges with faculty unions indicate that collective bargaining has already decreased their power. (See Table 19, Question A.) Still, an almost equal percentage feel that their power has not been affected. Only chief executives at private liberal arts institutions say they have either maintained or actually gained power. Union chairpersons, however, uniformly report great losses of administrative power at all institutions. Questioned about what might happen in the future, almost no union officials and only about one fifth of all presidents agree that "where it occurs, faculty collective bargaining will increase the power of the administration at the expense of the faculty." (See Table 20, Question A.) Administrators at two-year institutions perceive less hope for administrative gains than presidents of other institutions. This is not surprising since the union goal at two-year colleges is to enfranchise the faculty —at the expense of the administrators who previously dominated institutional decision making.

How realistic are these fears (or hopes, depending on one's perspective) of administrative impotence? Our observations show a complex, multifaceted picture. First, unionism can weaken administrative dominance at many two-year institutions, and administrators there can expect major changes. Second, we do not believe that unions have thus far jeopardized administrative authority on most four-year campuses. Most of

Table 19
Impact of Collective Bargaining on Unionized Campuses

	A. Power of the administration			B. Power of off-campus state agencies			C. Influence of faculty over administration issues		
	Increased	Remained Same	Decreased	Increased	Remained Same	Decreased	Increased	Remained Same	Decreased
Multiversities (N = 12)									
Presidents (N = 8)	0	67	33	50	50	0	0	88	13
Chairpersons (N = 9)	0	67	33	22	56	22	88	13	0
Public Colleges and Universities (N = 58)									
Presidents (N = 49)	10	51	39	57	37	7	31	57	12
Chairpersons (N = 42)	2	31	67	51	33	15	72	25	3
Liberal Arts Colleges (N = 20)									
Presidents (N = 11)	36	55	9	0	100	0	36	55	9
Chairpersons (N = 12)	8	33	58	10	90	0	67	33	0
Two-Year Colleges (N = 180)									
Presidents (N = 135)	14	42	44	30	66	4	42	44	14
Chairpersons (N = 126)	6	41	53	25	73	2	56	32	12
All Institutions (N = 270)									
Presidents (N = 203)	14	46	41	36	60	4	37	49	13
Chairpersons (N = 189)	5	39	56	30	65	6	62	30	9

Note: The question asked was "In your opinion, how has faculty collective bargaining affected the following areas of your institution?"

Table 20
Impact of Collective Bargaining on Administrative Activities Nationally

	Percent Agreeing[1]		
	Presidents, Nonunion Institutions (N = 134)	Presidents, Union Institutions (N = 204)	Faculty Union Chairpersons (N = 193)
A. Collective bargaining will increase the power of the administration at the expense of the faculty	21	22	3
B. System management is increasing all the time[2]	78	76	–
C. I prefer binding arbitration as a strategy for settling disputes	20	35	81
D. Collective bargaining will increase the influence of outside agencies (arbitrators, courts, or state agencies)	84	83	53
E. Collective bargaining will cause specialists such as lawyers and management specialists to replace generalists in campus administration	75	68	32
F. Collective bargaining will democratize decision making by allowing junior faculty to play a greater role	14	26	72
G. Collective bargaining will increase the effectiveness of campus governance	10	20	77

[1]Answer categories were "strongly agree," "agree," "neutral," "disagree," and "strongly disagree." Here "strongly agree" and "agree" are combined.
[2]The questionnaire for chairpersons did not contain this question.

Note: The table includes responses from both unionized and nonunion institutions, since the questions dealt with general trends and not necessarily the respondents' own institution.

the evidence seems to point to union—not administrative—weakness. Earlier chapters discussed the lack of union security agreements in most faculty contracts, the relatively limited scope of bargaining, controversy within faculty ranks about the idea of unionism, and the lack of effective union sanctions to apply against the administration. The picture may change, of course, as unions gain tactical experience and wider legislative support; at the same time, administrators may also gain similar political advantages. Our general conclusion is that although collective bargaining does complicate the administrative process, administrators do not appear to have lost power and potentially may be rewarded with more control.

Administrative Power Trends

It is questionable that administrative power at unionized schools is experiencing a net decline, yet it is evident that the locus of decision making within the administrative hierarchy has changed. At single campuses, we note a power shift upward, whereas in multicampus systems, "parallel power pyramids" seem to be developing.

Until recently, most large four-year institutions were decentralized, with departments, schools, and colleges traditionally involved in institutional decision making. Fiscal stringencies, however, have forced many governing boards to take a more active role in campus affairs—at the expense of both decentralized decision-making bodies and presidential authority. This pattern exists whether the institutions have unions or not. Although many trustees consider themselves novices and defer to the faculty in relation to academic affairs, they are confident about fiscal matters; thus, the present financial crises have moved trustees to the front line of decision making.

In both public and private institutions, coordination and centralization of policy making, particularly on economic issues, has moved upward from departments, to schools, to the central administration, and ultimately to off-campus authorities. In New York, for example, the grim forecast of limited funds, declining enrollments, and a surplus of advanced degree graduates has forced the Commissioner of Education to recommend phasing out some doctoral programs at both public and private institutions. As the Commissioner noted in 1975, "The old notion of complete institutional autonomy is out. Nobody can do as he exactly pleases."

In addition to these forces, faculty collective bargaining helps to push power upward, for boards and administrators function as "employers" involved in governance. It is conceivable that some administrations and boards may reclaim authority once granted to faculty senates in order to bargain effectively with a faculty union. For example, during the many months of the first contract negotiation at Hofstra University, the administration was unable to talk to the senate about matters under consideration at the bargaining table. This led the senate to comment in its annual report that "The opening of formal collective bargaining markedly reduced the capacity of the Senate and Faculty Meeting to function as spokesman for the faculty and university. . . . In other words, the more subjects included in formal collective bargaining, the fewer remain for existing university governance" (*Annual Report of the Senate to the University,* 1972-1973, pp. 8-9).

Because collective bargaining has so far concentrated on economic issues, which is the area of trustee expertise, unions are expected to stimulate increasing trustee involvement at individual campuses. A recent study of trustees at several unionized community colleges uncovered a new form of "shared authority": trustee participation in decisions that were once the president's prerogative (Channing, Steiner, Timmerman, 1973). Trustees are more inclined to ask questions, to be more aware of the ramifications of issues such as class size and faculty work load, and to take an active role in decision making alongside the union. A similar study of six upstate New York community colleges revealed that local government officials who become involved in bargaining tend to impose on the campus the industrial bargaining model with which they are familiar—at the expense of campus collegiality. A majority of campus administrators and faculty members surveyed in the study said that outside participation contributed to adverse relationships during negotiation (Falcone, 1975).

A union adapts to the organization it wants to influence; that is, it constructs a power pyramid parallel to the one in the organization. If the campus is organized locally, the union organizes locally. If the campus is part of a system, the union organizes systemwide; and system-level influence is growing. The Stanford survey asked presidents of nonunionized and unionized campuses to react to the statement, "System management is increasing all the time." The responses in Table 20,

Question B, show that about 75 percent of both two-year and four-year college presidents agree with the statement. In multi-campus systems, the bargaining unit is usually systemwide, with a membership that includes other academic employees as well as faculty. Large bargaining units inevitably force centralized boards to claim the bargaining authority over a wide range of issues.

Under these circumstances, there is concern that collective bargaining will generate demands that are beyond the control of local campus administrators. As the president at Michigan's Oakland University notes: "One of the temptations that will begin to emerge is [for campus administrators] to turn to legislatures and to governing boards, saying, 'Help us out.' Here we are—we're caught between declining state support and rapidly rising costs, particularly personnel costs through collective bargaining. We need some help, and the kind we can get is to turn to a central agency" (*College and University Business,* 1972, p. 39).

At public institutions, the intrusion of state officials into campus affairs is most likely to occur in the financial area. The difficulty is that economic and academic issues are hard to separate; thus, budget control may thrust state agencies directly into academic matters. To begin with, negotiations almost always occur at the system level. It is on the local campus, however, that adjustments to the daily give-and-take under the agreement will take place, and unresolved problems or major fights will inevitably set precedents and have ramifications for the whole system. Then, the system experts—lawyers and budget officers —will leap into action. The Stanford survey underscores the pattern of increased outside control. One question asked, "How has faculty collective bargaining affected the power of off-campus central agencies *on your campus*?" Few respondents feel that central power has decreased, and about half say it has increased as a result of collective bargaining. The results were fairly consistent for all types of institutions. Union officials were less pessimistic than presidents. (See Table 18, Question B.)

Our respondents also agree that "Wherever it occurs,

faculty collective bargaining will result in greater influence on campus decision making by outside agencies (e.g., arbitrators, courts, or state agencies)." (See Table 20, Question D.) In short, these responses indicate that collective bargaining is one more factor promoting centralized decision making. Up until now, collective bargaining has been a relatively weak force; it is still in its infancy. Yet, the reciprocal circle feeds on itself: power moves off campus to systemwide boards, the union organizes on a system basis to gain influence, and in turn this drives even more issues from the local campus into the hands of the system board.

Off-campus officials well versed in academic affairs may prove to be as effective in making decisions as are local faculty and administrators. Nonetheless, state officials not well-trained in the subtleties of academia might allow political demands and debts to interfere with the peaceful operation of institutions. This process could also expose campus administrators to increasing political pressures. Power shifts resulting from collective bargaining, then, need to be carefully assessed. As of yet, the decision-making authority of administrators does not appear to be usurped by unions, but there is a tendency for the authority to move off campus to centralized multicampus administrations.

Presidents as Middle Managers

Campus presidents are usually not considered middle managers, but the twin forces of system-level centralization and collective bargaining in large state systems may make them ones. Our survey data clearly show that presidents of unionized campuses within state systems see their power being divided between faculty unions and system management. In addition, they are becoming more accountable to an enlarging circle of evaluators: local union officials, system officers, and legislators with political ambitions. Will campus presidents fall between the cracks?

Centralized bargaining may cut both ways, sometimes helping the local presidents, sometimes hurting. A local campus president may sigh with relief that most of the conflict between administrators and union officials occurs at central headquarters and not in his office. Off-campus decisions leave more time for presidents to strengthen their academic and intellectual leadership. A CUNY central administrator says that despite the perceptions of local presidents, this is exactly what has happened within the system as a result of centralization of bargaining. Other benefits may result as well. In SUNY, collective bargaining has actually helped tie the sprawling system together. "Evidence abounds that local chief administrators are now accountable to the central administration in ways not deemed necessary before collective bargaining. And at the local units, employees now have information about budgets, salaries, etc., information difficult to acquire before the time of collective bargaining" (Doh, 1974, p. 39).

Not all the results are positive, however, and the costs can be high. By shifting power upward and off campus, centralized collective bargaining lessens the decision-making autonomy of administrators, schools, and departments on local campuses. In addition, the fragmentation of union groups leads to a "multiple adversary system," with many of the adversaries by-passing local administrators and appealing directly to whatever "employer" groups may influence bargaining. Elected officials, government bureaucrats, and campus administrators perform employer-like functions with little coordination and, frequently, with contradictory results. For both the union and the campus president, this proliferation of "bosses" poses complex problems. Both the union and president at CUNY, for example, have to deal in several arenas, including the Board of Higher Education of New York, the New York City administration, and the New York State legislature.

The intricate situation invites a round robin of buckpassing. An official in the Pennsylvania system calls it the "that's-your-problem" syndrome (Ianni, 1974, p. 295):

> The campus administrators ask the bureaucrats, "How can I pay the increases you have negotiated and continue programs and services at pre-

vious levels on the same budget as formerly?" and
receive the answer, "That's your problem." The
bureaucrats ask the legislature, "How can we fund
the pay raises we have negotiated if you insist on
cutting taxes?" and receive the answer, "That's
your problem." The bureaucracy asks the campus
administrators, "Why are there so many employee
grievances reaching the state level rather than being
resolved locally?" and receive the answer, "That's
your problem." The campus administrators ask the
bureaucracy, "Why are grievances lodged against
me on matters that I did not precipitate or do not
control?" and receive the answer, "That's your
problem."

A frequent criticism voiced during our study of the
CUNY institutions is that the system administrators seldom
acknowledge the vital role of local campus presidents. Bargaining is conducted without adequate local input, and as one
administrative spokesperson at Hunter College states, "The results show what a mess occurs when the boys downtown think
they know best, without even bothering to ask the local
people."

The problems generated by isolating presidents prompted
the Pennsylvania Department of Education to include them in
preparations for the second round of negotiations with the fourteen Pennsylvania State Colleges. One state official notes that
they learned the hard way under the first contract that input by
experienced local campus administrators is essential to successful bargaining. For this reason, they formed a Labor Policy
Committee that included several officials from the central
office, the chief negotiator for the system, and a representative
from the board of presidents. David W. Hornbeck, executive
deputy director of the Pennsylvania Department of Education,
discussed the committee in a speech (November 8, 1974):

That committee began to meet in early September some five months prior to the first formal
negotiating session. Stated simply, if we were going
to take this collective bargaining relationship seriously we were going to be prepared. During the

> course of those five months, we solicited and re-
> ceived the advice of all fourteen presidents, people
> within the department, the opinion of people con-
> cerned with affirmative action, and others. We then
> spent days wrestling with the old contract. We con-
> sidered proposed changes. We discussed our vision
> for the state colleges and how the contract might
> relate to that. We argued. We wrote position pa-
> pers. We did a statistical analysis of faculty ranks,
> wages, terms, and conditions of employment in a
> host of institutions in neighboring states similar to
> our fourteen institutions. The result was a com-
> plete proposed contract representing the best
> thinking of which we were capable.

In sum, the complexities of power sharing eventually may reduce local campus presidents to middle managers who execute policy but have little influence over decision making. Such an outcome, however, hardly appears to be in the best interests of higher education. Although faculties have viewed their presidents as adversaries in bargaining situations, they may regret losing their academic spokespeople when they are confronted with off-campus administrators. The example of the Pennsylvania system indicates that it is possible and desirable to involve local presidents, and other campus representatives, as much as possible in contract negotiations. Perhaps more effort and experimentation with new forms of local input can reverse the steady erosion of local campus authority in large state systems.

Outside Influence and Arbitration

One fear often expressed is that collective bargaining will result in a shift of decision-making power from the faculty and the administration to off-campus collective bargaining boards, arbitrators, and courts. Chapter Four discussed the difficulties that can occur when determinations about bargaining units and the scope of bargaining ignore important academic issues. Equally unsettling have been the initial experiences with arbitration as a dispute-resolving technique in higher education; the record has been a troubled one.

In the industrial sector, arbitration has been the preferred method of settling grievances under an ongoing contract. As the final step in grievance procedures, third-party arbitration can help to soften the political tone of controversies and give the process a quasi-judicial character. In this respect, collective bargaining can reduce conflict by directing disputes into acceptable channels for resolution. In actuality, however, arbitration has probably produced more, not less, conflict in higher education.

Experience in both industry and in higher education demonstrates that successful contract administration depends on the language of the agreement and the sensitivity of the arbitrators to the intentions of the parties. Arbitration is essentially interpretation. Therefore, the parties must construct precise, operational wordings to prevent arbitration from creating new contract language. Vague and general terminology, perhaps resulting from pressures to reach a final contract as quickly as possible, play into the hands of politically astute unions or administrators who want arbitration to achieve what could not be secured at the bargaining table.

The first contract at CUNY provides a classic example of imprecise wording pertaining to arbitration. The topic of this passage is grievance procedure relating to appointment, reappointment, tenure, or promotion: "In such case, the power of the arbitrator shall be limited to remanding the matter for compliance with established procedures. It shall be the arbitrator's first responsibility to rule as to whether or not the grievance relates to procedure rather than academic judgment. *In no event, however, shall the arbitrator substitute his judgment for the academic judgment. In the event that the grievant finally prevails, he shall be made whole*" (emphasis added).

Problems soon arose over the meaning of the last two seemingly contradictory sentences. The CUNY administration argued that the clause gave only powers of *procedural* review to the arbitrator, while the faculty unions maintained that the arbitrator had the power to change the *substance* of decisions, even granting tenure on the arbitrator's own judgment. Initial arbitration of the issue resulted in a decision favorable to the unions, and the administration promptly took the matter to court. The New York Court of Appeals eventually upheld the position of the administration, confining the arbitrator's review and remedial powers to procedural issues.

Needless to say, the second contract at CUNY left no loopholes for "creative arbitration." The relevant clause limits the arbitrator and upholds peer judgment processes: "In cases involving the failure to appoint, promote, or reappoint an employee in which the Arbitrator sustains the grievance, the Arbitrator shall not, in any case, direct that a promotion, appointment, or reappointment with or without tenure be made, but upon his finding that there is a likelihood that a fair academic judgment may not be made if normal academic procedures are followed, the Arbitrator shall remand the matter, including a copy of the Arbitrator's Award, to a select faculty committee of three tenured full or associate professors" (Section 20.5c, p. 23, of the 1973 Agreement between CUNY and the Professional Staff Congress).

Another difficulty with collective bargaining is that inadequate screening mechanisms result in a proliferation of grievances going beyond the first step of the grievance process. Although records have generally not been kept of the number of grievances processed before a contract has been signed, it seems likely that a larger number of grievances are processed during the first years of a contractual system than previously. The decline of available jobs occurring at the same time as the establishment of many contractualized grievance systems is one factor in this proliferation. Others are the divisive effect of the first bargaining election and the adversarial character of contract negotiation.

In the interest of stabilizing the grievance system and keeping administrative costs down, experience in the private sector suggests that controls on access to the grievance system are necessary: "Essential . . . to the functioning of the grievance system is the existence of effective screening and settlement procedures. In their absence, it becomes too expensive and too time consuming, placing demands on the arbitration process it simply cannot meet" (Feller, 1973, p. 755).

Why have screening devices not been included in contracts in higher education? The former Vice Chancellor for Faculty and Staff Relations at CUNY notes: "We had hoped a responsible union leadership would say, 'sorry buster, this is just not going to be grieved.' . . . in retrospect, no one anticipated that when the matter of tenure or job security came into the picture, with the potential loss of earnings of some two or three hundred thousand dollars involved in the issue of tenure for a single individual, that most rational human beings would be willing to invest twenty-five hundred or three thousand dollars to hire a lawyer and go through the whole process of arbitration in the hope of winning the larger prize" (Newton, 1973, p. 73).

Complaints about the inadequacy of lower stages in a grievance system also figure in union reluctance to impose controls. After a year of experience with the first contract, union representatives at SUNY reported a variety of complaints. Chief among them were the lack of adequate responses from campus administrators at the Step One level, the impression that what comments were made had been carefully checked out with higher level administrators who would themselves be reviewing grievances at Step Two, and that administrators rarely addressed the question of justice for the grievant. Administrators, according to the union viewpoint, found it impossible to shed their administrative robes. Additionally, union representatives complained about the limited scope of the grievance system. Since academic judgments could not be grieved, union officials were unable to do anything about the academic judgment of peers that seemed unfair but could not be appealed (Doh and Johnson, 1974, p. 71). Given these objections, it is easy to see why unions have been reluctant to settle a grievance short of the final step and why some grievances are filed that only remotely fall within the scope of the contractualized system. In any case, a fledgling union like the United University Professors at SUNY is not about to impose screening devices for fear of alienating faculty and losing support. Since most unions in higher education are weak, screening devices may be slow in coming.

The proliferation of grievances that go beyond the first step means arbitrators may have to contend with many matters that really could have been settled earlier. At CUNY, for example, despite a low grievance rate for the institution as a whole, many grievances were passed on to arbitrators by both union and administration that clearly represented losing issues (Benewitz and Mannix, 1974). The costs in time and money can be enormous. Further complicating the problem are the equal employment opportunity laws that permit grievances to be filed with local, state, and federal agencies—in addition to employing the contractual grievance process. As a result, an institution could conceivably be hit with a series of litigations pertaining to one grievance.

Despite the problems, most unions prefer arbitration to having a college president or board handle the final step of a grievance process. As Table 20, Question C indicates, over 80 percent of faculty union chairpersons say they prefer "binding arbitration as a strategy for settling disputes." Their administrative counterparts at both unionized and nonunion schools were much less supportive—35 and 20 percent respectively.

The reason why unions prefer arbitration to existing procedures is well illustrated by an experience at Rutgers. According to the 1970 contract, Step Four of the grievance procedure was a final hearing before a faculty University Appeals Committee (UAC), whose decisions "shall be considered advisory to the President and to the Board of Governors." This provision created problems when President Edward J. Bloustein began countermanding the decisions of the committee. The union president accused Bloustein of "replacing the thoughtfully constructed (and usually unanimous) underpinning supplied by the UAC with his own version . . ." (Laity, 1974, p. 2). As might be expected, the union called for binding arbitration as the final step in the grievance procedure during the 1974 bargaining.

A study of higher education arbitration awards up to the middle of 1974 reveals that nearly half are concerned with academic judgment issues. The report concludes that although the effect of these awards on academic governance has been minimal to date, the potential danger increases with growing use of arbitration as a dispute-resolving technique (Levy, 1975).

If arbitration is going to work in higher education, it must be adapted to the needs of the profession. *First, the scope of arbitral review must be clearly defined.* Do the parties intend the arbitrator to render substantive, as well as procedural, judgments? For example, can an arbitrator review a peer decision not to award tenure? So far, the scope of grievance arbitration in higher education has been limited. In a study of four-year contracts containing tenure provisions, Mortimer (1975) found nearly 70 percent restricted arbitration to nontenure matters. Of the remaining, a quarter restricted arbitration to procedural issues. In studying 94 community college contracts, Mannix (1974) finds that 68 provide binding arbitration. Over half of these limit the scope of the arbitrator's action, removing the right to review issues of academic judgment, appointment, reappointment, tenure, and personnel practices. It is important to realize that if normal academic processes are ineffective, job-conscious faculties will push unions to make the review and remedy power as broad as possible. Negotiators on either side who wish to restrain arbitrators should include both an affirmative statement outlining what is within arbitral review as well as a negative statement outlining what is not.

Second, the powers of remedy available to the arbitrator must be carefully specified. Can the arbitrator award back pay, reinstate people to jobs, reorganize discriminatory departments? Can the arbitrator command evidence, force witnesses to testify, obtain records? What may the arbitrator *not* do? For example, where faculty by-laws and similar governance documents are included as appendices to a contract, are they within the scope of arbitral review? The contract must spell out the appropriate procedures and the possible judgments.

Third, and perhaps most importantly, institutions must experiment with different arbitral models so that new concepts of arbitration can be applied to the needs of higher education with as little disruption and dissension as possible. For example, the second CUNY contract established a "select faculty committee" to determine alleged violations of academic judgment rather than allowing an outside arbitrator to make the substantive decision.*

*For a brief analysis of this innovation and of the complexities surrounding arbitration of academic judgment issues in general, see Benewitz, 1975. For a more provocative discussion from the union viewpoint, see the companion article by Morand and Purcell.

An interesting compromise on faculty grievances was suggested in Hawaii during the 1974 decertification campaign. There, the AAUP/NEA coalition extended the dual-track bargaining approach to faculty grievances (UHPA flyer, March 5, 1974):

> *Grievance handling* is crucial to contract enforcement. . . . *UHPA proposes that the dual role of faculty requires a separation of "faculty appeals" from "employee grievances"* . . . one track to handle appeals in academic matters, another to handle employment grievances in matters of economics, benefits, etc. Faculty appeals related to academic matters . . . would be processed by representative faculty committees. . . . Employee grievances would relate to matters covered by the contract. . . .
>
> *Binding arbitration* could be invoked by UHPA in the event of an impasse. . . . UHPA will also seek to establish an "Academic Arbitration Procedure." . . . This arbitration would involve external faculty and academic administrators who would be bound to apply national academic principles, such as the 1940 Statement of Principles on Academic Freedom and Tenure.

Not only is arbitration used in grievance disputes under the contract, it can be used to resolve impasses over the negotiation of contract terms (see Howlett, 1973). One innovative and increasingly used method of resolving impasses is "final-offer" arbitration. Rather than allow public employees to strike, each party is required to submit its last, best offer to an arbitrator. The arbitrator must choose between the final offers; he cannot arrange a compromise. "Item-by-item" final offer enables the arbitrator to choose between final offers on individual issues. In either case, final-offer arbitration is designed to force both sides to propose a reasonable solution or settle the dispute themselves rather than to risk losing everything through arbitration. A major criticism of this approach is that the arbitrator may be forced to choose between two equally flawed proposals, though item-by-item final-offer arbitration helps to mitigate this possibility. Experiences with final offer by whole package under Wisconsin law and by individual issue under Michigan law have been favorable. According to a person who has monitored both, "the final-offer arbitration process is working reasonably well . . . it is a valuable dispute resolution device with which other jurisdictions may wish to experiment" (Rehmus, 1975, p. 2).

Another collective bargaining innovation was recently proposed by a blue-ribbon study group in California: to substitute fact finding for arbitration. Normally, fact finding is an intermediate step in dispute settlement procedures, and the findings and recommendations are made public so that outside pressures will force the contending parties to arrive at an agreement; when they fail to do so, the parties are free to strike or are compelled to go to compulsory arbitration. Instead of this procedure, the California Assembly Advisory Council on Public Employee Relations recommended that for impasses that result in strikes dangerous to public health or safety, the recommendations of the fact finders be court-imposed. The rationale behind this novel approach is that the fact finders chosen by the parties will be more familiar with the technicalities of the dispute than a neutral arbitrator and thus will propose a better solution. The proposal also has the economic advantage of avoiding a full arbitration hearing.

To summarize, third-party arbitration is increasingly evident as a result of faculty collective bargaining. Inexact contract wording contributes to the tendency of arbitrators to interpret the contract in ways never intended by either party. Thus, controls are necessary to make sure that the exact function of arbitration is specified; also, screening devices should be established to ensure that the arbitration process is not misused, especially in relation to repeated litigations directed against an institution. If innovative arbitration procedures are encouraged, many of the drawbacks of current procedures may be avoided in the future. It is an aspect of faculty unionism that must be dealt with by all parties.

Changes in Campus Administration

As campuses have struggled with new problems and demands over the past several years, the character of campus administration has changed. One change has been an expansion in administrative ranks, for the growing complexity of campus management demands an increasing number of experts. Unfortunately, as many faculties have seen their own numbers level off or decline, they have become suspicious and resentful of "administrative featherbedding." On some campuses, faculty resentment has led to a new game—phone book research. Campus listings often show a greater percentage of administrators today than a decade ago, giving solid ammunition to those who complain that administrators are not sharing the consequences of retrenchment. There is a good explanation, however, for why the number of administrators is increasing and for why their tasks are changing. Collective bargaining, coinciding with a host of other demands, is producing a different kind of campus management.

Specialists Replace Generalists. One sign of the changing times is the influx of specialists into administrative ranks. Faculty generalists, from whose ranks most administrators have traditionally come, usually lack the experience and skills to cope with negotiating and administering a collective bargaining contract. To expect them to execute the detailed procedures of agreements is not only unwise but unrealistic.

A specialist critical to successful bargaining is the institutional researcher. At Central Michigan University, for example, a research team is considered necessary to prepare for negotiations by gathering background data on the institution and its faculty; to provide detailed and specific information to administrators engaged in negotiations, such as costing out a union retirement proposal; and to record grievances, questions, contract violations, and unexpected costs occurring during the administration of the contract. As one CMU official noted: "The consensus of the administration is that success is the direct product of planning and preparation. Preparation means investigating all possible proposals before those proposals come to the bargaining table. The bargaining team must know as much about policies, costs, and political ramifications so that nothing surprises them. Every possible issue must be identified and then a continuum developed from the 'best of all worlds' to the 'worst of all worlds.' Thus the team can identify the limits within which they can potentially agree" (Kieft, 1973, p. 6).

Lawyers are also essential to successful negotiation and are becoming more vital to contract administration, particularly in relation to personnel policy and practices. In addition, labor relations experts and budget officers are playing a larger role in educational administration. Although it may seem anomalous to be enlarging the administration when deficits demand cutting costs, hiring specialists may be a shrewd management technique. It may actually cut long-run costs, particularly those which, like fringe benefits, "pyramid" far into the future.

The Stanford survey asked respondents how collective bargaining has affected "the need for specialized administrative manpower (e.g., lawyers)" on their campus. Over 85 percent of the presidents say that the need has increased; not a single president reports a decrease. Of the union chairpersons, 60 percent agree the need for specialists has increased; and, like the presidents, the consensus was uniform across institutional types. Not only do presidents feel that more specialists will be needed, but they expect these experts eventually to replace the generalists; on this issue, however, the union officials disagree (see Table 20, Question E).

Dilemma of Department Chairpersons. A long-standing question that affects the nature of campus administration has been whether department chairpersons should be included in the bargaining unit. Because department chairpersons are neither employer nor employee, there is no simple answer, and yet they must be classified as one or the other. Department chairpersons themselves have not explicitly defined their traditional position. For example, at the University of Delaware, a poll conducted prior to the unit determination revealed that one third of the chairpersons considered themselves "managers" and preferred to stay out of the unit (Boyer, 1974).

Eliminating chairpersons from the bargaining unit has obvious consequences for shared governance: influential faculty leaders would be on the opposite side of the managerial fence from their colleagues, and peer decision making in the departments would undoubtedly be affected. The implications are greatest at institutions with a history of strong faculty influence over departmental policies, for the division of chairpersons and other faculty could paralyze departments, thereby encouraging critical decision making to be usurped by school deans.

If department chairpersons were to be included in the unit, however, they might very well be subject to pressures from all sides. Under most collective bargaining agreements, they are required to administer procedural aspects of the contract, such as faculty evaluation, workload adjustments, and grievance processing. At the same time, they must make substantive decisions regarding tenure conferral, dismissals, appointments, and so on. A new collective bargaining contract often produces a "shirtpocket contract mentality," with faculty members acting as quasi-lawyers, checking their ever-ready contracts against possible administrative violations. (Some contracts, like the SUNY-UUP agreement, is actually printed in pocket size for convenience.) This relentless and defensive faculty behavior can frustrate department chairpersons from imposing sanctions or making hard decisions. A reprimand or tenure denial may produce an instant confrontation with the union and possibly grievance action.

In the case of CUNY, departments in four-year institutions have been instrumental in hiring, promoting, and tenuring faculty, and department chairpersons have always played a key role. Under collective bargaining, the unit determination includes department chairpersons with the faculty. As a result, chairpersons wear three hats: as *supervisors,* they are expected by management to be accountable for careful decision making at a time of declining growth and "tenuring in"; as *faculty spokespersons,* elected department chairpersons are expected by faculty to be their advocates; and as *shop stewards,* they are expected by the union, which has battled with the administration to secure procedural guarantees in personnel decision making, to oversee contract provisions scrupulously.

Despite this last role, the CUNY union has often lodged grievances against department chairpersons. A study of the first three years under the CUNY agreement showed that over 80 percent of the grievances filed were against department chairpersons and other unit members—not against administrators (Benewitz, 1975, p. 276). And yet, the union does not want department chairpersons to be considered management, although the administration has defended department chairpersons against union attack. (While grievances are formally filed against the university, department chairpersons are usually called as administrative witnesses in hearings.) As one union spokesperson has said (Kugler, 1973, p. 69):

> The department should have an elected department chairperson *not* subject to the veto of management. This presiding officer then would be responsible *not* to management but to the department faculty. Under these conditions, department chairpersons are essentially *not* management. Administrators, however, seek to transform the department chairpersons into extensions of management. The faculty resists this, and the union will strive to keep the department as a democratic agent of the working faculty *even if the union has to defend a grievant against the department chairperson.*

At Rutgers, as at CUNY, department chairpersons are included in the bargaining unit. However, the Rutgers AAUP does not back grievances; instead, it seeks to play a facilitator's role: "The role of the AAUP representative is analogous to that of a court-appointed lawyer. He or she is expected to assist the grievant in any way that will make it possible to present the case in that light which is most favorable to protecting the rights of the grievant" (*Rutgers AAUP Newsletter,* March-April 1974, p. 1).

Playing a middle role has not been a complete success. In the words of a union past-president: "At Rutgers when you file a grievance, if it was your department that made the decision, the grievance is against the dean [grievances are always formally filed against the administration or the institution]. This clearly defines the adversaries. The department members who made the decision can then serve as witnesses for the dean in a formal hearing. But the thing that does disturb us is that it leaves us open to the accusation that we are evading faculty responsibility by acting as agents of the dean" (Laity, 1973, p. 71).

One escape for the department chairperson is to back out as a witness for the dean and to let the dean go to the university counsel for assistance. This suggestion by a CUNY union chairperson would essentially destroy peer review, for the right to demand that professional experts alone can judge professional performance is balanced by the professional responsibility to accept and support the decisions. However, such an escapist solution is almost unavoidable when the department chairperson is part of the union; the role is much too complex, and chairpersons are pulled in too many different directions.

Although the chairperson's behavior may change if he or she is included in faculty bargaining units, the attitude of the administration toward departmental effectiveness also may be altered. As one CUNY dean noted, the department chairpersons more and more "waffle and buck-pass where hard decisions are needed." As higher administrators begin to distrust the decisions being forwarded and as they shift administrative functions related to contractual provisions to higher level administrators, the power of chairpersons diminishes. When that happens, the first line of objective, serious decision making will not be done by the department, but by the school dean or school-wide faculty review committees.

Some institutions may formalize such a power shift by administrative reorganization. An administrator at the University of Scranton suggests eliminating departments altogether, consolidating them into several academic divisions administered by a new level of assistant deans. In our opinion, eliminating departments is unlikely because they are more than mere administrative subunits. They are the disciplinary homes of professionals trained in a particular world-view, and those professionals are not likely to surrender their identification for administrative convenience. Conceivably, departments might be combined into division units at small, single-campus institutions with little faculty participation in personnel matters. Such organizational changes would have to be made before unionization occurs and resists any structural realignment. *The most feasible course for campus administrations would be to add associate deans and other specialists to fill the administrative functions not effectively served by chairpersons.* Such a solution might solve the chairperson's employer/employee dilemma, but of course, even more administrative personnel would be added to the roster.

Middle Management Paranoia. Although the growth of middle management seems inevitable, our case studies reveal that deans, assistant deans, budget officers, and others within the middle management category feel frustrated, isolated, and insecure. In most instances, middle-level administrators are not included in either faculty bargaining units or at the bargaining table as part of the employer contingent. Yet, the decisions reached through bargaining affect their salaries and fringe benefits, their professional roles, and their managerial responsibilities. Middle-level administrators consequently fear being squeezed between the opposing forces of collective bargaining and economic retrenchment. At Rutgers University, an administrative official and his staff discussed their paranoia about the bargaining process, noting that most campus employee groups were unionized, and that students also had gained access to decision-making channels, so that only middle management was left out. "When the cut in personnel costs comes," said one staffer, "you can guess who will be forced to absorb that blow."

Indeed, there is growing concern within SUNY that middle management is rapidly losing ground relative to unionized groups. A recent comparison of salary increases shows that since 1973 nonunionized management has received consistently less in annual percentage increments than unionized employees. By 1974-1975, it would have taken nearly a 9 percent increase for nonunionized management personnel to stay even with the unionized group. They actually got a $250 one-time bonus, which shrank to $178 with deductions. One official in the Chancellor's office notes that strains are apparent within the system as the salaries of calendar year administrators fall behind many of the academic year instructional faculty.

With little involvement in faculty unions and tenuous identification with the top administration, middle-level administrators may be committed only half-heartedly to effective decision making. Middle managers and even deans may join department chairpersons in refusing to handle certain responsibilities if the benefits they receive do not outweigh the costs of increasing antagonism and conflict from co-workers. Such a response may be increasingly likely as they become aware that the trend toward administrative centralization has removed their ability to make effective decisions. As one dean says, "I'm damn sick of the vice president holding me accountable, yelling that I pass the buck, when everybody knows he long ago took away most of the deans' real power." Collective bargaining, then, reinforces already existing trends that have long been undermining middle management.

Most labor legislation excludes supervisors, but some state laws, such as the New York Taylor Law, allow middle management to form unions. Recently a study was completed of the contracts negotiated by administrative bargaining units at four community colleges in New York—Onondaga, Orange, Suffolk, and Ulster. The Ulster contract describes the bargaining unit as "all full-time professional administrative personnel with the exception of the President, Dean of the Faculty, Dean of Administration, and Dean of Students." Interestingly, the study of these four contracts concludes that they closely resembled contracts bargained for by faculty groups (The National Center for the Study of Collective Bargaining in Higher Education, 1975). Middle-level managers, faced with problems similar to those threatening faculty members, are likely to also seek the right to form unions—thus creating still another potential campus veto group. In conjunction with an increasing number of specialists and the problematic role of department chairpersons, this middle management discontent indicates that we can expect to see continuing changes in the nature of campus administration.

Positive and Negative Consequences

In our opinion, union impact on campus administration is both good and bad. We cannot evaluate the *overall* effect of faculty collective bargaining on campus administration because too much depends on institutional and individual characteristics, and on the ability and desire of those involved in bargaining to understand and control it. Whether the overall result is beneficial or not also depends on one's position in the system; obviously all observers have prejudices and vested interests. Nevertheless, we believe it is possible to identify several positive and negative impacts collective bargaining has had on campus administration.

One positive result, in our opinion, is that collective bargaining compels the administration to bargain with faculty union representatives in good faith, and it compels them to share information with the union—something administrators have been hesitant to do with faculty groups in the past. When administrators do not share information, effective faculty participation in campus decision making is curtailed. For example, a department cannot decide whether to add a seminar with twenty students or an introductory course with two hundred unless it has access to the budget allocations and to the long-range plans and priorities of the institution. As one author notes, "I fear that some administrative functionaries look upon information control as a major fulcrum of their authority and therefore seem reluctant to share it with faculty except upon a piecemeal basis. Whatever the explanation, administrators must come to realize that the free and candid exchange of fiscal information is absolutely essential during the bargaining process" (McHugh, 1972, p. 41).

The laws and the rulings of collective bargaining boards have made information exchange a mandatory requirement of the bargaining process. This requirement is one reason why faculties, frustrated by administrations reluctant to share needed information with governing bodies, turn to unionization in the first place. At unionized campuses, information sharing has resulted in an increased faculty impact on administrative decision making. The Stanford questionnaire asked whether collective bargaining has increased faculty influence over issues that were previously the domain of administrators on their campus. Roughly a third of the campus presidents indicate that the influence of the faculty has increased, with the highest level of agreement—42 percent—in two-year institutions; about twice as many union chairpersons indicate faculty influence has increased. Although many in both groups report no significant change in faculty influence, only a handful say that collective bargaining has decreased it (see Table 19, Question C).

A trend we term *the democratization of influence* could be considered both positive and negative. Power gains are not restricted to a few faculty members but are spread among many. Because bargaining units in higher education are comprised of many different kinds of academic employees, often from disparate institutional types, a "leveling" action has occurred. Large unionized units can democratize decision processes—sometimes at the expense of previous power holders. Judging whether this outcome is good or bad depends on one's values, the history of the institution, and one's beliefs about professionalism. At unionized schools, about 25 percent of presidents and 72 percent of faculty chairpersons agree that faculty collective bargaining will democratize decision making by allowing junior faculty to play a greater role (see Table 20, Question F).

As more groups become involved in decision making, some people fear that campus processes may grind to a halt because decision-making committees will be trapped by the competing claims of interest groups. In *The Lonely Crowd*, David Reisman popularized the term "veto groups"—groups in a complex society that cancel each other out, that can *stop* action, and that rarely cooperate enough to accomplish anything. Is it possible that veto groups are now expanding on our complex campuses? Are the environmental stresses and the economic problems generating so many conflicting demands and so many hostile interest groups that creative action may be stifled?

Unionism will probably contribute to a complex campus environment. Certainly, the respondents to our questionnaire have divided opinions on this issue. We asked for agreement or disagreement with the statement, "Collective bargaining will increase the effectiveness of campus governance." Presidents and union officials sharply differ in their answers: between 10 and 20 percent of the presidents agree, but an overwhelming 77 percent of the union chairpersons agree (see Table 20, Question G).

Bargaining, then, tends to increase faculty influence over administrative issues and to democratize faculty power. To the extent that this enfranchises the faculty in general and junior faculty in particular, it broadens participation in governance and also restricts administrative arbitrariness. However, to the extent that it produces another entrenched veto group on campus, it threatens to stalemate effective governance.

We also need to consider the advantages and disadvantages inherent in *administrative rationalization.* The economic crisis and collective bargaining combine to force administrators to perform a more efficient management function, and they must be able to rationalize their decisions. In order to conduct negotiations, the administration must analyze the cost of various proposals advanced by union bargainers and must project future impacts on the institution. As one authority on collective bargaining in the industrial sector notes, "Whether the union influence is weak or strong, it will always tend to force management to consider the probable consequences of its proposed decisions and to adjust those decisions accordingly" (Slichter and others, 1960, p. 952).

Since most union demands concern economic issues and personnel decision making, it is especially crucial that administrators consider the long-range consequences of accepting such proposals as a new fringe benefit plan or shortening the probationary period for tenure. Once these matters are settled, it is unlikely that the administration can successfully regain what might have been imprudently bargained away. Who, for example, ever heard of *reducing* salaries or fringe benefits except in the most dire financial circumstances? As the Chicago City College administration learned the hard way, what is decided at the bargaining table is not easily changed.

Although procedural regulations will help the administration to rationalize its decisions and protect the faculty from arbitrariness, the proliferation of organizational rules could create a situation best termed "the paralysis of the nitty gritty." It is an inescapable fact that a contract signed and ratified by union membership restrains the exercise of administrative authority. Faculty have turned to bargaining primarily to protect their jobs from arbitrary administrative action. The specific wording of employment rules in collective bargaining contracts provides concise guidelines for an insecure faculty. In addition, everyone from the president on down who discharges administrative duties must understand not only the implications of contractual provisions but also the explicit details. At SUNY-Cortland, for example, the first contract was quickly followed by related policy changes from the Board of Trustees and an additional "twenty-one typed, single-spaced pages of memoranda of understanding at the local level which have the force of the agreement" (Hedgepeth, 1974, pp. 11-12).

"Administering by the book" can dramatically affect administrators. Department chairpersons as well as campus presidents may be overwhelmed by paper work and complex procedural requirements. For example, one study suggests that an increasing amount of a community college president's work day is committed to contract-related noneducational matters. Chief among them is grievance processing, advising lower-level administrators, and planning for the new bargaining sessions. (Channing, Steiner, and Timmerman, 1973.)

To conclude, findings from the Stanford Project on Academic Governance indicate that, contrary to many campus presidents' belief, the power of higher-level administrators is increasing rather than decreasing as a result of faculty collective bargaining. At single campuses, the power has shifted upward, with trustees now exercising more control than ever before—especially because they are expert in the fiscal matters now commanding the attention of higher education. Although local administrators in multicampus systems might be losing some of their decision-making authority, they generally are losing more of it to centralized administration off campus than to unions.

Third-party arbitration might be the aspect of faculty unionism that will challenge local administrative authority more than anything else. If administrative bargainers are not careful, they may inadvertently allow inexact wording to be included in a contract; then, arbitrators at a later date may interpret the contract in ways detrimental to the administration. It is important to remember that what has been bargained away will not likely be reclaimed.

Changes in campus administration will inevitably result from the changing environmental scene, as well as from unionism. Specialists will replace generalists, faculty chairpersons will either be aligned on the side of faculty or management, middle-level administrators may themselves unionize. Whether these changes will be perceived as positive or negative will depend, to a great extent, on one's position in the system. What may be viewed as positive, however, is the administrative information sharing and decision rationalization that a contract would necessitate. Democratizing influence has both positive and negative aspects. What appears to be the major drawback of regulations resulting from unionism is the burgeoning bureaucratization with its overwhelming paperwork.

8

An Assessment of Faculty Collective Bargaining

In summarizing the overall costs and benefits of academic collective bargaining, it is helpful to review the basic assumptions we have made about academic governance and unionism. Recall that unionism is a powerful political tool, developed in the industrial sector to help workers gain some control over their working conditions or preserve benefits they had already achieved. As social and economic forces have threatened the position of academics, they—like many other groups—have turned increasingly to political tactics. Unionism is one of those tactics, and this phenomenon in higher education can best be understood by viewing academic governance as a political process.

The following nine assumptions recap our view of the political model: (1) Collegial, bureaucratic, and political processes exist side-by-side in academic organizations, with political processes dominating the picture today. (2) Conflict is normal in academic institutions and may even be a healthy sign. Environmental conditions and forces largely determine the level of internal conflict. (3) Educational institutions have many interest groups, each trying to gain concessions advantageous to their positions. (4) Unionism is a natural outgrowth of political processes in higher education. (5) As a political process, unionism can have enormous impact on the levels of conflict, the structures of bureaucracy, and collegiality; the impact may be positive or negative depending on specific circumstances. (6) Outside pressure groups and authorities play a large role in the political process. (7) Apathy dominates, because only a few people actually take the trouble to become involved in the political process. (8) Over time, political goals expand in scope. (9) In the political environment, a new image of leadership must develop, more along the lines of the "political strategist" than the old notion of the "bureaucrat."

It has been said that for every tough problem there is a solution: neat, simple, and wrong. Is collective bargaining the obvious, but wrong, answer to the problems faculties face? Or will the process really change things for the better? We believe the benefits of collective bargaining will be substantial if—and only if—faculty, administrators, and other policy makers can keep academic values uppermost and learn to harness the potential of collective bargaining to serve the academic process. The promises of collective bargaining are real. But so are the dangers.

Winners and Losers

In previous chapters, we have suggested some of the consequences faculty unionism will have on traditional governance patterns, personnel decision making, faculty senates, and campus administrations. In the process, we have touched on who will stand to benefit the most from unionism. Since unionism is a form of organizational conflict, some groups will gain at the expense of others. The winners and losers will not always be the same over the years, and they will vary depending on the local situation at individual campuses.

Disenfranchised and Average Faculty Members. It is obvious that making generalizations is a precarious business. From previous discussions, however, we conclude that the most disenfranchised—the nonteaching professionals at most institutions, community college faculty, and junior faculty at four-year and graduate institutions—will receive very real gains from collective bargaining. As a result of unionism, for example, the pay of community college faculty within CUNY rose sharply when parity with senior institutions in the system was achieved. Further, status differences between the disenfranchised and regular faculty are likely to be reduced as militants strive to dominate the union and establish union goals through the "majority rules" procedures. The NTPs with SUNY were able to win a faculty-like tenure policy in 1973, although by 1975 many came to fear the "up and out" character of the new regulations in the face of pending budget cuts. In our survey, over 65 percent of the union chairpersons agree that collective bargaining will reduce differences between junior and senior faculty on issues such as salary and workload. By contrast, only 30 percent of the presidents concur (see Table 21, Question B). These results suggest that union leaders will promote the interests of junior faculty, but that administrators may struggle to prevent major reductions in status differences.

Interestingly, these groups usually gain even if a faculty *tries but fails* to form a union. Discontented faculty who cannot quite gain a majority to elect a union may find both administrators and senior faculty trying to head off further unionization attempts by granting concessions. For example, at Albion College, a small Methodist Church-related institution in Michigan, changes made by the administration prior to the 1973 bargaining election helped diminish the faculty's resentment about their lack of policy influence and their fears about retrenchment (Lussier, 1974a). These changes undoubtedly played a part in the eventual "no-agent" victory at the polls. Continued administrative concessions seem likely, since Albion prefers not to have a faculty union.

The disenfranchised also will be likely to benefit from the collective bargaining threat to senates; in order to gain support, unions may compel senates to open their membership to junior faculty. In the process, unions may accidentally democratize faculty participation in senate governance.

Whether the average faculty member will be a winner or a

Table 21
Impact of Collective Bargaining on Various Issues Nationally

	Percent Agreeing		
	Presidents, Nonunion Institutions (N = 134)	Presidents, Union Institutions (N = 204)	Faculty Union Chair- persons (N = 193)
A. Collective bargaining will decrease the influence of students in decision making	69	60	15
B. Collective bargaining will reduce the difference between junior and senior faculty on issues such as salary and workload	31	38	66
C. Collective bargaining will increase the voice of the average faculty member in academic policy matters	9	17	72
D. Collective bargaining will result in more conflict in the governance process	70	74	42
E. Collective bargaining will formalize relationships between faculty and administration	87	96	89
F. If faculties bargain collectively, then students should have the right to do so as well	30	24	43
G. Collective bargaining will help improve the quality of educational services on campuses	4	7	77
H. Collective bargaining will improve the accountability and responsiveness of the institution to the community it serves	11	13	54
I. Collective bargaining will help safeguard faculty rights and academic freedom	9	32	95
J. The recent growth of faculty collective bargaining is beneficial and should be encouraged	5	15	95
K. Collective bargaining will stimulate greater faculty concern about state and local politics	35	55	84

loser is open to question (see Table 21, Question C). A lot depends on the nature of the campus. On campuses where the faculties have never played a major role in governance, the union may help. A study of six upstate New York community colleges in 1974 revealed that a majority of the faculty and administrative respondents believed that the union movement had enhanced the status of the faculty member, and that the union provided the political influence necessary to achieve equitable economic improvements that otherwise would not have been possible (Falcone, 1975). On campuses where traditional faculty participation in governance is threatened by increasing trustee involvement or administrators by-passing the senate, a faculty union may also help by erecting measures to assure that traditional channels are followed.

Despite the advantages, unionism can bring some problems for the average faculty member. He or she is likely to lose individual control over wages and benefits unless the union contract allows faculty to negotiate these issues individually. To some extent, the average faculty member loses power to pursue a grievance against the administration, for the union usually has the discretion to refuse to support a grievance. Assuming the average faculty member either joins a union or is forced to pay dues, he will see a hand outstretched for a portion of his paycheck. In return, he receives the benefits stemming from collective—not individual—agreement. These benefits usually outweigh the costs, but not always.

Traditional Governance Bodies and Administrators. With a union on campus, a new layer of bureaucracy—composed of union officials, staff, and perhaps an executive director—is added to the governance structure. This addition may make losers of certain campus groups. When a union gains a significant role in personnel decision making, it will be at the expense of departments and administrators. When a union gains power over issues previously controlled by a senate, such as curriculum or faculty workload, it will undoubtedly reduce the influence of the senate. In this manner, a union may influence policy in ways that rival traditional governance mechanisms. Since unions have a tendency to extend their jurisdiction at every bargaining session, they may eventually influence a wide variety of academic issues, even on those campuses where bargaining originally concerned only economic matters.

Middle managers are likely to be losers as a result of collective bargaining. Although their ranks are growing in response to the demands posed by faculty unionization, they will probably lose initiative and control to senior administrators. Contract negotiation, even at a single campus, is a highly centralized process, and the result may be a shift of decision-making power upward to those who ultimately have the final say.

In statewide higher education systems, this feeling of powerlessness may well extend to presidents of local campuses. Local presidents often feel centralized bargaining is yet another force causing power to shift upward. It is important to note, however, that this upward shift may not occur until after the bargaining process has gone on for some time; the central offices may flounder considerably before they work out effective methods for controlling the local campuses in respect to collective bargaining issues. Eventually, however, the central administrators will catch up. With centralized bargaining and the expansion of contracts over time, it is likely that the worst fears of local campus presidents will be realized—their power to develop policy may be substantially reduced. This will leave them in the supervisory role of ensuring that contract terms negotiated by higher officials are carried out at the local campus level. A somewhat comforting (but probably false) hope is that this centralized control will be directed primarily at economics and working conditions, and that it will thus free the local administrators to focus on real educational matters.

Looking at the whole picture, it is not entirely clear if faculty gain influence by resorting to a union, or not. Clearly, they gain some things—more control over personnel procedures and some economic benefits. It is also clear that a price is paid, for many traditional relationships are disturbed—as an example, faculty unionism generally decreases the influence of students.

Students. One concern of student radicals in the 1960s was to increase student participation in campus decisions. In response, some campuses started broad-based senates with administrators, faculty, and students together in a single body. It seemed to be a good way to democratize decision making and reduce alienation and conflict. The primary beneficiaries were students. Unfortunately, under collective bargaining, students now appear to be the most likely losers. To date, both federal and state collective bargaining laws limit bargaining to the employer and employee. Although some student groups have advocated student unionism, the laws do not consider them "employees"; consequently, they cannot legally use unionization as a political weapon. The one exception is student teaching and research assistants at a few public institutions where PERBs have ruled that they can be considered employees. For example, at the University of Michigan, the Graduate Employees Organization has won salary increases and tuition waivers—and has even resorted to a month-long strike in support of its demands.

The presidents who responded to the Stanford survey certainly feel unions will decrease student influence—over 60 percent agree. However, 85 percent of the union chairpersons disagree. (See Table 21, Question A.) Student leaders around the country seem to endorse the presidents' view, for they almost uniformly consider faculty unionism a threat. And perhaps with some justification. A recent review of two-year and four-year academic contracts by the National Center for the Study of Collective Bargaining in Higher Education noted only 28 percent contained references to student interests, and only 4 percent mentioned students more than once. Significantly, no student was present at the bargaining table during negotiations of the 145 contracts analyzed in the study (Shark, 1975). As Linda Bond, a lobbyist with the California Student Lobby, put it (1974, pp. 132-133):

> Our concern stems from the impact that collective bargaining has had, and will have, on the quality of university instruction and the participation of students in university governance. Students are concerned that increases in salaries and fringe benefits won by faculty unions will come out of students' pockets in the form of higher tuition. At a time when state dollars for higher education are being held constant, students are the most politically convenient source of increased revenues. Students fear that faculty strikes will interrupt their education and that faculty collective bargaining will freeze students out of their hard-won participation in campus decision making. Most important,

students are concerned that the quality of the educational product will be eroded. . . . Campus governance structures, once flexible enough to accommodate student involvement, are superseded by newly created joint administrative-faculty advisory committees rigidly defined by law. Educational policy issues are negotiated in secret behind closed doors. Course offerings may be reduced or entire programs phased out. Innovative educational programs that make use of community resources may be eliminated due to rigid definitions of faculty workload. Remedial and other support programs for minority students may well be the first to go because they add to faculty workload. Student needs for part-time learning opportunities on evenings and weekends conflict with faculty desires for more regular hours. Student-controlled courses and evaluations of their teachers are victims of faculty desires to limit such judgments to their peers. "Due process" clauses, which call for automatic promotion regardless of merit, further decrease the impact of evaluative mechanisms. . . . Out of sight and thus out of mind, students and their interests in educational policy remain either unknown or ignored. . . . Put simply, the situation can be interpreted as faculty power versus student power.

Whenever student leaders express anger at being left out of bargaining, they level most of the blame at the faculty union. One student leader at Central Michigan accuses the union of placing student welfare at the lowest priority. Since the union is economically based, said the student, its interests can be ranked in the following fashion: dollars, working conditions, student discipline, the profession, the students.

Union behavior often has reinforced student fears. In 1973, for example, students were given a role in bargaining at the City Colleges of Chicago, but the union refused to attend sessions when student representatives were present. Most of the time, said one administrative official, the union tried to argue they represented student interests—when the students were not present. The administration felt that bringing students into the negotiation sessions would expose them to all the issues and thereby "neutralize them as a factor in this power struggle." But the union felt this was "deadly" since most of their demands did not relate to students. "The few sessions where the union did allow the students to attend," said one administrator, "were enough to turn them around." Asked why his union opposed student involvement in bargaining, a union official gives three reasons: students lack expertise; the average student attends the City College only a year and thus has limited input to bring to bargaining; and students are a third party with interests of their own. The official does add, however, that student rights should be recognized. At Rutgers, an administrator who is intimately involved in bargaining reports, "In the countless hours I have spent at the bargaining table at this institution, I don't ever recall the students being mentioned."

At other campuses, administrators also come in for their share of criticism. Several student leaders feel they are "used" by the administration when they are included on the administrative bargaining team or allowed to attend bargaining sessions. Others feel the administration is paternalistic toward students. Union officials are especially critical of "administrative grandstand plays, always crying about the needs of the students—but really meaning to use the unwitting students as allies in administrative power grabs."

In the few instances where student input has been allowed, it has come in a variety of ways. In some cases, as at Ferris State College in Michigan, students have sat on the administrative side of the bargaining table. For a short time in Massachusetts, students had an independent status at the bargaining table in three state colleges. Although the "Massachusetts Experiment" was not a true example of tripartite bargaining since students had limited power to affect the agreement, the whole idea was jeopardized when the state collective bargaining law was modified to allow negotiation of economic issues beginning in 1974. Interestingly enough, until 1974, bargaining had been devoted to expanding student and faculty involvement in governance.

In the New Jersey state colleges and at Southeastern Massachusetts University, students have worked out agreements with the AFT faculty bargaining agents to consult with the union about its goals and activities. The National Student Association (NSA) has proposed creating a national student union, despite the fact that students are not employees. In short, the variety of *proposals* for student involvement is great, but *actual participation* is extremely limited. The Stanford questionnaire indicates that it will take a long time to change this situation, for neither presidents nor union chairpersons respond enthusiastically to the statement, "If faculties bargain collectively, then students should have the right as well" (see Table 21, Question F).

If students are not well received by administrators and union officials, they may try to gain influence in other ways— such as through lobbying. Students in California have used lobbying with some success on a variety of issues and have recently tried to influence the new collective bargaining laws. Created in 1970, the California student lobby recently was rated the twelfth most influential in the state by a sample of legislators. Ironically, tied for twelfth place in the survey was the California Teacher's Association, a NEA affiliate. In 1973, the students influenced the legislature to add this passage to the bargaining law that was later vetoed by then-Governor Reagan (*Assembly Daily Journal,* August 27, 1973, p. 7008):

> In negotiations over the terms and conditions of service and other matters affecting the working environment of employees in institutions of higher education, a student representative selected by the respective campus or systemwide student body association may be present at all times during which negotiations take place. . . . The student representative shall have access to all written draft agreements and . . . a copy of any prepared written transcripts of any negotiating sessions. The student representative shall have the right at reasonable times during the negotiating sessions to comment upon the impact of proposed agreements on the educational environment of students. . . . Prior to the entering into of a comprehensive agreement . . . a separate public report on the impact of

the proposed agreement on educational quality,
level of service to students, and direct costs to students may be prepared by the student representative.

Although the bill was vetoed, students have lobbied intensively
in every subsequent legislative session to include a similar clause
in the California legislation.

In 1975, the Montana student lobby successfully ob-
tained a stronger student role in faculty bargaining. The bill provides that students may be members of the administrative bargaining team, caucus with the administration, observe negotiations, and meet with the regents to voice their opinions before
the agreement is signed. Although students have previously participated in bargaining sessions by agreement of union and
administration (as in Massachusetts, at Ferris State, and at Long
Island University), Montana is the first state to grant them the
right to participate by law—unwilling unions or administrators
cannot keep them out! An even more successful lobbying effort
was achieved by the student lobby in Oregon in mid-1975 when
a new state law was passed giving students independent third
party status at the bargaining table. They are not aligned with
either side and thus have an independent right to comment, but
they have no vote. Although the Montana and Oregon legislation are minor breakthroughs toward student participation, and
similar legislation is being debated in several states, the general
pattern is nevertheless in the opposite direction: student influence has decreased as a result of collective bargaining.

In looking at some of the winners and losers of faculty
collective bargaining, it is hard to say whether the realities of
unionism balance out to overall faculty gain or loss. In order to
assess the costs versus the benefits more closely, we turn from
examining *who* wins and loses to *what* the positive and negative
effects of unions are for higher education in general.

Positive Aspects of Collective Bargaining

Some of the positive aspects of collective bargaining are
general in that they affect the entire academic profession. Issues

such as wages, fringe benefits, and working conditions fall into this category. Other benefits are highly specific to a local campus, such as local governance processes and personnel practices. Throughout the book, we have stressed that the impact of unionization will be different on different campuses. For instance, in some colleges collective bargaining may upgrade the quality of tenure evaluation, providing a certain degree of fairness, objectivity, and regularized procedure where none previously had existed. In other colleges with a strong tradition of careful peer evaluation, unionization may undermine the process by imposing such elaborate appeals procedures that sound peer judgments are overturned because of technical flaws in the complicated process.

Given that the impact of collective bargaining will be evaluated differently by people in varying situations, we nonetheless conclude that faculty unionism offers several positive contributions to higher education.

Promoting Economic Benefits. Few studies have been made of how much faculty collective bargaining affects wages and benefits. One reason, of course, is that faculty bargaining is a new phenomenon. Another is trying to determine how much wages would have increased if a faculty had not unionized. However, there has been one thorough analysis by a university chancellor. He set out to prove that unionized faculties are not paid more money than nonunionized; he found just the opposite. Between 1968 and 1972, the average compensation of unionized academicians at 88 institutions increased $777 more than faculty members at 88 similar institutions without unions (Birnbaum, 1974). The largest gains were made by unionized faculties in the four-year public colleges. Their increase over nonunionized faculty at comparable institutions amounted to almost $1200. Significantly, the Birnbaum study did not include the four-year campuses of CUNY because matches were not available among nonunionized schools. If CUNY institutions had been included, the increases for unionized faculties would show up even larger than they did, since CUNY has consistently been at the very top of the national salary charts for college professors. Other observers have found the economic benefits of bargaining less impressive (see, for example, Garbarino, Chapter Five, 1975). Based on the available evidence, however, it appears that bargaining has generally improved the economic condition of faculty members over their nonunionized counterparts. It is also another force pushing in the direction of equalizing economic benefits among faculty members and establishing parity between levels of institutions.

In the industrial sector, collective bargaining has long been viewed primarily as a means of maintaining gains already made and preventing labor underbidding, which is particularly likely in a buyers' market or in a time of economic scarcity. Without bargaining, some faculties may fall far behind other employee groups in the society who use it to *preserve,* as well as extend, economic benefits. A prime example is the University of Hawaii faculty, which was unable to agree on a union even though all other public sector employee groups in the state were quickly unionizing and securing contracts. As a result, from 1972 to the middle of 1975, the University of Hawaii faculty, in the words of one observer, "suffered singular economic defeat" given the economic picture of inflation and the high cost of living in Hawaii (Pendleton and Najita, 1974, p. 41).

Increasing Job Security. Aside from the examples of a few community college faculty and nonteaching professional groups, dramatic increases in economic benefits are not the main fruits of collective bargaining; rather, for most academicians, bargaining is the best means of securing job security. Almost all contracts negotiated in higher education have job security provisions, generally relating to procedural steps necessary to carry out personnel decisions. However, more and more contracts have provisions that at least indirectly affect the substance of the decision itself. So far, substantive provisions have taken the form of timetables and criteria to be used in making personnel decisions.

Personnel decisions, retrenchments, and layoffs are shaking many colleges. Administrators are struggling to make reasonable decisions in what are often impossible situations, and faculty are fighting to preserve their legitimate rights to jobs. In response, unions are trying to negotiate contracts that define such slippery issues as "financial exigency" (a common reason for layoffs) and that outline specific procedures in the event of terminations. Already some contracts state that a program cutback, for whatever reason, is subject to prior union consultation —and even agreement in some cases. Others outline procedures defining the order of termination in the event of serious financial exigency. The Temple University agreement, for example, mandates that the order of retrenchment be part-time faculty, nontenured faculty, and finally tenured faculty—providing the faculty with the least years of service to Temple University shall be released first. The agreement also provides for an alternative order of retrenchment where issues of affirmative action and the needs of a particular academic program are involved.

By the mid-1970s, over half of the negotiated contracts contained retrenchment clauses. Although the vagueness of these provisions meant that they were sometimes useless in actual situations, in general they are a step toward ensuring job security. A very likely outcome is that faculty will have more shelter, there will be fewer arbitrary actions, and in general there will be more procedural protection.

Legitimizing Authority. Collective bargaining helps to encourage the elaboration and codification of campus governance procedures. Even when the contract itself does not spell out the jurisdiction of campus groups in governance, the administration is likely to take the lead in demanding that governance responsibilities—such as senate jurisdiction, the role of student government, and the role of the faculty union—be clarified to prevent a chaotic situation from becoming even worse. The complexity is greatest in large state systems because the relationship between campus administrators and system officials must also be taken into account.

Administration activities are likely to become more consistent and predictable, for collective bargaining forces administrators to avoid *ad hoc* decision making. Decision makers must consider union response at the bargaining table and the costs of potential grievance suits. One by-product is improved communication and understanding within administrative ranks. For example, a study of several unionized community colleges reveals that trustees have a better understanding of the problems presidents face and are more willing to listen to their recommendations, especially those concerning bargaining and contract interpretation (Channing, Steiner, Timmerman, 1973). In many large systems, bargaining has forced a better understanding of the relationship between central offices and local campuses.

Contractual provisions, court decisions, and the rulings of arbitrators help rationalize and regularize campus decision making because they increase awareness of how decisions are reached; they contribute to the legitimacy of decisions by reducing the likelihood of arbitrariness; and they force administrators to be more accountable for their decisions by pinpointing responsibility. In short, collective bargaining may be the strongest internal factor promoting the regularization of decision-making procedures.

Increasing Faculty Influence in Governance. Faculty collective bargaining can *enfranchise* a faculty previously denied participation in campus governance. It can also *preserve* the influence of a faculty that has had a significant role in campus governance. But collective bargaining will not necessarily perform these functions solely by shoring up traditional decision mechanisms; rather, it almost surely will stimulate new forms and styles of governance in order to increase faculty influence.

Just the *possibility* of unionization may be enough to force administrators to pay more attention to faculty senates and committees. Administrators frequently seek to revitalize traditional faculty governance when it is apparent that a union organization campaign is beginning—often provoking charges that the administration is establishing a company union. Both the unfair labor practice filed against the Pennsylvania State University system and the establishment of the institutional senate at CUNY point to administrative efforts to coopt the opposition. Such efforts may also occur after a union is voted in and is negotiating contracts. Long after the establishment of a faculty union, the president of Central Michigan gave in to longstanding demands that the large number of administrators in the senate be reduced. The CMU administration also made a careful effort to direct policy deliberation on important issues toward the senate and away from the union. The response of the union was to file an unfair labor practice claim against campus administrators, charging them with failure to negotiate on a condition of employment, that of student evaluation of faculty members.

Many senate members on unionized campuses indicate that administrators have emerged as staunch friends of the senate, although many feel the friendship is superficial. "As long as senates and unions coexist," says one professor, "administrators will prefer to deal with senates where they can eventually obtain anything they want." Of course, the fear of being labeled a "company union" forces senate leaders to strive for greater independence from the administration. This fear was the motivation, for example, behind the desire of the Central Michigan senate to reduce administrative membership. In short, faculties will gain influence in campus decision making if unions pressure administrations to grant senates a larger role in governance. At the same time, the pressure may make senates open their membership to junior faculty and encourage faculty bodies to depend on the administration less than previously.

There are other ways, of course, for unions to gain more governance influence for the faculty. The most direct is through tough bargaining in contract negotiation. A less direct, although very important, process is through contract administration. At the local level, it may represent the first opportunity faculty representatives have had to consult with administrators as equals. Based on extensive questionnaire research, Doh and Johnson (1974) concluded that the consultative sessions between SUNY campus leaders and local union officials during the first year of the contract gave the faculty a new sense of participation. Unfortunately, despite greater opportunity to communicate, the same study also suggested that systemwide bargaining left both administrative and union leaders at the local level with only a consultative role.

Occasionally, the contract will legitimize the role of the union to work with administrators in ironing out complex problems not settled through the negotiation process. For example, at the Pennsylvania State College system, one contract provision establishes periodic "meet and discuss" sessions between the union and the state education department. During contract negotiations, both parties recognized that there were continuing complex problems. These problems included questions of retrenchment, affirmative action, workload, overload, summer employment, and retirement. Both union and administration resolved to continue discussing such items in monthly "meet and discuss" sessions. One state official noted, "After three sessions, it is clear that we are approaching these as *mutual* problems that must be solved for everybody's good. This way we avoid a rigid adversarial relationship." He added, "If our fourteen institutions are going to meet the challenges of 1974 and the years to come, we must learn to solve jointly the many problems facing us."

The resolution of such complex problems in informal sessions outside of normal bargaining meetings is a hopeful sign. In the industrial sector, such informal processes have allowed collective bargaining to identify points of conflict and channel their resolution. Unfortunately, such informal action can also reflect a union desire to monopolize faculty input in governance. In the Minnesota State Junior College system, the NEA union succeeded in abolishing senates in 1973, replacing them with a union committee structure at both the campus and system level. As to be expected, collective bargaining presents both problems and promises in relation to governance.

Managing Conflict. The political governance model assumes conflict is normal; it grows out of the very real, divergent desires of various interest groups. We do not subscribe to the widely held "communication gap" theory of conflict that assumes most conflict could be eliminated if only everyone had the same information, could reason together, and could be sensible. This position ignores the very real diversity of goals and values among campus constituents. Nor do we endorse the "maximum benefit" theory that assumes that conveying greater and greater benefits to unions and their members will pay off in reducing union militancy because "Where unions have broadened their concern with and bargaining over sources of attachment to work, they have increased the amount of their commitment to the work organization at the expense of their militancy" (Dubin, 1972, p. 12). Although there is undoubtedly some truth in the assertion, it certainly does not always work that way. Indeed, this was the course pursued in 1967 by the Chicago City College administration with their union, a course that did increase the scope of union-controlled activities but did not result in a dramatic lessening of conflict. To the extent that the faculty, the administration, and the students have different goals, they are engaged in a political struggle to determine the course of their lives at the university. The result is a persistent degree of conflict on campus, varying from place to place and time to time. Certainly the confrontations of the 1960s demonstrated that conflict existed on the campus and that existing mechanisms were inadequate to channel and resolve it. Now, in the 1970s, the growth of collective bargaining indicates that on many campuses administrations and faculties have different interests.

Many observers of higher education have come to believe that if a high level of conflict continues to characterize faculty-administrative relations, collective bargaining will be one means of controlling it. For example, one Carnegie Commission report concludes: "We may be involved in a long-term period of greater social conflict in society and greater tension on campus. If so, it may be better to institutionalize this conflict through collective bargaining than to have it manifest itself with less restraint. Collective bargaining does provide agreed-upon rules of behavior, contractual understandings, and mechanisms for dispute settlement and grievance handling that help to manage conflict. . . . Collective bargaining, thus, is one aspect of the rule of law, if and when a rule of law is required" (Carnegie Commission, 1973, p. 51).

Unfortunately, that "rule of law" can be more disruptive than helpful in early stages of faculty collective bargaining. As in the early day of industrial unionism, faculty grievances proliferate, threatening to overwhelm the fragile grievance/arbitration machinery. The contracts themselves are often limited in scope, leaving many matters to be handled in traditional ways. Sometimes contracts are poorly worded and generate conflict by their very existence. Nevertheless, these beginnings probably will lead to a more mature relationship between administration and union; the early conflict-stimulating experiences will give way to a conflict-managing process.

In its mature stages, collective bargaining manages conflict in three ways. First, the fixed-term contract stabilizes the responsibilities of the parties and limits their freedom of action regarding the substance of the agreement. Second, the grievance/arbitration provisions channel and resolve conflicts over the negotiation and administration of the agreement. Finally, over time, the developing relationship between the parties lessens the adversarial character of collective bargaining. In these ways, unionization can help channel and resolve the conflict that it initially helped to generate.

In some institutions studied in the Stanford project, the conflict-managing process was well under way. Collective bargaining has continued longest at the City Colleges of Chicago, and Chancellor Oscar E. Shabat believes conflict at the colleges has finally been reduced by the mechanisms established through collective bargaining. He argues, "The key to conflict management is learning to work out what is unclear. In a sense, the contract becomes a living document." The Chicago administration, notes Shabat, finally has started to work out a stable relationship with the union after years of deep division and hostility, although recent events there suggest otherwise.

At the City University of New York, both union officials and administrators agree conflict management is possible through collective bargaining. But, cautions one administrative official, the key to a successful relationship is the degree of responsible faculty participation in the union, and the strength and stature of faculty leadership. In addition, responsible union leadership must be matched by the administration. The maturing relationship at CUNY is illustrated by attempts to take a step away from the bargaining table and informally resolve common misapprehensions. For example, in 1974, twenty union grievance officers and their university counterparts attended a weekend conference on grievance processing. In one activity, they exchanged roles on hypothetical cases to develop an understanding of each other's expectations about the grievance procedures.

Other patterns of stable, conflict-resolving relationships have developed in some institutions. Mid-term bargaining, for example, is sometimes used, in which clauses omitted (perhaps inadvertently) from the scope of the agreement may be discussed subsequently. Mid-term bargaining may occur over particularly difficult problems, or the parties may agree to exempt some matters from bargaining altogether, preferring to establish joint study committees such as the ones at the Pennsylvania State College system and at Rutgers. There are limitations, however. For example, most of the issues studied by the Rutgers joint committees have not been academic in nature, nor are the procedures very stable.

Although we have been suggesting ways in which collective bargaining might reduce conflict, remember that collective bargaining is an intrinsically adversarial process. We do not wish to minimize the problem. Certainly our Stanford questionnaire shows that presidents and union chairpersons have mixed views about the conflict-managing properties of collective bargaining. Presidents generally agree that "Faculty collective bargaining will result in more conflict in the governance process." There is no consensus among union chairpersons—as many disagree as agree (see Table 21, Question D).

Remedying Past Discrimination. Fragmentation into interest groups, the process that in our opinion is the base of academic political conflict, is nowhere more apparent than in discrimination against minorities and women. Although employment discrimination is prohibited by many federal and state laws, the burden of enforcement falls on the individual, a burden that may be very great.* As the AFT *Negotiating Manual* points out, "Using the enforcement procedures of HEW and the complaint procedures of the EEOC and Department of Labor means lengthy proceedings, if not court trials. In many cases, enforcement agencies have a backlog of cases. Clear contract language, supported by binding arbitration, is a far more expeditious route."

---

*For an extremely enlightening review of the federal laws and important court decisions pertaining to employment discrimination, see Sandler (1975). This essay also discusses legal remedies women and minority groups could use against both union and employer in order to correct discrimination in higher education.

Increasingly, women and minorities are trying to use collective bargaining to promote their interests. As one leading women's rights advocate has written: "Collective bargaining mechanisms can and should be used to make the demands most women have come to agree are basic: equal pay and fringe benefits, appropriate medical insurance and care; maternity and parental leaves; day-care; clear and equitable standards for access to grants, supportive services, extra earning opportunities, promotion and tenure" (Reuben and Hoffman, 1975, p. ii). Women and minorities have an ally, because equal employment laws prohibit the union from unlawful discrimination and labor laws require it to offer fair representation to all members of the bargaining unit even if they are not union members.*

As a remedy against discrimination, collective bargaining presents both an opportunity and a challenge for minorities. For one thing, administrators often agree to bargain over these issues, for they do not want to be seen as unwilling to help cure discrimination, and they may be able to bargain toward a solution directly tailored to the particular needs of a campus. Yet, gaining enough clout within the union to force bargaining on these issues presents a distinct political challenge to minority groups. Unions work primarily for the interests of the majority, and without tight organization and concerted effort, women and minorities will be as powerless vis-à-vis the union as they have been vis-à-vis the institution. In order to use the union effectively as a political weapon, groups must first learn tactics to influence them. The key tactic is, of course, involvement. One woman member of the CUNY union attributes contract provisions promoting equality for women to "the hard work of a small group of women within the union who formed an *ad hoc* committee on the status of women, which later became a standing committee" (Croman, 1975, p. 29). Such involvement might promote debilitating strife within the union, but it is the only way for minorities to be effective.

*Susan Fratkin (1975), director of Special Projects for the National Association of State Universities and Land-Grant Colleges, provides an excellent review of three critical areas for unions regarding affirmative action laws and decisions: union practice of seniority rights, negotiated grievance procedures, and the union responsibility of fair representation.

So far, women and minority groups have had some success. Most agreements contain an affirmative commitment by unions to admit all eligible persons without regard to race, color, creed, national origin, sex, age, or marital status, and to represent all members equally regardless of whether they are union members. Groups in several institutions have worked hard to erase past discrimination against women. For example, a determined effort by women at Rutgers University succeeded in obtaining provisions in the 1972 contract that remedied salary inequities. At Oakland University in Michigan, women used collective bargaining to adjust salary inequities, promote a fairer sabbatical leave policy for women, achieve parity of the library faculty (mostly women) with other faculties, and secure a paid maternity leave. A woman union member at Oakland argues the union offers an avenue to leadership positions that is more accessible and democratic than the traditional governance structures (Schwartz, 1975, p. 11).

In summary, women and minority groups may find the union an effective political tool to help alleviate persistent discrimination. However, the task will not be simple; other competing interest groups also will be trying to capture the union for *their* goals. Internal conflict over union priorities will be fierce, and without persistent, organized pressure, discriminated groups will once again find themselves outside the power structure. Unions are no more likely to respond to demands merely because they are "just" or "right" than are other social institutions. The name of the game is politics.

All in all, then, the most positive aspects of faculty unions cover a fairly broad spectrum of individual, economic, and institutional benefits: economic gains, such as higher wages; job security, in terms of tenure and order of dismissal if retrenchment became necessary; legitimizing authority by forcing administrators to consider the consequences of their decisions; increasing faculty influence in academic governance, especially in relation to personnel decision making; managing the conflict inherent in academic institutions as vested interest groups fight for their goals; and, as we just discussed, remedying past discrimination directed at women and minorities. In the previous sections, we have noted that these gains are not without some "ifs"—a lot depends on particular institutions and circumstances, and the particular people involved. The positive aspects can be turned inside out and pose some very real problems.

Potential Problems

Since collective bargaining is a decision process with its own distinct characteristics, it cannot be superimposed on existing governance procedures without altering them. This section explores some of the dangers. However, before we discuss these issues, we need to sound the warning signals once again—unionism on campus is still new and conditions vary. Although some general patterns are emerging, changes may occur rapidly, and the events on any *specific* campus may not mirror the general trends. Thus, the dangers described in this section should be viewed as *potential,* not necessarily imminent, at the majority of institutions.

Polarizing Administrators and Faculty. Administrators have traditionally been identified with the faculty to whom they are accountable to a considerable degree. For their part, faculty generally have accepted administrators as faculty members engaged in the mundane task of seeing that the wheels of the academic red wagon turn. Presidents and other administrative officers have often been included in the faculty senate. They normally hold professorial appointments and occasionally they teach classes. Collegiality—not conflict—has been the accepted pattern of faculty-administration interaction. Even with exceptions to these general patterns, it is not too idealistic to say that faculty and administration have held similar academic values.

Recent times, however, have made it increasingly clear that the administrative and faculty roles are not always interchangeable. Beginning with the student rebellion of the 1960s and continuing with the economic crisis of the 1970s, administrators have been forced to make decisions frequently in opposition to faculty interests. Such events have, to some extent, placed the faculty and administration in a conflict relationship. Collegiality has been breaking down, and contributing to this breakdown has been centralization in the public sector—a process that siphons power off campus to central authorities and prevents informal relationships from developing between central authorities and those affected by their decisions.

Like centralization, collective bargaining helps to formalize relationships; it fosters a "we-they" mentality inherent in the bilateral legal framework. Unlike centralization, collective bargaining has a similar impact on single campus institutions as well as those tied into large state systems. The Stanford survey showed most respondents agree with the statement: "Where it occurs, collective bargaining will formalize relations between faculty and administration" (Table 21, Question E). The agreement was consistent for both union officials and campus presidents.

Collective bargaining clearly separates employer from employee at the bargaining table, and there is growing evidence the dichotomy continues during contract administration. The more faculty performance criteria are written into a contract, the greater the monitoring responsibilities of administrators. As a result, the problem mentioned earlier of a faculty "shirt-pocket contract" mentality is often matched by overly aggressive administrators. A recent study of unionized community colleges shows many presidents take a "watchdog" role over faculty under a contract, thereby perpetuating tension between the faculty and the administration. As an example, one trustee cites the president's responsibility to supervise faculty sick leave and make certain it is not abused. The same community college study shows that when things get tough during bargaining, board members view the faculty as the opposition and the president as the ally. This differentiation continues beyond the bargaining sessions. "It was interesting to note that the majority of trustees indicated that while their understanding of the president's role has increased in a positive sense, the 'status' of the faculty has diminished. . . . They certainly are not as likely to be influenced by them as they were in the past" (Channing, Steiner, Timmerman, 1973, p. 70).

The aggressive administration usually faces an aggressive union that cannot afford to allow its membership to be coopted. To maintain visibility, the union leadership must constantly seek out and publicize points of contention between administrators and faculty. Coupled with a worsening financial climate and tough bargaining, the constant repetition of the "we-they" theme may force the two constituencies into entrenched positions. Should bargaining turn into an impasse, the resulting polarization could have disastrous consequences for collegiality. Prolonged conflict between the parties, particularly where a strike is used, calls public attention to internal problems and may seriously damage the reputation of the institution. The consequences for fund raising and legislative support are obvious. Prospective students may avoid a campus where conflict has broken out into the open. The resolution of such an impasse through a strike (where it is allowed), or even through an outside arbitrator, may leave much bitterness on both sides and jeopardize the chances for the parties to work together effectively under an ongoing contract.

Polarization will also convince senior faculty that they must separate the academic senate from the administration as much as possible to avoid union charges that the senate is a "company union." Union charges of "company union" against the Central Michigan senate, in addition to the filing of unfair labor practice charges against the administration, were the prime factors behind the senate request that administrators pull out of the senate. This scenario is less likely within a large state system because systemwide bargaining does not occur on individual campuses. However, if central administrations and unions make decisions counter to the interests of local campuses, they compromise the workability of local campus collegial systems. Recall that within the CUNY system, several departments at Hunter College have found the 1973 contract provisions unworkable. At SUNY-Cortland, centralized bargaining has contributed to an erosion of mutual trust between state level administrators and local campus personnel and has compromised the governance responsibilities of the campus senate (Hedgepeth, 1974).

Giving Disproportionate Power to Unions. Collective bargaining is an effective weapon for interest groups because it allows them entry to the decision-making arena and compels the employer to bargain under highly regulated and externally supervised conditions. As mentioned previously, due to traditional professional allegiances, professors who have high status and good working conditions are unlikely to be union advocates; the most disenfranchised are usually the ones who mount the drive to form unions. The latter are most likely to dominate union ranks and thus control union affairs.

Given its legal backing, a union knows that the administration risks court action by dealing with nonunionized groups, including academic senates, and thus these groups often lose influence. For example, since most students do not have the option of joining a union because they are not employees, union power may increase at their expense. The recourse for nonunionized interests is to withdraw, to struggle to maintain other avenues of influence, or to join the union. Ironically, the possible dominance of unions coincides with the movement in the academic community to open up decision-making channels to a broad range of campus interest groups. In the words of one commentator, "That a model of decision making which greatly constricts such participation should win approval just at this moment must be seen as a great historical irony" (Ping, 1973, p. 106). To be fair, of course, it must be noted that open, shared participation has rarely been a reality on those campuses where unions have emerged.

The important point is that collective bargaining is a *bilateral* decision process that historically has never included nonunionized parties. The inevitable result is that unions gain governance power at the expense of nonunionized groups. Where unions are systemwide or nationally based, they often have enough clout to affect the outcomes of *legislative* processes as well as the outcomes of bargaining with employers. In such cases, collective bargaining becomes a double-barreled weapon for unions—and a double headache for those who are not or cannot be unionized.

Increasing Centralization. Although the drive toward centralization and coordination of public higher education occurred before unions appeared, collective bargaining and centralization are ready-made stimulants for each other. In order to be effective, unions must deal directly with the power centers. It should come as no surprise, then, that systems of education tend to have systemwide bargaining. There has to be a union power center equivalent to the central administrative offices— and vice versa. The result is that centralized bargaining stimulates the trend toward centralized control. Moreover, where the central administrative office is not the funding source, unions must move to where the financial power lies. There may be increased contact and conflict with, or lobbying against, noneducational agencies such as the governor's office or the legislature.

Interestingly, the movement *toward* collective bargaining in the first place partly reflects faculty anxiety over the erosion of local autonomy by statewide boards and coordinating agencies. Many faculty have embraced collective bargaining as a weapon to use against economy-minded legislators and trustees who insist upon cost reductions and improved accountability. Yet, ironically, collective bargaining *promotes* centralization through large bargaining unit determinations and by focusing on economic issues that must be settled off campus. Thus, the circle is complete: anxiety about system control stimulates unionism, and unionism accelerates system control.

Another threat to local autonomy is the *standardization effect* collective bargaining agreements have on campus operations. For example, the evaluation scheme for junior faculty in the second CUNY/PSC contract is very difficult for large departments to carry out, yet all departments are forced into the same mold in evaluating personnel. In the SUNY system, there is only one master contract despite the great geographical separation and divergent educational missions of the campuses. A master contract covering a few systemwide matters such as salary and benefits, coupled with a secondary contract worked out at the local campus level, might ameliorate the trend toward standardization. However, such master-secondary arrangements have not been adopted, at least to date.

Although there are clear trends toward centralization, the long-term effect of unionization on institutional autonomy is certainly not settled. In concluding this discussion, we simply list the opposing forces that will probably determine the long-run patterns. *Forces contributing to centralization* include: (1) large bargaining units; (2) a limited choice of bargaining agents; (3) common problems, such as desires for greater economic benefits and job security, that provoke common responses; (4) the centralizing and standardizing effect of master contracts; (5) the decision making of legislatures, PERBs, and courts that rarely grant higher education separate treatment. *Forces safeguarding diversity* include: (1) the voluntary nature of collective bargaining (it is not imposed from outside the campus, with the important exception of the multicampus bargaining unit); (2) the restriction of unionization largely to the less prestigious faculties and institutions; (3) variations within the legal framework such as management rights clauses and arbitration procedures that produce different styles of campus bargaining; (4) the professionalism and tradition of academia that helps confine bargaining largely to economic rather than governance issues at many campuses. In short, there are many contradictory pressures that make it difficult to say positively what the impact of unionization will be. The danger of increased centralization as a result of unionization, however, is very real.

Increasing Bureaucratization. Collective bargaining introduces new bureaucratic factors to campus governance. First, there are the complexities of the union itself; union policies must be established by internal operating procedures. Second, bargaining is a slow process, for both union and administration must consider their constituents. Third, after a contract is ratified, grievances and changes in administrative policies usually involve the union and require its consultation. For all of these reasons, the union becomes yet another bureaucratic feature of campus governance.

After the bargaining phase, the contract contributes to bureaucratization because it sets forth rules and regulations for personnel decisions and other organizational processes. Since a contract often requires that other documents, such as board by-laws and senate constitutions, be reworked completely, it contributes to burgeoning bureaucratization throughout the institution. As the contract grows more detailed—as is inevitable—more red tape is produced to complicate the routine of campus administration.

The consequences of increased bureaucratization can be very serious. First, the proliferation of rules and regulations now *makes it much easier for unions to challenge negative personnel decisions* through the grievance process than previously. The obvious danger is that personnel decisions that depend on subjective, subtle, and nonquantifiable academic judgment will be harder and harder to make. This means that merits may be sacrificed to egalitarianism. Where the discretion of peer judgment is curtailed by increased bureaucratization, status differences among faculty related to rank, publications, degrees, and experience will be reduced.

A second consequence is that increased procedural complexity *may seriously hamper institutional innovation and change.* The contract can become a straitjacket on any changes that affect past practice or the jobs of union members. For example, we noted earlier that the first contract at the City Colleges of Chicago prohibited *any* changes in past practices at *any* of the seven campuses. We also discussed the constraints unions seek to place on administrations trying to cope with economic problems. In their study, Channing, Steiner, and Timmerman (1973) found that a majority of trustees at unionized community colleges agreed that institutional change had slowed down. Before a college could undertake a new program, the union had to be consulted, the contract provisions studied, and many rules and regulations negotiated. In general, administrators and trustees felt that unionization slowed down the time it took the institution to respond to new situations and that it hampered attempts to introduce new educational practices. Where unions and senates coexist, a senate may find its ability to initiate change confined to academic areas and then subject to indirect union veto where personnel and conditions of work are affected.

On the other hand, contracts, of course, can be written to promote innovation and change. For example, a policy of giving merit awards for superior teaching or for program innovation can be written into the contract, as it was at the Pennsylvania

State College system. A really creative union and administration can develop new ways to stimulate sound educational practices without hurting faculty job security or working conditions. Unfortunately, such cooperation is not likely to occur in those conflict-filled early days when unionization is just beginning— and that is the stage of most faculty unionization today. The immediate likelihood is for unions to be a barrier to innovation; hopefully, that likelihood will change in later phases of collective bargaining.

Affecting the Quality of Educational Services. We asked presidents and chairpersons to agree or disagree with this statement: "Where it occurs, faculty collective bargaining will help improve the quality of educational services on campuses." The overwhelming majority of presidents at both nonunionized and unionized institutions disagree. By contrast, nearly 80 percent of the union chairpersons agree (Table 21, Question G). Presumably, union chairpersons believe that greater institutional benefits will result in a greater amount of high quality work. Unfortunately, it is doubtful that such a positive correlation exists. In our interviews, for example, administrators at the City Colleges of Chicago say they learned the hard way that "there is no correlation between dollars spent and educational improvement." Admittedly, this is a biased administrative viewpoint, but there is at least a grain of truth in the statement; without guarantees, it is doubtful that increased faculty benefits will improve the quality and effectiveness of educational service. A study by Lindeman (1974) substantiates this doubt, for he finds that faculty sympathetic to unionization at a large state university want a greater role in governance, but at the same time, they do not want to be held accountable for their decisions. The 1974 Stanford survey asked respondents to react to the statement, "Where it occurs, faculty collective bargaining will improve the accountability and responsiveness of the institution to the community it serves." As might be expected, only union chairpersons agree frequently with the statement. A large percentage of all respondents are neutral—but that is understandable, given their brief experience with faculty unionization (Table 21, Question H).

In light of the potential problems outlined above, it seems obvious that administrators must demand that high standards of educational service be established in exchange for meeting union demands. It may actually be easier for experienced administrators to achieve greater academic productivity and hence efficiency with collective bargaining than without it. Not only does bargaining promote wide-ranging discussion about campus operations, it promotes trade-offs between the parties. As Garbarino (1975, p. 237) points out:

> Forms of productivity bargaining are more likely to be achievable since a faculty concession on workload, for example, can be linked to higher pay or other benefits. Faculties enjoy the protections of many well-established "work rules" that might be difficult to challenge directly through traditional procedures, but that might be changed as part of a bargaining package. Sophisticated administrations may in the next decade be able to take advantage of these characteristics of bargaining to make more changes more easily than they could through traditional structures.

The trade-offs go both ways, of course; the union may be just as successful at making changes and securing concessions from administrators. It may be that the pressure collective bargaining places on administrators to be effective managers will improve educational services. In the last analysis, the value of collective bargaining must be judged by its impact on the educational process. Bargaining is under the control of the parties who use it. Presumably, a concerned faculty and skilled administration can tailor it to improve the educational process and at the same time increase the accountability of both professors and administrators to the students they serve. Shaping unionism to benefit higher education poses a very real challenge to both faculty members and administrators; it is the challenge of statesmanship.

A Call for Statesmanship

Although many people—including students, trustees, legislators, and parents—will be affected, the day-to-day challenges of collective bargaining will fall most heavily on the faculty and administration. In large part, these people will determine whether long-term academic values will be nurtured and protected, or whether unionism will undercut them.

We have argued repeatedly throughout this book that academic governance is a political process, a complex dynamic by which divergent interest groups try to gain their objectives. Unfortunately, the political imagery too often carries the connotation of unprincipled action, or "the ends justify the means" mentality—in short, that "politics" means "dirty politics." The image is very ingrained, and in the post-Watergate era it is particularly difficult to shake.

There is another political image, however, that is just as deeply ingrained as the negative one, and it also has deep roots in our tradition. It is the image of *political statesmanship*. It is true that politics is frequently used by unscrupulous people to gain purely selfish ends. It is just as true that at its best, politics is used by statesmen to strive for the common good. Every person's cherished values and fond hopes for society are inevitably linked to the political process. Because this is so, we want to mount a call for *academic statesmen,* people who will meet the challenges of collective bargaining, fight for the promises it holds, and not be afraid to struggle against its misuse.

Challenges to Faculty Statesmen. If a union election comes to the campus, faculty members will have to make their own decisions about whether to vote for unionism, whether to support a particular union, and whether to become a union member. Academic statesmanship will mean different things in different situations, and different actions will be appropriate. However, in all settings, the statesman *will get involved.* Most people are apathetic on most issues. In our 1971 survey, we found that only 21 percent of the faculty said they regularly got involved in campus governance; is it surprising, then, that most academicians complain of having little impact on campus affairs? Further, it is not unusual for fewer than half the eligible members of a faculty bargaining unit to actually join; of those that do, only a handful take the time and energy to participate in establishing union policy. Often a union is "captured" by the most discontented people, and they often are not well established in their profession and do not subscribe to traditional academic values. Unless the mainstream faculty become involved, they will lose control of their own union—to the detriment of themselves, their institution, and the academic profession as a whole. Our respondents indicated that collective bargaining in public institutions will stimulate greater faculty concern about state and local politics (Table 21, Question K). If this concern is translated into faculty lobbying, faculty matters such as hours, wages, and tenure will receive increasing publicity. The result may be greater faculty involvement in and responsibility for union affairs.

Being involved means more than attending union meetings. Conscientious union members will also strive for positions of union leadership, even though these positions may not be among the most highly coveted ones on campus. The failure of recognized faculty leaders to run for union office may leave the union either in the hands of less skilled leaders or may exalt the role of paid union professionals. Quality union leadership is critical to the outcomes of bargaining, and the stakes are too high for faculty members to abandon the matter. Certainly, it is asking too much to return a particularly effective leader to office year after year. Like campus administrative positions, the demands on union leadership are too great for most individuals to sustain over long periods without reduced effectiveness. We believe that union administration demands that the most capable faculty participate and that highly trained paid professionals be hired when they can be afforded.

Assuming faculty do get involved, they will have an opportunity to shape union policies and priorities, and in this effort there are many opportunities for statesmanship. First, student needs must be considered constantly. Second, academic senates, collegial processes in departments, and faculty committee networks must continually be supported and strengthened. A union cannot, in our opinion, be a substitute for these traditional mechanisms. The legal setting, the democratic environment of unions, and the adversarial nature of employer-union relations all undermine the possibility of the union playing the professional role that traditional governance processes usually play. In some circumstances, the union may actually work hard to *strengthen* the traditional governance mechanism, and that is one of the more positive aspects of unionism. However, the faculty should be constantly alert to any attempts by union leaders to *undercut* the governance processes. Promises about the ability of the union to govern more effectively than other bodies should be carefully examined. In short, we believe that "dual-track" bargaining, in which economic union matters are separated from academic professional matters is an idea worth fighting for—even though the fight will be a hard one.

Finally, faculty statesmen must defend academic quality and excellence. In the face of union egalitarianism and political pressure, it will be increasingly difficult but nonetheless necessary to make hard personnel decisions, to insist on the validity of subtle academic judgments even if they are unquantifiable, and to stress the legitimacy of strong professional standards.

Challenges to Administrative Statesmen. Faculty statesmen must be joined and supported by administrative statesmen. With more of the institutional resources and power under their control than ever before, administrators have a unique trusteeship. They must learn to rise above the petty hostilities and arbitrary actions that unfortunately have characterized initial reactions of administrations against unionism. There are too many important things to be done to get caught up in small circles of bitterness and mutual recriminations that have regrettably colored many unionized campuses. What are some of the actions that can move administrators beyond such pettiness and demonstrate administrative statesmanship?

First, the administration must take a strong lead in supporting the dual-track governance concept. They must deal with unions fairly and carefully on economic matters, yet they must also insist that academic governance and curricular policy are the role of senates, departments, and faculty committees. This dualism will erode rapidly unless it is constantly guarded. Often, due to the apathy of the faculty and the aggressiveness of the union, the task of guarding traditional governance processes will fall to administrators.

If the goal is to maintain a dual-track system, then the

administration cannot afford to be paternalistic to the senate, nor can it perpetuate practices that ensure the senate will remain ineffective. One conclusion from our case studies is that administrators are quite supportive of senates and the opportunity they provide for collegial deliberation of significant issues. However, administrative motives are often suspect, for faculty members, including those who hold positions of authority in the senate, complain of administrative hypocrisy. To repeat one typical reaction, "Senates get support because they are manipulable." If the dual-track concept is to survive, such administrative double-dealing must be avoided and sincere efforts to foster campus governance must be mounted. Since administrative arbitrariness is one of the forces stimulating unions in the first place—especially in colleges without strong governance traditions—it must be guarded against; it can be at least as big a threat to dual-track bargaining as an aggressive union.

Second, the administration must take the lead in clarifying governance roles. The more groups influencing governance, the more confusion and inefficiency are likely. It is primarily up to the administration to sort out the confusion of overlapping assertions of authority and establish clear areas of responsibility. At Hofstra University, for example, there are three formal bodies participating in governance: the AAUP, the senate, and the university faculty. Which group is to do what? Since the Hofstra administration participates in senate deliberations, acts on the recommendations of the university faculty, and bargains with the union, it has a unique opportunity to promote—even insist upon—a clarification of roles.

The legal framework of collective bargaining is an important impetus to role clarification. Recall from Chapter Six that the faculty union may charge an unfair labor practice against an administration if it consults another group, such as the senate, about a matter also negotiated with the union. To keep formal charges from being filed, administrators should take the lead in establishing guidelines governing intra-institutional power structures. The campus governing structure must be adapted to the labor laws, and, in a sense, the administration must do the adapting.

Third, it is the job of the administration to maintain a strong bargaining stance in order to restrict the scope of bargaining. Unions have a tendency to expand the scope of bargaining. Collective bargaining is a political process designed to provide ever-increasing benefits for union members who, in turn, keep union leaders in office. Thus, jurisdictional extension by unions should be expected at the bargaining table, and demands for negotiation over many nonmandatory subjects of bargaining will arise. Where senates have a strong tradition of effective influence over academic, personnel, and other issues, unions will naturally hesitate to intrude. The last thing a union wants to do, especially in the absence of an agency shop, is to alienate its members. In such a situation, administrators will not find it too difficult to resist union advances. If, however, the senate is weak, the administrators should consider resisting union expansionism at the bargaining table. One of the most effective, yet little realized, forces for shaping collective bargaining is the conduct of the administration, both at the bargaining table and during contract administration.

Fourth, the administration must take its case to the public to influence legislators, trustees, and state agencies. Unions make no pretense about their persistent use of lobbying. Neither should administrators. Boards of trustees and administrators must get involved in communication off campus in order to help public employment boards, state legislators, courts, and the general public understand the uniqueness of the educational enterprise and the challenges posed to it by collective bargaining. There is no question that off-campus agencies unfamiliar with higher education welcome assistance. As one member of the National Labor Relations Board has noted, "The board is not in need of *more* information—just *better* information. We cannot tailor our decisions to the unique concerns of a particular university until we know how that university is structured and how it operates" (Kennedy, 1974, p. 313). The most significant attempt by administrators to influence the outcomes of collective bargaining to date was by the Regents Task Force at the University of Wisconsin to establish a state law tailored to higher education. After months of deliberation, including a national contest to devise the best legal framework, the Task Force released its report, opting for a separate and special statute that "recognizes and protects the traditions and practices of shared governance in Wisconsin higher education" (Report of Regents Task Force on University Governance and Collective Bargaining, March 1975). Whether the proposals of the Task Force will actually become law is unclear at this point, for competing legislation is now being proposed to the Wisconsin legislature by much more powerful groups.

Concerted administrative action can go a long way to counterbalance the power of unions and affiliated labor groups. For one thing, administrators are probably closer to the value system of arbitrators and judges than are union spokespersons. In any case, lobby action is important because it enables administrators to make some impact, however slight, on those agencies whose decisions determine much of the character of collective bargaining at the campus level.

Finally, administrators must share responsibility with the faculty to protect student interests. Unions are generally opposed to including students in bargaining, because unions have vested interests that often conflict with student interests. As "institutional custodians," however, administrators have no such vested interests. Therefore, they should guard student interests constantly and work to open avenues of student participation. So far, administrators have apparently done little in this area aside from voicing a few platitudes aimed at securing student support. Persistently advocating student interests, articulating institutional responsibilities for students, and assessing the impact of collective bargaining on educational services— these are among the prime obligations of administrators.

Postscript

We would like to close on a personal note. When we began planning this book and researching faculty unionism, we were, by our own accounts, mildly pro-union. Our chief assumption was that unions were necessary to protect the academic profession against an increasingly hostile environment. In addition, we unquestionably held a strong pro-faculty stance. From this pro-faculty stance, we saw the value of unions as strong counterforces to what we believed was often arbitrary and capricious administrative behavior. We relished the thought that unions could bolster the power of the faculty.

Gradually, as the research and the book continued, we began shifting our positions slightly. Toward the end of the project, we both shed our faculty gowns and took over administrative desks—and it is at least possible that the transformation made us view the situation differently! However, our vision of the problems in unions were sharpened not only by our changed roles but also by persistent problems that we noted in our case studies and in our questionnaire research. The weaknesses of unionization and the dangers that it poses became as evident as its advantages.

As we end our study, we feel that we are neither strongly pro-union nor strongly anti-union. Interestingly enough, the prepublication reviewers of the manuscript frequently attributed prejudices to us based on their own positions. Administrators usually believed we were pro-union, while union officials generally believed we were anti-union. We believe we basically are neutral. It seems to us that the positive features of unionization are enormous—but so are the dangers to the academic enterprise. This leads us to our final point. If higher education is to be healthier and stronger because of faculty collective bargaining, then it will require genuine statesmanship on all sides. We have said countless times that academic governance is a political process. If we expand the analogy, the language of statesmanship is always linked to the language of politics. In the political battles to come, there will be union members and administrators who are petty and contentious; there will also undoubtedly be those in both camps who are creative leaders with goals of preserving the spirit of campus community and assuring that the profession serves the needs of its clients. In large measure, the fate of higher education depends on which style of leadership accompanies faculty collective bargaining.

References

Academic Collective Bargaining Service. *Special Report 17.* Washington, D.C., 1975.

Altman and Weil, Inc. *Survey of Corporate Law Department Salaries.* New York, 1973.

Andes, J. O. *Developing Trends in Content of Collective Bargaining Contracts in Higher Education.* Washington, D.C.: Academic Collective Bargaining Information Service, 1974.

Aussieker, B. "Community Colleges Without Community." In J. W. Garbarino (Ed.), *Faculty Bargaining: Change and Conflict.* New York: McGraw-Hill, 1975.

Baldridge, J. V. *Power and Conflict in the University.* New York: Wiley, 1971.

Baldridge, J. V., and Deal, T. E. *Managing Change in Educational Organizations.* Berkeley, Calif.: McCutchan, 1975.

Benewitz, M. C. "Contract Provisions and Procedures." In J. P. Vladeck and S. C. Vladeck (Eds.), *Collective Bargaining in Higher Education: The Developing Law.* New York: Practicing Law Institute, 1975.

Benewitz, M. C., and Mannix, T. M. "The CUNY Grievance and Arbitration Experience: What Does It Teach Us About Collective Bargaining?" In M. C. Benewitz (Ed.), *Proceedings, Second Annual Conference, April 1974.* New York:

National Center for the Study of Collective Bargaining in Higher Education, Bernard Baruch College, 1974.

Birnbaum, R. "Unionization and Faculty Compensation." *Educational Record,* Winter 1974, *55,* 29.

Blair, P. N. "Union Security Agreements in Public Employment." *Cornell Law Review,* 1975, *60,* 183.

Bloustein, E. J. "Collective Bargaining in the Halls of Academe." *Liberal Education,* May 1973, *59,* 187.

Bok, D., and Dunlop, J. T. *Labor and the American Community.* New York: Simon and Schuster, 1970.

Bond, L. "Impact of Collective Bargaining on Students." In D. W. Vermilye (Ed.), *Lifelong Learners—A New Clientele for Higher Education: Current Issues in Higher Education 1974.* San Francisco: Jossey-Bass, 1974.

Boyer, W. W. "The Role of Department Chairmen in Collective Bargaining: The University of Delaware Experience." *Journal of the College and University Personnel Association,* April 1974.

Brown, R. C. "Federal Legislation for Public Sector College Bargaining: A Minimum Standards Approach." *Toledo Law Review,* 1974, *5,* 681.

Burton, J. F., and Krider, C. "The Role and Consequences of Strikes by Public Employees." *Yale Law Journal,* 1970, *79,* 418.

Byrnes, J. F. "The Existence of Both Academic and Union Models of Governance at Rider College." *Journal of the College and University Personnel Association,* July-August 1975, *26,* 41.

Carnegie Commission on Higher Education. *Governance of Higher Education.* New York: McGraw-Hill, 1973.

Carr, R. K., and VanEyck, D. K. *Collective Bargaining Comes to the Campus.* Washington, D.C.: American Council on Education, 1973.

Center for Health Services Research and Development of the American Medical Association. *Profile of Medical Practice.* Chicago, 1974.

Channing, R., Steiner, S., and Timmerman, S. "Collective Bargaining and Its Impact on Board-Presidential Relationships." In M. Brick (Ed.), *Collective Negotiations in*

Higher Education. Washington, D.C.: ERIC Clearinghouse for Higher Education, 1973.

Cheit, E. F. "Systems Need Not Threaten 'Academic Style.' " *The Chronicle of Higher Education,* Oct. 15, 1973.

College and University Business. "A Roundtable: How to Live with Faculty Power." Dec. 1972, 33.

Commission on Academic Tenure in Higher Education. *Faculty Tenure.* San Francisco: Jossey-Bass, 1973.

Croman, C. "Women and Unions." In E. Reuben and L. Hoffman (Eds.), *Unladylike and Unprofessional: Academic Women and Academic Unions.* New York: Modern Language Association Commission on the Status of Women, 1975.

Doh, H. "Collective Bargaining in SUNY: The Story of the Senate Professional Association." *The Journal of the College and University Personnel Association,* Jan. 1974, 25.

Doh, H., and Johnson, S. "Collective Bargaining in SUNY: The Experience of 50 Local SPA Leaders During the First Year." *Journal of the College and University Personnel Association,* April 1974, 25, 2.

Dubin, R. *Organizational Bonds and Union Militancy. Technical Report No. 14.* Washington, D.C.: ERIC Clearinghouse for Higher Education, 1972.

Duryea, E. D., Fisk, R. S., and Associates. *Faculty Unions and Collective Bargaining.* San Francisco: Jossey-Bass, 1973.

Enarson, H. L. "University or Knowledge Factory?" *The Chronicle of Higher Education,* June 18, 1973.

Faculty Participation in Academic Governance. Washington, D.C.: American Association for Higher Education, National Education Association, 1967.

Falcone, M. A. *Collective Bargaining: Its Effects on Campus Governance.* Washington, D.C.: Academic Collective Bargaining Information Service, 1975.

Feller, D. E. "A General Theory of the Collective Bargaining Agreement." *California Law Review,* May 1973, 61, 663.

Finkin, M. W. "Book Review: 'Collective Bargaining Comes to the Campus.' " *University of Pennsylvania Law Review,* 1974a, 123, 217.

Finkin, M. W. "The NLRB in Higher Education." *University of Toledo Law Review,* Spring 1974b, *5,* 608.

Fratkin, S. "Collective Bargaining and Affirmative Action." *Journal of the College and University Personnel Association,* July-August 1975, *26,* 53.

Garbarino, J. W. "Emerging Patterns of Faculty Bargaining." In J. P. Begin (Ed.), *Academics at the Bargaining Table: Early Experience.* Washington, D.C.: ERIC Clearinghouse for Higher Education, 1973.

Garbarino, J. W. *Faculty Bargaining: Change and Conflict.* New York: McGraw-Hill, 1975.

Gee, E. G. "Organizing the Halls of Ivy: Developing a Framework for Viable Alternatives in Higher Education Employment." *Utah Law Review,* 1973, *1973,* 233.

Goodwin, H. I., and Andes, J. O. *Collective Bargaining in Higher Education: Contract Content, 1973.* Morgantown, W.Va.: Department of Educational Administration, 1974.

Hedgepeth, R. C. *An Exploratory Analysis of the Consequences of Collective Bargaining in Higher Education: The Role of the Faculty.* Washington, D.C.: ERIC Clearinghouse for Higher Education, 1974.

Hepler, J. C. "Timetable to Takeover." *Journal of Higher Education,* Feb. 1971.

Hodgkinson, H. L. *The Campus Senate: Experiment in Democracy.* Berkeley: Center for Research and Development in Higher Education, 1974.

Howlett, R. G. "Contract Negotiation Arbitration in the Public Sector." *University of Cincinnati Law Review,* 1973, *42,* 47.

Ianni, L. "The Critical State of Collective Bargaining in Higher Education." *Intellect,* Feb. 1974, *102,* 294.

Kadish, S. H. "The Theory of the Profession and Its Predicament." *AAUP Bulletin,* June 1972, 120.

Katz, E. "Faculty Stakes in Collective Bargaining: Expectations and Realities." In J. H. Schuster (Ed.), *Encountering the Unionized University.* San Francisco: Jossey-Bass, 1974.

Kay, W. F. "The Need for Limitation Upon the Scope of Negotiations in Public Education, II." *The Journal of Law and Education,* Jan. 1973, *2,* 155.

Kemerer, F. R. *Issues of Collective Bargaining at the University of California, Berkeley.* Washington, D.C.: ERIC Clearinghouse for Higher Education, 1973.

Kennedy, R. E. "The Educator's Role in Educating the NLRB: Requirement of a Complete Record." *Journal of College and University Law,* Summer 1974.

Kieft, R. N. *Collective Bargaining: Its Impact for Institutional Research.* Washington, D.C.: ERIC Clearinghouse for Higher Education, 1973.

Kugler, I. "Creation of a Distinction Between Management and Faculty." In M. C. Benewitz (Ed.), *Proceedings, First Annual Conference, April 1973.* New York: National Center for the Study of Collective Bargaining in Higher Education, Bernard Baruch College, 1973.

Ladd, E. C., Jr., and Lipset, S. M. *Professors, Unions, and American Higher Education.* Berkeley: Carnegie Commission, 1973.

Laity, R. W. "The Grievance Procedure: A Serious Problem Threatens Its Continued Success." *Rutgers AAUP Newsletter,* March-April 1974, *5,* 2.

Laity, R. W. "Resolving Faculty Grievances at Rutgers University." In J. P. Begin (Ed.), *Academics at the Bargaining Table: Early Experience.* Washington, D.C.: ERIC Clearinghouse for Higher Education, 1973.

Leslie, D. "Conflict Management in the Academy: An Exploration of the Issues." *The Journal of Higher Education,* Dec. 1972.

Levy, H. "Academic Judgment and Grievance Arbitration in Higher Education." Washington, D.C.: Academic Collective Bargaining Information Service, April 1975.

Lindeman, L. W. *University Goals and Collective Bargaining.* Norman, Okla.: The Center for Studies in Higher Education, University of Oklahoma, 1974.

Lozier, G. G. "Changing Attitudes Toward the Use of Strikes in Higher Education." *Journal of the College and University Personnel Association,* April 1974.

Lussier, V. L. *Albion College Votes "No Agent": A Case Study.*
Washington, D.C.: Academic Collective Bargaining Information Service, 1974a.

Lussier, V. L. *National Faculty Associations in Collective Bargaining: A Comparative Discussion.* Washington, D. C.:
Academic Collective Bargaining Information Service,
1974b.

McHugh, W. F. "Faculty Bargaining: Practical Considerations."
In T. N. Tice and G. W. Holmes (Eds.), *Faculty Power:
Collective Bargaining on Campus.* Ann Arbor: The Insti-
tute for Continuing Legal Education, 1972.

McHugh, W. F. "Faculty Unionism and Tenure." In M. Brick
(Ed.), *Collective Negotiations in Higher Education.* Washington, D.C.: ERIC Clearinghouse for Higher Education,
1973.

Mannix, T. "Community College Grievance Procedures: A Review of Contract Content in Ninety-Four Colleges." *The
Journal of the College and University Personnel Association,* April 1974.

Morand, M. J., and Purcell, E. R. "Grievance and Arbitration
Processing." In J. P. Vladeck and S. C. Vladeck (Eds.),
*Collective Bargaining in Higher Education: The Develop-
ing Law.* New York: Practicing Law Institute, 1975.

Mortimer, K. P. "Research Data on Tenure and Governance
Under Collective Bargaining." Washington, D.C.: ERIC
Clearinghouse for Higher Education, 1975.

National Center for the Study of Collective Bargaining in Higher
Education, The. *Newsletter,* March-April 1975.

National Education Association. *Due Process and Tenure.* Washington, D.C., 1974.

Newton, D. "CUNY: A Grievous Story." In James Begin (Ed.),
Academics at the Bargaining Table: Early Experience.
Washington, D.C.: ERIC Clearinghouse for Higher Educa-
tion, 1973.

Newton, D. *Unionization in Academe: Another View.* Unpub-
lished, 1973a.

Olsen, J. K. "Governance by Confrontation: Adversarialism at
the University." *Intellect,* March 1974, *102.*

Olson, M., Jr. *The Logic of Collective Action: Public Goods and the Theory of Groups.* Cambridge: Harvard University Press, 1971.

Park, D., Jr. "Tenure Shock." *The Chronicle of Higher Education,* June 4, 1973.

Pendleton, E. C., and Najita, J. M. *Unionization of Hawaii Faculty: A Study in Frustration.* Honolulu: Industrial Relations Center, University of Hawaii, 1974.

Ping, C. J. "On Learning to Live with Collective Bargaining." *The Journal of Higher Education,* Feb. 1973, *44,* 102.

Rehmus, C. M. "Alternatives to Bargaining and Traditional Governance." In T. N. Tice and G. W. Holmes (Eds.), *Faculty Power: Collective Bargaining on Campus.* Ann Arbor: The Institute of Continuing Legal Education, 1973.

Rehmus, C. M. "Constraints on Local Governments in Public Employee Bargaining." *Michigan Law Review,* 1969, *67,* 919.

Rehmus, C. M. "The Final Offer Arbitration Example." *New York State Public Employment Relations Board News,* Jan. 1975, 2.

Reuben, E., and Hoffman, L. (Eds.) *Unladylike and Unprofessional: Academic Women and Academic Unions.* New York: Modern Language Association Commission on the Status of Women, 1975.

Sandler, B. "Equal Employment Opportunity on The Campus." In J. P. Vladeck and S. C. Vladeck (Eds.), *Collective Bargaining in Higher Education: The Developing Law.* New York: Practicing Law Institute, 1975.

Satryb, R. P. *Faculty Grievances at SUNY: The First Two Years Under a Negotiated Contract.* Washington, D.C.: Academic Collective Bargaining Information Service, 1974.

Schuster, J. H. (Ed.) "Encountering the Unionized University." *New Directions for Higher Education,* Spring 1974, *5.*

Schwartz, H. "Women Faculty and the Union at Oakland University." In E. Reuben and L. Hoffman (Eds.), *Unladylike and Unprofessional: Academic Women and Academic Unions.* New York: Modern Language Association Commission on the Status of Women, 1975.

Seidman, J., Kelley, L., and Edge, A. "Faculty Bargaining Comes to Hawaii." *Industrial Relations,* Feb. 1974, *13,* 5.

Semas, P. W. "Union Is Given 50-50 Chance at University of Massachusetts." *The Chronicle of Higher Education,* Nov. 12, 1973.

Shark, A. "Current Status of College Students in Academic Collective Bargaining." Washington, D.C.: Academic Collective Bargaining Information Service, July 1975.

Shaw, L. C., and Clark, R. T., Jr. "Determination of Appropriate Bargaining Units in the Public Sector: Legal and Practical Problems." *Oregon Law Review,* 1971, *51,* 152.

Shulman, H. "Reason, Contract, and Law in Labor Relations." *Harvard Law Review,* 1954-1955, *68,* 999.

Slichter, S. H., Healy, J. J., and Livernash, E. R. *The Impact of Collective Bargaining on Management.* Washington, D.C.: Brookings Institute, 1960.

SUNY College of Arts and Sciences at Geneseo. "Viewpoints on the Goals of the College at Geneseo." Institutional Research Report No. 75-2. May 1975.

Tice, T. N., and Holmes, G. W. (Eds.) *Faculty Bargaining in the Seventies.* Ann Arbor: The Institute of Continuing Legal Education, 1973.

Vladeck, J. P., and Vladeck, S. C. (Eds.) *Collective Bargaining in Higher Education: The Developing Law.* New York: Practicing Law Institute, 1975.

Walters, D. E. "Collective Bargaining in Higher Education: Its Impact on Campus Life and Faculty Governance." In J. P. Begin (Ed.), *Academics at the Bargaining Table: Early Experience.* Washington, D.C.: ERIC Clearinghouse for Higher Education, 1973.

Wellington, H. H., and Winter, R. K., Jr. "The Limits of Collective Bargaining in Public Employment." *Yale Law Journal,* 1969, *78,* 1107.

Wellington, H. H., and Winter, R. K., Jr. "Structuring Collective Bargaining in Public Employment." *Yale Law Journal,* 1970, *79,* 805.

Williams, B. J. "Faculty Bargaining: Exclusive Representation and the Faculty Senates." *Journal of the College and University Personnel Association,* Sept. 1973.

Winkler, K. "Teaching: Historians Act to Upgrade It." *The Chronicle of Higher Education*, July 7, 1975.

Wollett, D. H. "The Bargaining Process in the Public Sector: What is Bargainable." *Oregon Law Review*, 1971, *51*, 177.

Wollett, D. H. "Historical Development of Faculty Collective Bargaining and Current Extent." In M. C. Benewitz (Ed.), *Proceedings, First Annual Conference, April 1973*. New York: National Center for the Study of Collective Bargaining in Higher Education, Bernard Baruch College, 1973.

Zeller, B. "Bargaining at the City University of New York." In T. N. Tice and G. W. Holmes (Eds.), *Faculty Power: Collective Bargaining on Campus*. Ann Arbor: The Institute for Continuing Legal Education, 1972.

Index

244

98223

DATE DUE			

DISCARDED